THE FACE OF
AMERICA

Books by Children's Theatre Company
Published by the University of Minnesota Press

The Face of America: Plays for Young People
Peter Brosius and Elissa Adams, Editors

Fierce and True: Plays for Teen Audiences
Peter Brosius and Elissa Adams, Editors

THE FACE OF AMERICA

AMERICA

PLAYS FOR YOUNG PEOPLE

CHILDren's THeaTre company

PETER BROSIUS AND ELISSA ADAMS, EDITORS

UNIVERSITY OF MINNESOTA PRESS
MINNEAPOLIS
LONDON

The plays in this anthology were supported by The Harold and Mimi Steinberg
Charitable Trust and the Minnesota State Arts Board, through an appropriation
by the Minnesota State Legislature and a grant from the National Endowment
for the Arts.

Published by the University of Minnesota Press
111 Third Avenue South, Suite 290
Minneapolis, MN 55401-2520
http://www.upress.umn.edu

Library of Congress Cataloging-in-Publication Data
The face of America : plays for young people / Children's Theatre Company;
Peter Brosius and Elissa Adams, editors.
    p. cm.
Four plays commissioned, developed, and produced on the Children's Theatre
Company stage.
ISBN 978-0-8166-7312-4 (hc : alk. paper)
ISBN 978-0-8166-7313-1 (pb : alk. paper)
1. Young adult drama, American. 2. Teenagers—United States—Drama. 3. American
drama—Women authors. I. Brosius, Peter. II. Adams, Elissa. III. Children's
Theatre Company (Minneapolis, Minn.).
PS625.5.F33 2011
812'.60809282—dc22

2011015736

Printed in the United States of America on acid-free paper
The University of Minnesota is an equal-opportunity educator and employer.

18 17 16 15 14 13 12 11   10 9 8 7 6 5 4 3 2 1

CONTENTS

Peter Brosius

Children's Theatre Company is committed to creating a new canon of plays that speak to the contemporary reality of young people and their families. A significant portion of the theatre work being done for young people is drawn from classics of children's literature, and we feel it is equally important to embrace the realities young people presently face in a world that is complex and in a state of profound and constant change.

New play development is a serious priority for us. We commission artists from around this country and the world to create their best work—work that we hope speaks to young people in ways that challenge, uplift, inspire, and excite. We want to make theatre that is vital, that is alive, and that honors the extraordinary audience that we serve.

With this collection, *The Face of America: Plays for Young People,* we bring you four plays commissioned, developed, and produced on the Children's Theatre Company stage. These works began with our invitations to extraordinary playwrights with unique and powerful theatrical voices to capture the reality of young people's lives—their yearnings, disappointments, optimism, and humor. All women, they are as different in aesthetic as they are in their life experiences. What they have in common is a passion for speaking to young people in a theatrical language that is fresh, surprising, and endlessly inventive. We asked these playwrights to explore issues of identity and who we are as a nation. Who owns the language, the discourse, the right to call oneself an American? The results have been remarkable. The plays they have created speak in language both direct and poetic, in startling images, and in searing and heart-breaking scenes that show us how fragile our notions are of who is an American. They let us feel how fractious our national conversation about this can be and how these questions can never fully be resolved. The United States will always be a work in progress. It will always be defined by change, by immigration, by an epic wrestling match with the reality of who we are and the myths that inhabit our national psyche. The questions about who is an American continue to dominate the news and spur debate. We know that the conversations about race and identity that we have had for centuries are not resolved, will not be resolved, and must be part of an ongoing discussion if we are ever to truly move forward.

We are deeply grateful to playwrights Lynne Alvarez, Kia Corthron, Larissa Fasthorse, and Melissa James Gibson for sharing the gift of their voices with a young audience. These plays invite that audience to dive into worlds of ideas, images, characters, and stories that will inhabit the heart, challenge the thinking, upset established notions, and incite conversation.

INTRODUCTION
Elissa Adams

O pen this book to any of the four plays collected here and the face of America will be reflected back to you. The faces are Somali, Russian, Native American, West Indian, Puerto Rican, Caucasian, Mexican. These plays represent a passionate, intentional effort on the part of the Children's Theatre Company (CTC) to commission and produce plays that highlight and celebrate the diversity of the American landscape.

Since 1998, when artistic director Peter Brosius established Threshold, CTC's new play development program, the theatre has created and produced more than thirty new plays. It has enlisted many of the nation's leading playwrights to expand the canon of plays for young audiences, inviting them to use their unique voices and their artistic and political sensibilities to create plays that will educate, challenge, and inspire young people. The plays in this anthology represent some of the fruits of that labor.

The richness and relevance of these plays—what makes them seem particularly fresh and necessary additions to the canon of plays for young audiences—arise from the complex and multifaceted portrait of diversity and cultural collision they paint. None of these plays focuses on a lone person or family of color making their way through white America. These playwrights are observant enough to know that the American landscape is much more colorful, varied, and complicated. In *Snapshot Silhouette,* the tension between Najma, a Somali-born refugee, and Tay C, the Minnesota girl in whose home she is living, is heightened because Tay C isn't just American, she is African American. Najma and Tay C may share the same skin color, but that doesn't mean they understand each other. The ESL class Najma attends at school is particularly (and hilariously) complicated because there are almost as many languages and countries of origin as there are children in the class. When Sasha, in search of a pen, ventures out into her building's hallways in *Brooklyn Bridge,* she must forge new connections with neighbors who are Puerto Rican and West Indian while worrying that she is losing connection with her Russian mother. In *Esperanza Rising,* Mexican immigrants who come to work in the migrant camps legally must wrestle with whether they owe allegiance to the illegal immigrants they work alongside as well as navigate the threat posed by the Okies—the poor, largely white farmers looking for work in the camps. In *Average Family,* the character who knows the most about the Dakota way of life is the daughter of a white family.

Our goal and the playwrights' goal is, first and foremost, to tell compelling stories. Each play here grew out of conversations with the writers about which stories they wanted to tell to a young audience. Only in retrospect did we realize that many of the young protagonists in these plays are recent immigrants. We did not consciously set out to create a body of work about the immigrant experience, but that it happened is not surprising. Immigration is one of the defining narratives of the contemporary American experience (since 1965, the number of first-generation immigrants in the United States has quadrupled). Recent immigrants face urgent questions: What is this new world? How will I make my way through it? How do my choices reflect who I am and who I will become? Many of the characters in *The Face of America* cannot return home. They must make do, find their way, survive. The stakes are high. This makes for a good play.

In *Average Family* by Larissa Fasthorse, the Roubidouxs, an urban family living in Minneapolis, and the Monroes, a hard-core back-to-nature clan from northern Minnesota, sign up to face off in a reality TV show. Their challenge: to survive three months as an 1840s frontier family on the Minnesota prairie. When the Roubidouxs, whose Native American heritage plays no part in their fast-paced lives, are cast as the "Indians," they realize the key to surviving the summer and keeping their family together is to embrace the teachings of their Dakota ancestors.

Sasha arrives home to an empty apartment in Melissa James Gibson's *Brooklyn Bridge.* Her Russian mother cleans offices in the big Manhattan buildings Sasha can see from her window. Faced with a looming deadline to complete her research paper for school and unable to find a pen or pencil, Sasha heads out the door of her apartment in search of a writing utensil. In a journey that takes her through the doorways and hallways of her building, Sasha encounters, for the first time, her neighbors. Like her and her mother, they have come from different places in the world to make their way in America. By the end of the play, Sasha has found a pen and finished her paper, but more important, like the famous bridge she is writing about for school, she has forged connections and created a community within the walls of her building.

Lynne Alvarez's adaptation of Pam Muñoz Ryan's novel *Esperanza Rising* opens with the privileged life of party dresses and servants of Esperanza, born into a rich ranching family in northern Mexico in the 1930s. But when her father is killed by revolutionaries, her mother sends Esperanza north to America with the family who had been her servants. They settle in a camp for migrant farm workers in California, where money is scarce, work is hard, and the threat of a workers' strike hangs over everyone.

In *Snapshot Silhouette* by Kia Corthron, Najma, a refugee recently arrived in Minneapolis, is taken in by an African American mother and daughter while she awaits the arrival of her mother, who is trapped in Somalia waiting for her immigration papers to clear. Najma's struggles to assimilate to life in Minneapolis—to school, to the weather, to the joys of Girl Scout cookies and Kanye West, and to the sorrows of remembering her little sister who died in Mogadishu—are compounded by the tensions between her and Tay C, the African American girl in whose home she is staying.

The world of young people today is exhilaratingly global. It is enriched and enlivened by the influences of many different cultures. With that comes the need for children to retain confidence in their own unique identity and heritage and attain the ability to empathize and communicate with people who can seem very different from them. The protagonists in these four plays struggle to, and eventually make great strides toward, achieving that balance. Sharing their stories onstage serves as a way to support and inspire young people to seek that balance too. It puts both the burden and the opportunity for doing so in their hands. In all of these plays, the challenges and the possibilities of finding a place in a new world are shouldered by young people. Parents are literally or figuratively absent. Adults are mired in the past. It is the young characters who must find solutions, forge connections, make a new place.

A culturally plural society can be a place where people stand on different sides, separated by a perceived chasm of unfamiliarity and supposed differences. But bridges can be built to span the chasm and connect those sides. In the words of *Brooklyn Bridge*'s heroine, Sasha:

> The worth of the bridge is that it links geographies
> The worth of the bridge is that it links populations
> . . .
> And when things aren't enough in one place
> All you have to do is cross a bridge to another place to find
> the thing that
> will be enough.

The bridge is a bridge . . .
And bridges are necessary things.

It is our hope that the plays gathered here serve as bridges.

AVERAGE FAMILY

Larissa Fasthorse

Directed by Peter Brosius

The world premier of *Average Family* opened on September 7, 2007, at Children's Theatre Company, Minneapolis, Minnesota. *Average Family* was funded in part by The Marshall Group.

CREATIVE TEAM

Scenic and costume design: G. W. Mercier
Lighting design: Geoff Korf
Sound design: André Pluess
Fight choreography: Ted Sharon
Video production: Ron Halpern of Moxie Productions
Stage manager: Chris Schweiger
Assistant stage manager: Megan Traina
Assistant director: Leah Starr
Assistant lighting designer: David Riisager

ORIGINAL CAST

DEBRA ROUBIDOUX	George Keller
NATHAN ROUBIDOUX	Steven Monés
RODNEY MONROE	Reed Sigmund
JACK PARK	EJ Subkoviak
MIKAL' ROUBIDOUX	Jack Wyatt Jue
MIKENZIE ROUBIDOUX	Raven Bellefleur
MARSHEL ROUBIDOUX	Noah Kol Balfour
SARAH MONROE	Elaine Patterson
LUKE MONROE	Mitchell Perry
JONATHAN MONROE	Connor Flanagan

CHARACTERS

NATHAN ROUBIDOUX

DEBRA ROUBIDOUX

MIKENZIE ROUBIDOUX

MARSHEL ROUBIDOUX

MIKAL' ROUBIDOUX

JACK PARK

RODNEY MONROE

JONATHAN MONROE

LUKE MONROE

SARAH MONROE

A brief video montage features four different families. This can be re-created with voice-overs.

~~~~~~~~~~~~~~~~~~~~~~~~~~~~~~~~~~~~

ACT ONE

Scene 1

A nice living room is illuminated downstage center. NATHAN ROUBIDOUX, *forty and Native American, enters wearing a business suit and carrying a briefcase. He plops himself tiredly on the couch.*

NATHAN: Anybody home?

The slam of a door is heard. MIKENZIE, *ten and Native with a distinctive Avril Levine/skater girl look, storms through the light and yells without noticing her father.*

MIKENZIE: Where are you, Shelly!?!

Another door slam is heard from the opposite side of the stage. MARSHEL, *fourteen with a jock attitude, saunters into the light trying not to look bothered.*

MARSHEL: Don't be sayin' that.

MIKENZIE *gets in his face.*

MIKENZIE: What'd you tell Keyanna Brian?
MARSHEL: Who?
MIKENZIE: Keyanna Brian, the queen of seventh grade? If you said anything to her, then she'll decide to hate me, which means the whole seventh grade will hate me, which means the whole sixth grade will really hate me, and my whole life at middle school will be over, and I haven't even gotten there yet.
MARSHEL: Would I seriously let anyone know I'm your brother?

NATHAN *sinks into the couch, shaking his head.*

MIKENZIE: Don't tell them we're related, fine by me.
MARSHEL *starts to turn away.*
MARSHEL: I tell people you're from Pluto.
MIKENZIE: Well, maybe you want everybody in your new high school to know your nickname is Shelly.

MARSHEL *snaps, she got him.*

MARSHEL: You know high school kids? I don't think so, Freak Face.

MIKENZIE *flips out.*

MIKENZIE: Where'd you hear that, Shelly?
MARSHEL: Shut up, Mikenzie.
MIKENZIE: Shelly, Shelly, Shelly . . .

MIKAL', *a six-year-old regular kid with an explosive energy, runs into the room, indignant.*

MIKAL': Don't tell her to shut up!

MIKAL' *launches over the back of the couch and at* MARSHEL. NATHAN *is too stunned to react. Pandemonium.*

MARSHEL: Get off!

MIKAL': Take it back!

MIKENZIE: Mikal', stop it. I can fight for myself.

Grabs for MIKAL', *who holds on to* MARSHEL.

MIKENZIE: Take it back, Shelly.

MARSHEL: Off. I'm serious.

MARSHEL *spins to dislodge* MIKAL' *just as* MIKENZIE *grabs his leg. They all fall in a tumble.* NATHAN *jumps up.*

NATHAN: Stop! What is wrong with you kids? It never ends, and I'm sick of it!

All three kids freeze and notice their dad for the first time.

MIKAL': What're you doing here?

NATHAN: I live here.

MIKAL': But it's only like five o'clock.

NATHAN: Mikenzie, get off your brothers.

MARSHEL: Tell her to stay away from my life.

NATHAN: Mikenzie, high school is an important time.

MIKENZIE: But he called me . . . *(She stops herself.)*

NATHAN: That's enough. Where's your mother?

MIKAL': It's Wednesday—she goes to yoga after work.

MIKENZIE: You always take Mar-SHEL's side.

Storms out, upset.

NATHAN *(calls after* MIKENZIE*)*: Would it kill you to be a better example for your little brother?

Behind NATHAN'S *back* MARSHEL *mouths "freak" to* MIKENZIE. MIKAL'
sees and shoves MARSHEL; *he shoves* MIKAL' *back.*

NATHAN: Mikal'. Marshel. That's enough fighting.
MIKAL': But he's like four people bigger than me.
MIKENZIE (*offstage*): This house is so unfair!

Door slam.

MARSHEL (*to* MIKAL'): I've got four chicks texting me. Go watch TV in
    your room, Mikey.
NATHAN: Good . . .

The boys go, punching each other in the arm. NATHAN *drops back on
the couch.*

NATHAN: Wait, shouldn't you be doing home . . . (*He's alone.*) work.
    Never mind. I should've stayed at work. Less stress.

NATHAN *feels for the remote and aims it toward the audience. A
commercial comes on two screens on either side of the stage. On-screen
we see* JACK PARK, *fifty, wannabe car salesman, but* JACK *is not nearly
smooth enough. He has a tendency to ramble and sells RVs.* JACK, *in a
brown polyester suit from the 1980s, wears a safari hat in his RV lot. He's
standing in front of a banner that reads, "Jack's All American RV Super
Safari, New Ulm MN." He's obviously reading off cue cards.*

JACK: Do you feel like you and your family never talk anymore?
    (NATHAN *listens closely.*) Do you feel like your kids don't
    appreciate you? (NATHAN *nods.*) Do you long to go back to a
    simple time, free of the rat race? Get back in touch with who you
    really are as a family?
NATHAN: Yeah.
JACK: Well, here at Jack's All American RV Super Safari in New
    Ulm, Minnesota, we've always been about family togetherness.

So we're embarking on something big, yes, bigger than our thirty-nine-foot 2007 Fleetwood Bounder. *(Gestures to an RV.)* I'm producing the first cable access family reality show right here in Minnesota. That's right. *(Pulls off safari hat and replaces it with big cowboy hat.)* We're taking two real families back to the frontier. Yes siree, live off the land, working together for a reward of simple joys. *And* a brand new RV for the winning family, fully equipped with all the latest electronics, mechanics, and luxury. Compliments of Jack's All American RV Super Safari in New Ulm, Minnesota, now open for our Midnight Madness sale! Time's almost up to send in your application tapes. Here are some of the great *(finger quotes)* "Average Families" we've already screened. Call the number on the screen to apply.

NATHAN *pulls a pen out of his shirt pocket and scribbles with a smile on his face. The stage lights go dark while the screens continue. The picture switches to grainy, amateur video. A generic house with a picturesque yard appears. The camera, obviously handheld, shakily pans to a really clean-looking family of six standing in the driveway by a white Saab station wagon.*

VOICE OFFSCREEN *(loud whisper)*: You're on.

The family smiles at once and waves to the camera. The dad speaks in a nervous monotone; he sneaks peeks at note cards in his hand.

DAD 1: Hi. We are the Hogan family. We live here *(awkward gesture to the house)* in Shakopee. *(Checks card.)* Minnesota. We would be a super Average Family. As avid bird watchers, we spend a great deal of quality time outdoors.

The screens switch abruptly to a log cabin in the northern woods. A woman stands alone wearing a Little House on the Prairie—*type outfit.*

MOM 1: Welcome to our home.

The windows and doors open, revealing three kids and a dad, each in different costumes, Davy Crockett, cowboy, and so on.

MOM 1: We're the singing Randalls!

The family breaks into a poor but enthusiastic rendition of "Oklahoma!" Change to a family at the Renaissance Festival in full courtly apparel doing a maypole dance.

DAD 2: Thee kindly gentle folk would be greatly enriched by the courtly presence of ye olde Masters family.

Screens change, and a family in Oktoberfest getups appear. The dad plays an accordion while the kids do the chicken dance.

MOM 2: Guten Tag. We're the Feidelhofsters, and we love authentic history, ya.

The screens go dark.

Scene 2

The lights come up on the prairie; bright sunshine, blue skies, tall prairie grass, some cottonwoods and other trees leading off upstage right to indicate water, but nothing else in sight. Both screens show endless, empty prairie. Center stage is a podium decorated with balloons and bunting. JACK, *wearing his cowboy hat, puts the finishing touches on his decorations. On either side downstage are two mounds covered with tarps. The stage-left mound is quite a bit larger. Also, slightly upstage, are two of those paper frames that football teams run through, one on each side. They look very homemade. The stage-left one says "*MONROE*"; the right, "*ROUBIDOUX.*"* NATHAN *enters alone, looking nervous.*

NATHAN: Mr. Park, um, Jack?

JACK *rushes over to him.*

JACK: Nathan! Where have you been? We're ready to start the opening presentation.

NATHAN: Yeah, I had a few questions about this contract we had to sign. *(Pulls contract out of pocket.)*

JACK: What isn't clear?

NATHAN: The part where we owe you ten thousand dollars if we drop out.

JACK: I thought that was especially clear. There are only two families. If one leaves, the show is over. Ten thousand dollars doesn't even cover what I lose if this ends early. *(Puts pieces together.)* Are you planning to drop out?

NATHAN: No, but that's a lot—

JACK: Then it isn't an issue. *(Grabs the contract from NATHAN.)* Where is your family?

NATHAN: They're waiting in the SUV.

JACK: Oh. Don't they want to come out and meet everyone?

NATHAN: Not so much. I think it's better if we just start, no introductions.

JACK: OK. Then let's go. I want you behind your entrance, then when I say your name, you burst through. Very dramatic. The other family is standing by.

NATHAN: That's good. Let me get everyone, and we'll just go right into it, no talking, right?

JACK: Sure, whatever.

JACK *returns to his finishing touches.* NATHAN *gestures offstage right for the family to come. Nothing. He gestures more emphatically.*

NATHAN *(to self)*: They whine about being in the car, now they won't get out. *(Calling offstage.)* Look, we aren't getting dinner until we're done here so you may as well come out.

DEBRA *(offstage)*: Come on, kids. I'm sure there's more to your father's surprise than . . . whatever this is. *(She enters, well dressed and Native with a city flair.)* Right, dear? I mean New Ulm was charming, and this back-to-nature moment is nice, but it's not exactly the trip to New York we had discussed.

NATHAN *guides her behind the paper.*

NATHAN: Just trust me. Hey, kids, I'm locking you in the car in ten
    seconds. Ten, nine, eight. (MIKAL' *runs in.*) Seven.
MIKENZIE (*offstage*): Mikal', you traitor!
MIKAL' (*to* MIKENZIE): I told you I need to go to the bathroom.
NATHAN: Stay right here, behind the screen thing.
MIKAL' (*behind screen*): Mom?
DEBRA (*behind screen*): Let's give your father a chance.
NATHAN: Seven, six, five, four.

MARSHEL *saunters in and past his dad as if he isn't even there.*

MARSHEL: Let's get this over with.
NATHAN: That's my boy. Three, two, one. Mikenzie? Fine.
Frustrated, NATHAN *marches back offstage. The alarm chirps twice.*
MIKENZIE (*offstage*): Hey! I chose to stay in there.
NATHAN (*offstage*): I've chosen to bring you outside with your family.
NATHAN *enters, pulling the reluctant hand of* MIKENZIE. *They are all
behind the paper frame now.* JACK *listens to all of this with interest.*
NATHAN: OK, go, Jack.
JACK: Okeydokey. (*He looks into the audience.*) Roll it!
DEBRA: What is going on?
JACK: Welcome, people of New Ulm and the surrounding cable access
    area, to *Average Family*! Over the next three months you will see
    our (*finger quotes*) "average" families tough it out together. And
    boy, do we have two great families for you, the Monroes and the
    Roubidouxs!

The MONROE *clan bursts through their paper. They are three huge men:
the father* RODNEY, JONATHAN (*twelve*), *and* LUKE (*ten*), *with one small
girl,* SARAH (*eight*). *They are all dressed in appropriate clothing for the
period. The men tear through the paper at once, knocking the whole frame
over. Meanwhile,* NATHAN *punches through and steps through the paper
carefully, not too much tearing. He reaches back and pulls his family after
him. They just stand there in shock. It's so quiet you can hear crickets.*

JACK: The rules are simple. No outside help. Nothing allowed that was not available before 1840. You must maintain a campsite of some kind the entire three months. Breaking any of these rules will quit the competition. In the end the team who makes the most new stuff, including food, wins the brand-new RV!

MONROES: RV! RV! RV! Victory!

The ROUBIDOUX *family turn as one and glare at* NATHAN.

NATHAN: Surprise.

All the ROUBIDOUX*s talk at once.*

DEBRA: I don't understand.

MIKENZIE: Three months? That's our whole summer vacation.

MIKAL': We'll be cowboys!

MARSHEL: I'm going to basketball camp.

JACK: Hey. *(Loud whisper.)* We're still rolling! Shhh.

The ROUBIDOUX*s look into the audience.* MARSHEL *moves away from his family as if they aren't together.* MIKENZIE *covers her face.*

MIKAL': Cool, cameras. Hi.

He smiles and waves. MIKAL' *makes faces at the "cameras."*

MIKENZIE *(to* NATHAN*)*: Have you gone completely insane?

JACK *(to* MIKAL'*)*: Stop it, kid. Never look at the cameras. That goes for everyone.

MIKAL' *stops reluctantly.*

DEBRA: Is this some kind of joke, Nathan?

NATHAN: Please, Debra, just give me ten more minutes. Then if you don't want to stay—

DEBRA (*to* NATHAN): Ten minutes.

RODNEY: What is going on, Jack?

JACK *motions for* RODNEY *to be quiet.*

JACK (*to* RODNEY): Shhh. This should be good.

RODNEY *shakes his head, but waits silently with his kids.*

MIKENZIE: You're trying to ruin my whole life!

NATHAN: Don't speak to me like that, young lady.

MARSHEL: I'm out of here.

MARSHEL *starts to go.* MIKENZIE *and* MIKAL' *follow him.*

NATHAN: Marshel, stop.

MIKENZIE: This isn't a dictatorship.

NATHAN (*losing it*): I am your father, and I am telling you to stop. Hate me if you want, but we are going to become frontier people and prove to the world of cable access that we are as average as anyone. Now that is final.

MARSHEL *turns and stares down* NATHAN. *The other kids are waiting to see who wins.* DEBRA *watches silently.*

NATHAN: Please, Marshel. Just hear it out.

This cracks LUKE *up.*

LUKE: Puleeze.

JONATHAN *looks directly at* MARSHEL *and laughs with his brother.* MARSHEL *pretends he didn't hear them, but he's standing straighter. He stops, aware of his siblings following him.* MARSHEL *waits.* NATHAN *jumps at his hesitation and pastes his smile on.*

NATHAN: Keep going, Jack.

JACK *isn't sure.* MIKENZIE *sulks.*

JACK: OK . . . um . . . *(checking his note cards).* On my left is the
    Monroe family.
RODNEY: Family roll call!
LUKE: Luke!
JONATHAN: Jonathan!
RODNEY: Rodney!
SARAH: And . . . Sarah!
MONROES: Monroe!
JACK: The Monroes are no stranger to reenactments. You may
    recognize them from Fort Snelling and rendezvous all over the
    area. To my right is a very special family from Minneapolis, the

Jack Park (EJ Subkoviak) announces his new cable access reality show, *Average Family,* during the world premiere of Larissa Fasthorse's play *Average Family* in 2007. Photograph by Rob Levine.

Roubidoux clan: Nathan, Debra, Marshel, Mikenzie, and Mi-cal, Meekal, Mike. (*Sincere to the family.*) We really are honored that you are sharing your knowledge with us. It will be quite an education. Here are your supplies.

JACK *steps forward dramatically and pulls the tarp off of the larger mound. A pile of goods are stacked there.*

JACK: For our homesteaders, exactly what would have fit in a wagon. You have tools, furniture, household basics, and food including flour, corn meal, corn cobs, sugar (white and brown), bacon, dried apples, coffee, pickles, canned goods, dried beef, salt, rice, dried fruit, seeds to plant, two cows, five chickens, and a rooster.

The MONROEs *nod at their things approvingly. They immediately start sorting through their goods.*

JACK: And . . . ta da!

JACK *pulls the other tarp away revealing a bundle of eight long, slender tree trunks still full of bark and branches; a pile of fur that looks like something dead; several leather bags; and a few small items. Everyone stares at the pile, not understanding. The* ROUBIDOUXs *look especially confused.*

JACK: Eight lodge poles, skins, and canvas to make your home, personal items for each of you, trade beads for Debbie, two bows and arrows, and—
DEBRA: You've got to be kidding.

Distressed, JACK *looks to* NATHAN.

JACK: Didn't we do it right? Sorry, I don't know Indian stuff, but you can fix it?
MIKAL' (*realizing, and not happy about it*): We're not cowboys, we're Indians!

JACK: Of course you are. You're my *(finger quotes)* "average" Indian
   family.

RODNEY'S *clan are suspicious; they weren't ready for this.*

MIKAL': But the Indians are the losers. I want to be a cowboy.
NATHAN: Hold it. There's been a huge misunderstanding.
JACK: On your application tape you said you were Indians. I know
   you did.
DEBRA: Did you, Nathan?
NATHAN: I mentioned our ethnicity is Native American, because . . .
   well . . . I thought it might help us get on the show.
DEBRA: But I haven't been to my reservation since I was a child.
NATHAN: I know. *(To* JACK.*)* I didn't mean we wanted to be *Indian*
   Indians, like this.
JACK: Well, you are Indians so . . . you're the Indians. Here's the
   best part: *(grabs bows and arrows)* no permits and no limits.
   I arranged it so you can shoot anything that moves. Wait till
   you change into the buckskin though. It'll be amazing for the
   cameras. Maybe paint your faces or something.

He hands the bows to MARSHEL *and* MIKAL', *who immediately start to
pretend shooting things.*

RODNEY: Wait, can we hunt?
MIKENZIE: No one should hunt. This is unethical. Mikal', stop it.

MIKAL' *keeps playing.* MARSHEL *checks out the bow; it's OK.*

DEBRA: She's a vegetarian.
JACK: Oh, one of *those.* *(To* RODNEY.*)* You have all this stuff.
RODNEY: I see. They can hunt because they are Indians.
JACK *(uncomfortable)*: It's the law, Rodney. Treaty rights and all.
DEBRA: This has gone far enough. Go to the car, kids.
NATHAN: No. You promised me ten minutes. Just let me fix this.

DEBRA: Fine. But there's nothing to fix. We aren't going to be this man's token Indians.

DEBRA *checks her watch and waits.*

JACK: What kind of Indians are you then?

NATHAN: Jack, I've lived in the Twin Cities all of my life. We can't survive with just *(gestures to their sad pile)* this.

MIKAL': Yeah, they've got way more stuff.

JACK: Oh, for goodness sake, animals provided everything your people needed. You lived off the land.

NATHAN: But I've never seen half these things before.

JACK: Look, this is the deal. Take it or leave me a check. I'll be back in an hour to collect your things.

DEBRA: Leave what?

JACK *grabs his podium and rushes offstage.* NATHAN *looks to* DEBRA; *it's scary.*

NATHAN: I've got a couple more minutes, Deb.

He flees toward RODNEY.

DEBRA: Nathan! Wait.

NATHAN *extends his hand to* RODNEY. DEBRA'*s had enough. She rejoins her kids.*

NATHAN: Rodney, hello. I guess we may be neighbors.

RODNEY: I'm not trying to be rude or anything, but I've seen your kind a thousand times. You want to reclaim your roots, feel family togetherness, then go back to your comfy city life. So you need to know two things. One, we may look like a bunch of hicks to you, but we live this life every day, so respect it. Don't make a joke out of it. Two, we want that RV, and we have to beat you to get it, so don't quit.

NATHAN (*annoyed*): We have no intention of quitting.

RODNEY: I didn't get that impression. But if you stay, you'll want to quit, but don't. (*Before* NATHAN *can respond,* RODNEY *turns to his kids.*) Who are we?

KIDS: The Mighty Monroes!

RODNEY: Frame up, Monroes!

The MONROE KIDS *have sorted out their stuff. Amazingly, a whole frame is erected in front of our eyes. The sides of the cabin pop up, fully intact. The kids fasten everything into place while* SARAH *hangs their cooking pans around a fire pit, complete with wood benches. While they work, they sing their Monroe song.*

MONROES: *We are the Mighty Monroes. We're home anywhere we go. Frame the house and lift the wall, wood or sod we do it all. Cowboy, frontier, we are there. We even grow authentic hair. That is why the song still goes: we're the best, the Mighty Monroes!*

The ROUBIDOUXS *are awestruck. The* MONROES *settle into their home.* DEBRA *speaks quietly to the kids.*

DEBRA: Kids, go to the car please. Time's up, Nathan.

MARSHEL *and* MIKENZIE *are happy to go.* MIKAL' *keeps his bow. Over the following* MIKENZIE *wrestles for it.*

NATHAN: You haven't given it a chance.

DEBRA: You can't be serious about this.

NATHAN *dives into their pile of things and sorts. He avoids her eyes.*

NATHAN: I should have told you, but I didn't think you'd come.

DEBRA: My job. I can't just leave.

NATHAN: I arranged everything. You're on family leave right now.

DEBRA: You went to my boss behind my back?

NATHAN *doesn't know what to say. The kids are almost gone.* NATHAN *looks to* RODNEY, *who glares back. The* MONROES *are contentedly putting final touches on their little cabin. This is* NATHAN'S *last chance. He chases down the kids and drags them back under loud protest.*

DEBRA: I'm not finished speaking with you.

NATHAN: I know.

MIKENZIE: Stop it.

MARSHEL (*aware of* JONATHAN *watching*): Don't touch me.

MIKAL': Ow!

NATHAN (*sincere*): But this is about all of us. I'm sorry. I did this wrong, and I know it's desperate, but . . . we need something desperate to save this family. Look at us. We're five strangers under the same roof.

The truth touches DEBRA.

DEBRA: I know. But for you to do something like this . . . we make decisions together.

NATHAN *looks to the kids. This is one of those conversations they'd usually have without them.*

NATHAN: We haven't in years. I have a life, and you have a life, and sometimes we cross paths. I know you feel it too.

DEBRA *becomes equally uncomfortable in front of the kids, who watch intently.*

DEBRA: Of course I do. But . . . this is crazy.

NATHAN: We were crazy once.

DEBRA: Can't we figure this out at home?

NATHAN: We've tried, and now it's almost too late. Please, Debra. Give us this chance to save our family. Save us.

DEBRA (*struggling*): But like this?

NATHAN: Come on, Deb. Are you with me?

DEBRA (*she breaks*): Of course I'm with you. I just didn't expect it to be on the prairie.

NATHAN *is greatly relieved. He grabs* DEBRA *in a hug. The kids don't know how to react. It's weird to watch your parents as a couple.* DEBRA *turns to them and switches into pep-talk mode.*

DEBRA: Kids, you know I'm the last person to want to spend my summer as a farmer or camper or whatever, but your father is right.

MIKENZIE: Mom!

DEBRA: We'll give it a try. Maybe it can work.

MARSHEL: I'm not going to look like a loser.

MIKAL': Yeah, look at all their stuff.

Disheartened, they look toward the MONROES, *then at their own small pile.*

DEBRA: Who are you people? Not my kids. My kids are intelligent, successful, and self-sufficient. Look at these amazing things. (*Kneels down and pulls out clothes.*) Marshel, I can see you as a young warrior. (*Hands it to* MARSHEL.) A leader. Girls dig that.

MARSHEL: "Dig"? You people need help.

DEBRA: Please. Your brother and sister need you. Try it on?

MARSHEL: This is a free trial, no guarantees.

DEBRA: Thank you.

MARSHEL (*looks around*): Where do I go?

NATHAN *pulls up one of the skins.*

NATHAN: Use this.

MARSHEL *takes it and goes off to one corner. Through the following he tries to change by holding the skin as a robe, around his waist, etc. He finally manages to change.*

DEBRA: Mikal', this could be your chance to have a pet. Maybe find a frog or . . .

MIKAL': A pet squirrel that rides on my arm?!

DEBRA: You never know.

MIKAL': That would be the coolest ever!

He grabs an outfit and dives under a skin to change. He wiggles on the ground under the skin.

DEBRA *(pulls out a buckskin dress)*: You would be so beautiful in this, Mikenzie. Like Pocahontas.

MIKENZIE *(sarcastic)*: Perfect, my life dream.

DEBRA: My grandmother gave me a dress like this when I was your age. I wonder what happened to it.

MIKENZIE *meets her mother's eyes. She knows this is emotional blackmail, but she won't be the one to say it.*

MIKENZIE: You can save the guilt. It's not like I have a choice.

MIKENZIE *takes the dress and a skin as her brothers come out. They are in their roles and dig into the supplies.* NATHAN *hands* DEBRA *an outfit.*

NATHAN: You are amazing.

DEBRA: They didn't make me a partner for nothing.

NATHAN: Mikenzie, help your brothers figure out how to make a tepee. I guess we're going to be Indians.

NATHAN *and* DEBRA *go behind the paper frame to change, leaving the kids alone.*

MIKENZIE: This is so gross.

RODNEY, JONATHAN, *and* LUKE *leave stage for a moment to survey things.* SARAH *checks to be sure they are gone and approaches* MIKENZIE *shyly.*

MIKENZIE *ignores her and keeps trying to change, while the boys stack their lodge poles and sort their bags.*

SARAH *(quietly)*: Hi. I'm Sarah.

MIKENZIE: Yeah, I got that. We won't be sticking around long.

SARAH: But what about the RV?

MIKENZIE: You actually want an RV?

SARAH: Have you seen it? We went to the RV lot; it's beautiful. It even has a TV and DVD player and a microwave and everything.

MIKENZIE: You live in the woods or something?

SARAH: Yeah, in a cabin on the north shore of Lake Superior. *(Suddenly aware.)* I guess you guys have all that stuff already.

MIKENZIE *finishes changing.*

MIKENZIE: Yeah. Excuse me. *(Joins* MARSHEL *and* MIKAL'.*)* We can't do this. This is too weird. They're some kind of woods people, or hillbillies, or something.

MARSHEL: That's kind of sad.

All look to SARAH.

MIKENZIE: It's not like we want an RV.

MIKAL': I do!

MIKENZIE: We need to go home. Then they get the RV, we get our lives back, and it's all good.

SARAH *(jumping in)*: No. You heard Dad. We only get the RV if we win. It's the rule. If you don't play, we can't win.

MARSHEL: Look, kid, I'm a winner, so if we play this thing, we win. It's a fact.

SARAH: I don't know. My brothers want that RV pretty bad. We've never had a microwave before.

MARSHEL: I'm not worried about your brothers.

JONATHAN *and* LUKE *return.*

JONATHAN: Sarah, it isn't historically accurate for you to be talking to the enemy.

The huge boys stand protectively behind SARAH, *homesteaders facing Indians.*

MARSHEL (*trying not to look intimidated*): I'm Marshel. He's Mikal', and that one's Mikenzie.

LUKE: Why do you have such weird names?

MIKENZIE: Why are you so freakishly big?

JONATHAN: Look who's calling us freaks.

MIKENZIE: Hey!

MIKENZIE *makes a move toward the boys.* MARSHEL *grabs her easily and yanks her behind his back. He tries to front with the guys.*

MARSHEL: Ignore her, that's what I do. So, you guys must have some serious football skills, huh? What high school? Maybe I've seen you play. (*Both boys laugh.*)

LUKE: High school? I'm in fifth grade.

JONATHAN: Seventh.

MARSHEL (*a little rattled*): Whoa.

RODNEY *enters.*

RODNEY: Come on, Monroes. Leave the special family with their special rules alone.

JONATHAN (*to* MARSHEL): We don't cheat.

MARSHEL: What does that mean?

RODNEY: You can hunt; we can't. That's two sets of rules for one game.

MARSHEL: We didn't ask for this.

RODNEY: Know what I think? I think you're scared that if me and my boys could hunt like you, we'd win this thing hands down.

MARSHEL (*standing up to* RODNEY): I'm not scared of you.

RODNEY: But you're scared of losing. I can see it in your eyes.

MARSHEL *holds* RODNEY'*s gaze.*

MARSHEL: No one calls me a loser.

RODNEY: You want to play by the same rules? No hunting? (MARSHEL *holds out his hand to shake.)* What about your dad?

MARSHEL: Don't worry about him.

RODNEY: Then it's your choice, son. They shake firmly.

MARSHEL *feels like "the man."*

MARSHEL: We've made our choice. Right team?

MIKAL': Yeah, keep your crummy special rules!

MARSHEL: Mikenzie?

MIKENZIE: No hunting? Yeah, sure.

Satisfied, RODNEY *and his clan go back to their camp.* MARSHEL *is totally amped up.*

MARSHEL: Come on, Team Roubidoux!

JACK (*to the sound booth*). Tepee music!

MARSHEL *grabs a pole and stands it up.* MIKAL' *tries to and nearly topples over.* MIKENZIE *steps in to save him.* NATHAN *and* DEBRA *return and jump in. Soon they each have a pole stood up, and lower them together. They form a nice tepee-looking shape. The* ROUBIDOUXS *let go and high-five each other over their accomplishment. Even* MIKENZIE *feels good.*

NATHAN: That's right. We're the R . . . rr . . . rockin' Roubidouxs!

They throw the skins at the poles. They struggle at getting the heavy skins to "stick." The skins fall back on their heads, catch on branches. They work through the following.

DEBRA: Should it be open like that?

NATHAN: Well . . . it's a shelter.

MIKAL': When's dinner? I'm hungry.

NATHAN *and* DEBRA *exchange a look.* DEBRA *moves to their small pile of belongings and searches.*

NATHAN: I guess we better learn how to use these bows.
MARSHEL: I made a deal with Rodney. We're not hunting if they can't.
NATHAN: You did what?
DEBRA (*to* MARSHEL): Honey, I understand how you feel, but there's just dried fruit and some kind of jerky product here. It's barely enough for a few days.
MARSHEL (*resolute*): We don't need charity. I shook on it.
NATHAN: We haven't made that decision.
MARSHEL: If you want us to stay, we don't hunt. Period.
NATHAN: We need food.
MIKENZIE: You said you wanted us to be a family and do this together. The family voted against hunting. So, either we're smart and everything Mom said, or we should give up now.

Finally most of the skins are hanging in various degrees over the poles. It's rough but livable. NATHAN *and* DEBRA *start to see the potential monster they've created.*

DEBRA: I guess they're right. There have to be other options for food, right?

NATHAN *sees his kids and the tepee. It's a start.*

NATHAN: OK. We'll figure things out the Rockin' Roubidoux way.

He puts his hand out to stack hands. The kids look at him, then each turns away and works at dragging their stuff inside. NATHAN *stands alone with his hand out.*

DEBRA: Don't push it, dear.

In the other camp the MONROES *assemble around their fire humming the Mighty Monroe song. The stage lights and screens go dark.*

MIKENZIE: Get off!

MARSHEL: You're on my foot!

MIKAL': I don't have enough room!

DEBRA: Go to sleep!

Scene change

Confession cam. Screens come up with MIKENZIE *sitting alone in front of a black curtain. She looks sulky.*

JACK (*off camera*): It's a confession cam. Every week you just come and talk.

MIKENZIE: About what?

JACK (*off camera*): Anything, like what it's like being an Indian?

MIKENZIE: I don't know. I've never thought about it before.

JACK (*off camera*): Really?

MIKENZIE: I don't know what being Indian's supposed to mean. I don't feel different, I mean not 'cause of that. (*Suddenly more uncomfortable.*) I don't want to do this.

Scene 3

She leaves. The screens go dark. The screens show the prairie at daybreak. Birds chirp. The stage lights come up to early morning light. NATHAN *and* RODNEY *are alone, talking downstage. (Right now they are the only ones onstage, but otherwise family members can always be working in the background or entering and exiting their homes.)*

NATHAN: If you don't let me do this, we may as well start packing.

RODNEY: It can't be permanent.

NATHAN: Of course not. I work for you, you pay in food. Once we get our feet under us, it stops.

RODNEY: We choose the food we pay you with. And the work you do.

NATHAN: It's a deal.

They shake on it.

RODNEY: First thing we need is an outhouse. Start digging.

RODNEY *hands* NATHAN *a shovel.* NATHAN *takes it, yuck.* DEBRA *and the kids emerge from the tepee.* NATHAN *puts on a brave face and approaches them. The* MONROES *enter and exit doing morning chores.*

NATHAN: Good news. I'm using the Rockin' Roubidoux thinking already. I've got a job working for Rodney.
DEBRA: What does that mean?
NATHAN: We get paid with food at the end of the week. You'll have to manage until then. Got to get to work.

NATHAN *goes to* RODNEY'S *camp. Through the following scene* NATHAN *works in the background.*

MIKENZIE: What do we do now?
DEBRA: Well, I will investigate our water and bathing situation. You kids focus on ways to improve our tepee. Brainstorm some ideas together by the time I get back.

She picks up her belongings and makes her way off toward the trees. The ROUBIDOUX KIDS *pull a few skins off.* MIKENZIE *stops and surveys their situation.*

MIKENZIE: Nice family togetherness.
MARSHEL: Nothing's changed but the scenery.
MIKENZIE (*a little sad*): Guess so.

They sit with two skins and pull out an awl and some long leather strips. The kids stare at the foreign items, completely lost. MARSHEL *looks around.*

MARSHEL: There's gotta be berries or something out there. See you later.

MIKENZIE: Mom said—
MARSHEL: Men bring food. Women sew. Welcome to history.

He takes off. MIKAL' *looks to* MIKENZIE *hopefully.*

MIKENZIE: Fine, go with him. Stupid boys.
MIKAL': I'll pick some berries for you.

He runs after MARSHEL. MIKENZIE *tosses the stuff away from her, defeated.* SARAH *approaches carefully.*

SARAH: I thought maybe you could use this.

She hands a book to MIKENZIE. MIKENZIE *looks at it suspiciously.*

MIKENZIE: Is this a trick? Like to get us in trouble?
SARAH (*distressed*): No! I got it from a rendezvous, but it's about the
    1840s and just made with paper, so I think it's OK, not cheating
    or anything. Sorry. I wanted to help.

SARAH *flees.* MIKENZIE *feels a little bad. She reads the cover.*

MIKENZIE: "The Dakota and Their Ways."

MIKENZIE *makes sure she's alone, then pages through the book. She stops suddenly and studies a page. She finds the awl and holds it next to the book and names her find.*

MIKENZIE: Awl. Like a needle but different.

She studies another page, then puts the book down, pulls a skin over it, and starts pounding holes in the skin with the awl. DEBRA *enters and watches.*

DEBRA: How did you know what that was for?

MIKENZIE *considers the hidden book.*

MIKENZIE: It just made sense.

DEBRA: Good problem solving, Mikenzie. You kids don't even need us.

MIKENZIE *enjoys her mother's praise. She makes a couple holes then strings the leather through to sew the pieces together.* MARSHEL *and* MIKAL' *return empty-handed.*

MARSHEL: We didn't see like . . . strawberries or anything.

MIKAL': I'm hungry.

DEBRA: We'll eat a little of our food now, but we should be careful to make it last.

MIKENZIE: What if we can't find anything to eat?

DEBRA: I don't know. But we only have to last the week.

They all look to NATHAN *working very hard for the* MONROES. *Stage lights go dark.*

Scene 4

Confession cam with a grumpy MIKAL'.

MIKAL': This has been the longest two weeks of my entire life. No one wants to do anything fun. All Rodney gave us for food was crummy corn and rice. Dad says it'll be better this week. I hope so. It's scary being hungry all the time.

The screens go black. Lights and screens up on a bright, hot day. The finished tepee juts onto stage right. MIKENZIE *stands over a fire, watching it nervously. She looks hot and tired. She makes sure she is alone, then pulls out her book and checks a page.* MIKENZIE *tucks the book back under her dress as* DEBRA *enters.* MIKENZIE *reaches into the edge of the fire and pulls out an ear of corn. It's hot, she drops it, and it falls into the fire. A puff of black smoke goes up.* DEBRA *is upset.*

DEBRA: Mikenzie! That corn was half of our food.

MIKENZIE: Sorry.

DEBRA: You said you knew how to do this.

MIKENZIE: It was too hot.

DEBRA: Now we have nothing left to eat tonight. Do you understand?

MIKENZIE: Yes.

DEBRA (*trying to calm down*): Sorry. I should have done it myself.

DEBRA *leaves* MIKENZIE. *Dejected,* MIKENZIE *backs away from the fire, fanning herself.* MARSHEL *walks in holding something. He's a little on edge but covering.*

MARSHEL: Found another brown one. (*Holds up a feather.*) I only need six more to finish my shirt.

MIKENZIE *busies herself using water and dirt to put out the fire.*

MIKENZIE: Could you help a little?

MARSHEL: Help you screw up? Don't think so.

MIKENZIE: I'm the one who figured out how to sew the tepee and start the fire. What are you doing, Shelly?

MARSHEL: I'm a warrior. I'm looking the part. It's better than . . . him.

They both look toward the MONROES' *area as* NATHAN *carries firewood for the cabin. The kids are embarrassed.*

MARSHEL (*continuing*): Rodney's screwing with us, and Dad keeps taking it.

MIKENZIE: This sucks.

MARSHEL: He's making us all look bad.

MARSHEL *takes off, frustrated.* MIKENZIE *feels bad; she's thinking it may be true. She pulls out her book and searches for something to help. The lights go down.* MARSHEL *comes up in the confession cam, lots of attitude covering the truth.*

MARSHEL: I may not be shooting hoops, but don't worry, coach, I'm totally in shape. All day I'm walking and running. There's a lot of carrying stuff, so my arms are good. The heat is killer, so my system's totally getting stronger. I'm on a diet. *(The armor cracks; he's scared.)* I've maybe lost a little too much weight, but I'll get it back. I swear. I'll get it all back.

Scene 5

The lights come up on the stage. MIKENZIE *and* MARSHEL *are sitting on opposite sides of their area, completely at a loss.* MIKAL *runs in from the* MONROES' *area wearing a huge pioneer shirt over his leggings.* MIKENZIE *turns her frustration on him.*

MIKENZIE: Where'd you get that shirt?

MIKAL' *(excited)*: It's Luke's old one. Isn't it cool? He and Jonathan said maybe they'd give me a pair of jeans next week.

MIKENZIE: What'd they make you do for it?

MIKAL' *(defensive)*: Stuff.

MIKENZIE: Like what? *(Sees something on his neck and grabs him.)* What happened to your neck? It's all red.

MIKAL' *(really small)*: Cowboys need to practice roping, so I was the cow so they could practice. Their cow just stands there.

MIKENZIE *(furious)*: They threw a rope around your neck? You're never going over there again.

MIKAL': I can if I want to.

MARSHEL: They're using you, bro.

MIKAL': I'd rather be with them than a dumb Indian here. *(Runs in the tepee.)*

MIKENZIE: I'll take on Jonathan and Luke together.

MARSHEL: Don't be stupid.

NATHAN *and* RODNEY *walk into the background having a discussion that gets more heated.*

MIKENZIE: Then do something, Marshel!

MARSHEL: I'm the man around here. Don't give me attitude.

MIKENZIE: What makes you the man? This isn't home, Marshel. No one cares if you can hit a three pointer.

NATHAN (*overlapping*): We had a deal!

MARSHEL: Shut up, Mikenzie.

The kids stop fighting to listen.

RODNEY: We still have a deal, but it has to change to fit the current situation.

NATHAN: That's not fair. You promised to pay us!

RODNEY: We're giving you half the garden. When it comes up, you get paid.

NATHAN: But that takes . . . ah . . . a long time. My kids are hungry. We'll have to go home.

RODNEY: I knew you'd quit. You said this was temporary, but you aren't doing any better, so I've got to protect my own.

RODNEY storms off. DEBRA *comes out of the tepee with* MIKAL'. NATHAN *turns to his family, embarrassed.*

DEBRA: Without food, we're done.

MIKAL': But they have tons of food.

NATHAN: We can't go. We don't have ten thousand dollars to spare right now.

DEBRA: Ten thousand dollars? Why?

NATHAN: That's how much we have to pay if we quit. It's in the contract.

DEBRA: You signed a contract without showing it to me? I'm an attorney.

MARSHEL: We're trapped here?

DEBRA: There has to be a way out of it. This isn't a game anymore. Our children are going hungry.

MARSHEL (*to* NATHAN): We look like losers. Stand up to Rodney. Make them pay.

NATHAN (*snaps at* MARSHEL): You made the deal not to hunt, so you figure something out, because I'm out of ideas.

NATHAN *storms off;* DEBRA *follows him. His words hit* MARSHEL *hard.*

MIKENZIE: Marshel . . . maybe we could use this. (*Pulls out her book.*) It says here—
MARSHEL: A dumb book isn't going to help us. (*Grabs the book from* MIKENZIE *and tosses it away.*) The Monroes broke the deal. Anything's fair now.
MIKENZIE: You promised no hunting!
MARSHEL: I'm keeping my word. But Dad put me in charge, so we're gonna get what we're owed.

The lights go dark. The confession cam comes on the screen. JONATHAN *and* LUKE *sit squashed together reading off of a piece of paper.*

JONATHAN: When we win the RV, these are the top ten things we want to cook in the microwave until they explode.
LUKE: Or catch fire.
JONATHAN: Hot dogs, those plastic cups of soup, a watermelon, two frozen teriyaki bowls—
LUKE: If Dad'll let us buy them.
JONATHAN: A bag of Cheetos, bananas, a can of shaving cream—
LUKE (*shakes head*): Metal.
JONATHAN: Right. (*Thinks.*) If we can find a plastic one, otherwise a tube of toothpaste, walnuts, a tennis ball, and, of course, a persimmon.
LUKE (*smiles*): Sweet.

The screens go dark.

Scene 6
The stage is barely lit by moonlight. A half moon shines over the prairie in the screens. The ROUBIDOUX KIDS *huddle center stage.*

MIKENZIE: We're going to get in trouble.

MARSHEL: Mikenzie, we've been over this. It's not stealing because it's the stuff they owe us. It's ours.

MIKENZIE: I don't know . . .

MARSHEL: For once in your life, will you be a cool sister and not embarrass us?

MIKENZIE: What about Mom and Dad?

MARSHEL: Since when do you care about Mom and Dad?

MIKENZIE (*he's got a point*): Let's go.

MARSHEL: OK. We're only grabbing some food. Don't go crazy and get caught. We don't want 'em to know we're there.

MIKENZIE: I want the water bucket. We need another container.

MIKAL': I want a chair.

MIKENZIE: What would you do with a chair, stupid?

MIKAL': For Mom. She misses chairs.

MARSHEL: Only essentials, little bro. Let's go.

The kids sneak over to the MONROES' *area. They hesitantly pick up a bucket and canned goods. They creep back and stash the stuff. They all look at each other anticlimactically.*

MIKAL': That was easy.

MARSHEL: Yeah. May as well snag some more.

MIKENZIE *shrugs. They walk back, bolder, to grab more stuff including a glass jar of canned fruit. They return and open the jar, eating hungrily. They run back, having fun now.* MARSHEL *unties a big burlap sack. The kids suppress a laugh as* MIKAL' *triumphantly lifts a chair over his head. Not to be out done,* MIKENZIE *goes off left. After a moment a chicken squawks loudly, then all the chickens and the rooster start screaming.*

MIKENZIE *runs back in, eggs in both hands.*

MARSHEL: Run!

Commotion is heard in the cabin. MARSHEL *and* MIKENZIE *run across the stage and try to hide the stuff behind the tepee.* RODNEY *and* JONATHAN *stumble out.* RODNEY *easily catches* MIKAL', *struggling with his chair.*

RODNEY: Stop, you little thieves!
MARSHEL: Let him go.

NATHAN *and* DEBRA *rush out.* LUKE *and* SARAH *stumble in sleepily.*

NATHAN: What on earth are you doing, Rodney?
DEBRA: Let go of my son.

They gather their kids.

JONATHAN: That's our stuff.

The Roubidouxs (Steven Monés, Raven Bellefleur, and Noah Kol Balfour) square off against the Monroes (Reed Sigmund, Elaine Patterson, Connor Flanagan, and Mitchell Perry) as the competition heats up. Photograph by Rob Levine.

NATHAN *realizes it's true.*

NATHAN (*to his kids*): Why would you steal?
MARSHEL: You quit, so I figured it out, just like you told me to.
RODNEY: You sent your kids to steal for you?

RODNEY *marches back to his cabin and grabs his rifle.*

NATHAN: No. I didn't tell them—
RODNEY: If that's how you want it . . . (*Lowers his rifle threateningly.*)
    If I see any of you on my land, I'll shoot first.
NATHAN: Rodney! You can't be serious!
RODNEY: Food's life and death on the frontier.

DEBRA *grabs the kids close to her, horrified.* NATHAN *seems to snap.*

NATHAN: I provide for my family a lot better than you! (NATHAN *grabs
    the bows and arrows and hands one to* MARSHEL.) You stay away
    from us, or I'll shoot!

NATHAN *and* MARSHEL *aim their bows toward* RODNEY *and* JONATHAN.

DEBRA: Nathan, stop.
MIKAL': Go, Dad!
MIKENZIE: Yeah!
MARSHEL: You heard him, Jonny baby.
RODNEY: You asked for this. (*To* LUKE.) Luke!

RODNEY *grabs the table from their area and overturns it in the middle of
the stage. He takes the chair* MIKAL' *stole and piles it on top.*

RODNEY: If you're staying, then stay right there.

JONATHAN *and* LUKE *help stack a wall between the camps.* NATHAN *and*
MARSHEL *keep their bows on them.* SARAH *stays back, watching sadly.*

DEBRA (*disbelieving*): Are you trying to put us on a reservation?

RODNEY: I'm trying to protect my family.

NATHAN: So am I.

RODNEY *stacks the line around the front of the tepee.* NATHAN *and* MARSHEL *stay on guard.*

MIKAL': Hey! That's not fair, you have more room.

RODNEY: You aren't making use of the land. We are, so we deserve more room.

MIKENZIE: They can't keep us in here!

MIKENZIE *rushes around the barrier before her parents can stop her.* JONATHAN *lowers the gun toward her.* MIKENZIE *freezes.* NATHAN *reaches across and pulls* MIKENZIE *back.* RODNEY *stands menacingly with his ax.*

RODNEY: This is your last warning. Don't cross this line.

RODNEY *rushes upstage and chops at a tree.* NATHAN *speaks to his family.*

NATHAN: I don't want you kids out unless you are with me or Marshel. It's dangerous.

MIKENZIE *and* SARAH *lock eyes across the barrier.* DEBRA *grabs* MIKENZIE *to get her attention back.*

DEBRA: Promise us, Mikenzie.

MIKENZIE: Fine, I won't go off the Rotten Roubidoux Reservation.

Suddenly a tree comes CRASHING down between the camps, enclosing the ROUBIDOUXS. *The realization of their new situation sinks in as the lights go to black.*

End Act One.

After intermission: on-screen we see the Average Family logo.

JACK: And now we return to the continuing story of the Monroes and the Roubidouxs on . . . Average Family. Brought to you by Jack's All American RV Super Safari in New Ulm, Minnesota.

Confession cam comes up on-screen. NATHAN *sits in front of the camera, waiting.* JACK *pops his head up in front of the camera, too close, looking at the lens, tough interview style.*

JACK: So, Nathan, we're one-third of the way. How are things?

JACK'S *head drops below camera.*

NATHAN: Fine.

JACK (*head back in*): But you lost your job, you're in a war with your neighbors, and your kids were caught stealing. Is that how you expected this experience to go?

NATHAN: No, of course not.

JACK: What do you need to change to stay in the game?

NATHAN: I'm working out a new idea . . .

The shot zooms in dramatically on NATHAN'S *face. Then it suddenly goes too far and quick zooms up his nose.*

JACK (*off camera*): Oops. That's not right.

The shots widens at a dizzying speed. JACK'S *head pops up as he reaches toward the camera.*

JACK: Whoa. Let's try that again.

The camera's light comes on glaringly bright, right in JACK'S *face.* JACK *yells and jumps up, blinded.* NATHAN *shields his eyes.* JACK *loses his balance and falls on* NATHAN'S *lap.* NATHAN *jumps up in surprise, and they both tumble into the curtain. One of their feet hits the camera. The lens whips around the booth wildly. We hear noises of their struggle, then the screens go dark.*

Scene 1

The curtains open to reveal the wooded clearing around the pond. The light is filtered through the leaves of the cottonwood and other trees. Soft cotton occasionally floats through the air. The screens show prairie. MIKENZIE *sits by the pond studying her book. She sounds out words.*

MIKENZIE: He un . . . kee . . . ye—

She hears something and tucks the book into her dress. SARAH *enters with two water buckets. She stops short and checks to be sure they are alone. Through the following* SARAH *gets water.*

MIKENZIE: You going to tell on me for being off the reservation?

SARAH: Dad knows you need water too.

MIKENZIE: How nice of him.

SARAH: You did steal from us, you know.

MIKENZIE: He didn't pay us, you know.

SARAH: Dad's not mean, just real serious. We've lived like this a long time.

MIKENZIE: What's up with that anyway?

SARAH: We were normal, until my mom died.

MIKENZIE (*genuine*): Oh, sorry.

SARAH: It's OK. She died when I was a baby.

MIKENZIE: Do you miss her?

SARAH: I didn't meet her so I can't really miss her. But I wish I knew what a mom is like. Before, Dad was a truck driver so he was gone a lot. Jonathan said Mom wanted to live in the forest. After she died, Dad flipped out, and when he quit flipping, he moved us to the woods. We've been together ever since.

MIKENZIE: Wow, that's so Everwood of him.

SARAH: Huh?

MIKENZIE: You know the TV show—never mind.

SARAH: Mostly I like how we live, but sometimes I wish we could be a normal family. Like you.

MIKENZIE: Ha. Trust me, if we're normal, the world is in bad shape.

SARAH: Why?

MIKENZIE: We live in the same house, but it's like we're on different planets and none of them know what mine's really like.

SARAH: But you get to go to school and have friends.

MIKENZIE: I don't have any friends. I'm called Freak Face at school, so no one will talk to me in case they're called Freak Face too.

SARAH: Why would they call you that?

MIKENZIE: I don't know. One day some girl walked up to me and called me Freak Face and that was it. I didn't even know her name.

SARAH: That's so mean.

MIKENZIE: Yeah. Mom and Dad don't know, so . . .

SARAH: I won't tell.

MIKENZIE *and* SARAH *exchange a smile. They hear* DEBRA *and* NATHAN *approaching.*

MIKENZIE: Great. I'm busted.

MIKENZIE *waits, defeated.*

SARAH: Don't just stand there. Hide.

SARAH *pulls* MIKENZIE *behind a rock.* MIKENZIE *is touched by* SARAH'S *concern.* NATHAN *and* DEBRA *enter. He has one of their bags under his arm. They are in the middle of a disagreement.*

NATHAN: But the Native Americans traded with settlers all the time.

DEBRA: These are regular farmers who know nothing about this show. Why would they want to trade food for our things?

NATHAN: I'll just try at the closest farm. I'll be back by dark.

DEBRA *still isn't happy with this. But stays silent as* NATHAN *leaves. She heads back to the tepee.* MARSHEL *and* MIKAL' *enter upstage left as* MIKENZIE *and* SARAH *come out of hiding.*

MIKENZIE: Thanks, Sarah.

The tension is obvious when the boys see SARAH. MIKENZIE *feels caught.* SARAH *understands and leaves quietly.* MARSHEL *watches her until she is gone.*

MARSHEL: Zee, we've been looking everywhere for you.

MIKENZIE: You said we were going to the pond so I went to the pond.

MARSHEL: No more screwing around. We've wasted a whole month not working as a team. This stops today. Agreed?

MIKAL': Agreed.

MIKENZIE: Did you know Dad's gone?

MARSHEL: Of course. That's why it's up to us to make this work. Obviously I'm team captain—

MIKENZIE: Big surprise.

MARSHEL: No more sarcasm. I've got the most experience on winning teams, and I'm the oldest, and I've made a plan of attack. Either of you guys have a plan?

MIKENZIE *and* MIKAL' *look at each other.* MIKENZIE *feels her book under her dress. She pulls together a little confidence and speaks up.*

MIKENZIE: Actually, Marshel, I've found some roots I think we can use for soup.

MARSHEL: Roots? You think we're going to win this on roots? It's gone way past that. What they've done to us isn't right. We've gotta stand up for us and our people. Right, Mikal'?

MIKAL' (*jumping up and down*): Right. Yeah!

MIKENZIE: Stop getting him all excited. What's the big plan?

MARSHEL (*excited*): This's sweet. We're gonna tax the water.

MIKAL: Huh?

MARSHEL: They come across our land to get to the pond, right?

MIKAL': Yeah.

MARSHEL: So we charge them. They want water, they gotta pay in food.

MIKENZIE: But we don't own the water.

MARSHEL: It's the frontier. You just claim it. (*Grand gesture to the pond.*) I hereby claim this water to belong to the Roubidoux family for eternity, or at least the next eight weeks. There. It's ours.

MIKENZIE: I guess so. But how do we get them to pay?

MARSHEL: That's the fun part. I've studied this area and made a bunch of battle plans in case they don't want to pay. There's only one good way to get to the pond, and with this tree and these rocks it's easy to defend.

MIKENZIE (*concerned*): We're gonna fight them?

MARSHEL: No. We'll encourage them that it's better to pay the tax.

The lights go dark.

Scene 2

Lights up on the empty clearing. LUKE *enters with water buckets.* MARSHEL *jumps up from behind a rock.*

MARSHEL: New rules. You want water, you gotta pay the water tax.

LUKE: Or else what?

MARSHEL: Glad you asked. Mike.

From the tree above MIKAL' *dumps a bucket of "water" on* LUKE. LUKE *sputters.*

LUKE: What was that for?

MARSHEL *bends over and picks up another bucket from behind a rock and holds it threateningly.* MIKENZIE *comes out from the tree behind* LUKE, *holding one of the water bags.*

MIKENZIE: You're surrounded. Give us some food, and you're free to get all the water you want.

LUKE: You can't do this.

MARSHEL: Yet we are. Got food or not?

LUKE *glares at* MARSHEL. MARSHEL *raises the bucket higher.* LUKE *pulls a sandwich from his pocket and throws it at* MARSHEL.

LUKE: It's wet now anyway. You'll be sorry for this.

MARSHEL: Thanks. Take your water, tell the others, and don't run to daddy. This is between us.

LUKE *fills his buckets quickly and storms off. The* ROUBIDOUX *kids laugh excitedly. The lights go out.*

Scene 3

The confession cam comes on-screen with MARSHEL *alone and very amped up.*

MARSHEL: I seriously didn't think it'd work this well, but with Dad gone, Mom's too busy to notice. It's been like two weeks already. See these? *(Points to lines on his tunic.)* One for each time we force them to pay. Like a real warrior.

Scene change

Early morning in the glen. NATHAN *strides across the stage carrying two of their supply bags.* DEBRA *rushes in after him.*

DEBRA: Going away for a day was one thing, but this—

NATHAN *stops.*

NATHAN: What I got from that farm helped, but it's not nearly enough. I've got to try other farms.

DEBRA: Leaving your family for days on end can't be the only way.

NATHAN: You're more than capable of taking care of things. Please, Debra, I got us into this mess, let me try to fix it.

DEBRA *gives up reluctantly.* NATHAN *touches her arm, then continues off.*

Scene 4
The lights come up on the pond. MARSHEL, MIKAL', *and* MIKENZIE *wait with their buckets.* MARSHEL *watches offstage.*

MARSHEL: Here she comes.

The kids spread out with MARSHEL *blocking the pond.* MIKENZIE *stands behind the boys trying to wave off the approaching target.* SARAH *enters unhappily. She doesn't make eye contact with anyone so misses* MIKENZIE'S *warning.* SARAH *silently hands a covered plate to* MARSHEL *and starts to move past him.*

MARSHEL: Wait. This isn't enough.
SARAH: Those cookies were the end of our sugar. There isn't any left for us either.
MARSHEL: What about the veggies you owe us?
SARAH: They aren't grown yet. I can't get anything else, Dad'll know.

She looks to MIKENZIE *for help.* MIKENZIE *looks away, guilty.*

MIKENZIE: Marshel, it's enough.
MARSHEL: No it's not. You want to go hungry again? (MIKENZIE *doesn't answer; to* SARAH.) Go get something else.

SARAH *doesn't know what to do. She turns and runs away.*

MIKENZIE: Come on, she's just a kid.
MARSHEL: She's one of them. You remember how they roped Mikal' and were going to let us starve?
MIKENZIE: Yes.

MARSHEL: You're with us or you're against us. *(Listening.)* Shhh? Hear that?

MIKAL': No.

MARSHEL: Someone's coming. Attack position three. Go.

MARSHEL *crosses the stage and hides behind a large tree trunk. He slides a long pole across the earth to a rock.* MIKAL' *grabs the other end of the pole and holds it on the ground while hiding behind the rock.* MIKENZIE *sighs and bends to fill a bucket from the pond. She changes her mind and scoops up mud from the edge of the pond into her bucket. She climbs into a tree that hangs over the edge of the pond just past the lodge pole on the ground. We hear whimpering offstage.* JONATHAN *strides onstage pulling the still upset* SARAH *after him.*

JONATHAN: I know you're here. *(No response.)* She brought cookies, even though I told her not to. Now we get our water. *(To* SARAH.*)* Give me the bucket.

SARAH *holds the bucket at arm's length toward him but doesn't move.* JONATHAN *grabs the bucket and moves to the pond. When he gets to the lodge pole,* MIKAL' *and* MARSHEL *stand quickly holding the pole.* JONATHAN *tries to jump out of the way, but the pole is too high and he trips and falls forward.* SARAH *screams and runs. Before anyone realizes what is happening,* JONATHAN *jumps up and grabs the lodge pole. He twists it hard pulling it out of* MIKAL'S *hands as he falls forward. Caught off guard, the pole hits* MARSHEL *in the side and slams him into the tree.*

MIKENZIE: Hey, creep!

JONATHAN *looks up as* MIKENZIE *dumps her bucket of mud in his face.* JONATHAN *drops the lodge pole and sputters to wipe off the mud.* MARSHEL *recovers and leaps at* JONATHAN, *shoving him hard.* MIKAL' *jumps onto* JONATHAN *from behind.* MARSHEL *pulls* MIKAL' *off.*

MARSHEL: Mikal', stop.

JONATHAN *takes advantage of the moment and dips a bucket of water before taking off.*

JONATHAN: You're dead!

MIKENZIE *scrambles out of her tree as* MARSHEL *stands* MIKAL' *up.*

MARSHEL: You OK?

MIKAL': Yeah, just ripped my hands up.

MIKENZIE: He seemed pretty mad.

MARSHEL: Not as mad as I am.

MIKAL': Me too.

MIKENZIE: This is getting dangerous. He could have hurt Mikal'.

MARSHEL: I know. *(Smiling.)* You seriously earned your first stripe, little bro.

MIKAL' *(proudly)*: I coulda taken him.

MIKENZIE: Marshel, don't encourage him. We need to try something else.

MARSHEL: It's too late. I'm pissed now.

Scene 5

The lights come up on the glen. MIKENZIE *cleans a pile of roots in the pond.* DEBRA *enters.*

DEBRA: Where are your brothers?

MIKENZIE: Being stupid somewhere. Am I in trouble again?

DEBRA: You're not in trouble. We just want you to be safe.

MIKENZIE: We're fine. *(Awkward silence.)* Do you want something?

DEBRA: I liked having you kids around the tepee, and now your father's gone. I just . . . I thought I'd come find you.

MIKENZIE: OK. Well, here I am.

MIKENZIE *goes back to cleaning her roots.* DEBRA *doesn't know what to do. She bends down and helps. As* DEBRA *handles the roots, memories come back to her.*

DEBRA: Where did you get these?

MIKENZIE: In the prairie. They're called prairie turnips.

DEBRA: Huta.

MIKENZIE: What?

DEBRA: That's what my grandmother called them. How did you know what they were?

MIKENZIE *considers her mother a moment, then pulls out her book and hands it to* DEBRA *reluctantly.* DEBRA *scans it.*

MIKENZIE: Sarah gave me this in the beginning. So I'm a big faker. I didn't figure out any of that stuff.

DEBRA *recognizes* MIKENZIE *sinking into her old sulk.*

DEBRA: You aren't a faker. You learned from this book like I learned from my grandmother. You aren't born knowing this.

MIKENZIE: Do you remember any of it?

DEBRA: Sort of. When I was growing up, I believed you could never be successful if they knew you were from a reservation. So I let it go, forgot. Fitting in was very important then.

MIKENZIE: It's pretty important now.

DEBRA: Yeah, I guess it is.

MIKENZIE *meets* DEBRA'S *eyes. As she studies her daughter, a new understanding passes between them.*

DEBRA: I should have found you sooner. I'm sorry.

MIKENZIE: It's OK. (*Takes her book back and finds a page.*) Do you know how to pronounce these words? I've been trying to teach myself a Dakota song, but I don't know if it's right.

DEBRA: I'm rusty, but I think we can figure it out together.

Mother and daughter look over the words. The lights fade to black.

Scene 6

Lights come up on the pond. MIKAL' *watches excitedly as* MARSHEL *puts an arrow in his bow and shoots it offstage.*

MIKAL': Cool! That one almost hit the tree!

MIKENZIE *hands a leather thong to* MIKAL'. *He carefully wraps it around an awl in his hand.* MIKENZIE *helps him tie a knot.* MARSHEL *is antsy.*

MIKENZIE: You have to dig your own bait. I don't do worms.
    Remember, we only fish for what we need and—
MIKAL': Thank the fish for giving us the food. Yeah, yeah. Look,
    Marshel, this is a great fishing pole, only without the pole.
MARSHEL: It's been days. Where are they?
MIKAL': Guess we scared them good, huh?
MARSHEL: I don't know. Something's up.
MIKENZIE: We can't sit here waiting for them twenty-four hours a
    day. We won't get anything else done.
MARSHEL: Jonathan won't give this up that easily, and neither will I.

MARSHEL *grabs his arrows and heads off.*

MIKENZIE: What are you going to do?
MARSHEL: I don't know. But a warrior would do something, not just
    wait. Watch Mikal'.

MARSHEL *storms off.* MIKAL' *practices casting his line.*

MIKENZIE: Boys. I don't get them.
MIKAL': I don't get girls either.
MIKENZIE *(smiles)*: That's fair. I'm going to get some more prairie
    turnips to go with your fish.
MIKAL': Say it in Indian.
MIKENZIE: It's Dakota, Mikal', not Indian. I only know "huta"; that
    means root.
MIKAL': It's so cool you're learning all this.

MIKENZIE: It's cool stuff. If we'd just work together like our ancestors did, we wouldn't need Rodney's old food.

MIKAL': Maybe if you told Dad . . .

MIKENZIE: You know how it is. Dad never listens to me. Marshel can have us stealing, and he doesn't even get in trouble.

MIKAL': I guess.

MIKENZIE: I'm going to do some digging.

MIKAL' (*worried*): Should I be left alone?

MIKENZIE: They haven't been around for days. I'll be right back.

She exits right. MIKAL' *looks around apprehensively. He digs for bait, then hears a noise. He jumps up.*

MIKAL' (*quietly*): Mikenzie?

MIKAL' *edges closer to a tree to hide.* LUKE *comes in from upstage left.*

LUKE: Looks like you're all alone, little Indian.

MIKAL' *turns and runs downstage left, toward home. Before he makes it off,* JONATHAN *jumps out and grabs him.* MIKAL' *screams for help.*

MIKAL': Zee!

JONATHAN: Hurry, tie him up.

LUKE *helps tie* MIKAL'.

LUKE: Where's Mikenzie?

MIKAL *stops yelling.*

JONATHAN (*shaking* MIKAL'): Keep calling her. (*Nothing.*) Whatever. Luke, scream like a girl, she won't know the difference.

LUKE (*in a high-pitched voice*): Zee, help me! Help!

MIKAL': I don't sound like that.

MIKENZIE *rushes back on.* LUKE *and* JONATHAN *burst out laughing.* MIKENZIE *freezes when she sees what's happening.*

LUKE: Guess you do.

MIKENZIE: What're you doing to him?

JONATHAN: Getting your attention.

MIKENZIE: You've got it. Let him go.

JONATHAN: We're settling this tonight. Tell your brother to be here right before sunset, when no one else is around. Just us.

MIKENZIE: OK, give me Mikal'.

JONATHAN: Nope, that's our insurance that you'll come back, alone.

MIKAL': You're keeping me all day?

LUKE *stuffs a rag into* MIKAL'S *mouth.* MIKENZIE *is shocked.*

MIKENZIE: Are you crazy? He's just a little kid.

LUKE: You're the crazy ones, stealing, throwing water all over me, attacking Jonathan—

MIKENZIE: We're sorry, it was stupid, but no one got hurt.

JONATHAN: Show up tonight. Don't follow us.

JONATHAN *and* LUKE *pull* MIKAL' *back through the trees.* MIKENZIE *rushes after them.*

MIKENZIE: Wait!

JONATHAN *turns to her and punches* MIKAL' *in the arm.* MIKAL' *pulls away; it really hurt.* MIKENZIE *freaks and runs at them.* JONATHAN *grabs her at arm's length and roughly tosses her to the ground. Before* MIKENZIE *can recover,* JONATHAN *holds his fist up, threatening to punch* MIKAL' *again.* MIKENZIE *is stunned. She stays on the ground as they retreat offstage. Once they are gone,* MIKENZIE *falls apart, crying.*

MIKENZIE: It's all my fault. Marshel's gonna kill me.

After a moment, MARSHEL *enters. His sister's distress scares him. He runs to her.*

MARSHEL: What's wrong? You hurt? Where's Mikal'?

MIKENZIE: I'm so sorry. I should have never left him.

MARSHEL: I told you to watch him. Where is he?

MIKENZIE: Jonathan and Luke kidnapped him and said we have to meet tonight or . . . I don't know what, but they hurt Mikal' and tied him up.

MARSHEL (*a steely anger rises to the surface*): They've gone too far.

MIKENZIE: He said no parents, but maybe we should tell.

MARSHEL: Tell them what? That we've gotten our six-year-old brother kidnapped?

MIKENZIE: But what if Mom notices Mikal' is gone?

MARSHEL: I'll get him back. Mom's clueless.

MIKENZIE: Because we don't tell her.

MARSHEL (*snaps*): A warrior takes care of his own business. They've taken our advantage, so we take it back.

The stage lights go black. The confession cam comes up on-screen. SARAH *sits alone looking nervous.*

SARAH (*whispering*): I can't tell you what Jonathan and Luke did, but it's bad. I took some food out to—what they did so that it wouldn't be as scary. Jonathan said this is all part of it, but this isn't right— (*Scared.*) Someone's out there. I'd better go so they don't think I tattled.

SARAH *steps out of the booth. We hear her scream, then silence.*

Scene 7

Sun sets on the glen. MARSHEL *and* MIKENZIE *are stashing something behind a tree.* MIKENZIE *looks really freaked.*

MIKENZIE: I'm sorry. (*To* MARSHEL.) This is all so messed up.

MARSHEL: We didn't have a choice. Be ready.

JONATHAN, *leading* MIKAL' *without his gag, and* LUKE *enter from the trees.* JONATHAN *looks really mad. They square off across from* MARSHEL *and* MIKENZIE.

JONATHAN: Give her back!
MARSHEL: Get her.
MIKENZIE: Marshel, I can't do it.

MARSHEL *backs away from* JONATHAN *and pulls* SARAH *out from behind the tree. She is tied like* MIKAL'. *Both captives seem really scared.*

MARSHEL: Now we're even. Just give us Mikal' and you can have Sarah.
JONATHAN: You can't blackmail us anymore. Give her back!
MARSHEL: No!

JONATHAN *doesn't know what else to do, so he holds* MIKAL' *in front of him and shakes him.*

MIKAL': Ow! Help!

Pissed, MARSHEL *reacts by doing the same to* SARAH. MIKENZIE *screams. All the kids yell on top of each other.*

KIDS: Stop! Give 'em back! You first! You started it! *(Etc.)*

JONATHAN *reacts and gives* MIKAL' *a hard shove, almost knocking him over.* MARSHEL *does the same almost instantly.* JONATHAN *grabs* MIKAL' *roughly and punches him. Without hesitating* MARSHEL *punches* SARAH *in the arm. She crumples in his grip.* JONATHAN *and* LUKE *completely freak.* JONATHAN *throws* MIKAL' *to the ground.* MARSHEL *does the same, then sees* JONATHAN *preparing to kick the defenseless boy.* MARSHEL *dives over* SARAH *and slams into* JONATHAN. *All the kids erupt into yelling as* MARSHEL *and* JONATHAN *roll into a fight. It's realistic, sloppy, fighting. They pull and push at each other and roll around until one of them breaks, and they scramble to their feet. The kids keep screaming as they go at it again. Surprisingly,* MARSHEL *starts to get the upper hand. He knocks* JONATHAN *off his feet and dives on top of him. They wrestle until* JONATHAN *tosses him off. Instead of attacking* MARSHEL, JONATHAN *crawls away as fast as he can.* MARSHEL *struggles to his feet and starts to go after him, when he realizes what* JONATHAN *is going toward.* MARSHEL *sees a rifle leaning against a tree.* MARSHEL *turns and runs back toward* MIKENZIE.

MARSHEL: Get down!

MIKENZIE *freezes. The other kids are still yelling.* MARSHEL *shoves* MIKENZIE *aside as he ducks behind the tree where they had kept* SARAH. JONATHAN *reaches his rifle, turns, and fires. The gun goes off with a deafening blast that silences everyone.* MARSHEL *comes from behind the tree with his bow and arrow. Before he can aim, he lets the arrow fly across the stage. The shot is wild, nowhere near the kids. The kids are all frozen in fear.* MARSHEL *and* JONATHAN *meet eyes for a moment. Then each one rushes to reload before the other.* MIKENZIE *realizes they are going to shoot again. As both boys take aim, she jumps between them and opens her mouth. The strong, haunting wail of a traditional Dakota song fills the stage. It's enough to break the moment. Both boys stop and stare at her.* MIKENZIE *keeps singing.*

MIKENZIE: He unkiyepi. He unkiyepi.
MARSHEL: What was that?

MIKENZIE *stops, suddenly self-conscious.*

MIKENZIE: A song Mom taught me. I didn't know what else to do.

RODNEY *and* DEBRA *rush in from stage left.* NATHAN *runs in from the right, carrying his bags.*

DEBRA: Nathan, what's going on?
NATHAN: I was on my way back and heard a shot—

DEBRA *sees* MIKAL' *and* SARAH *still bound. She's horrified.*

DEBRA: Oh my God! The children!

MIKENZIE *unties* MIKAL'. DEBRA *runs over to free* SARAH. RODNEY *grabs his daughter and makes sure she's OK. He turns back to* NATHAN *angrily.*

RODNEY: What did you do to my daughter?

JACK *finally rushes in all askew in a pair of lederhosen.*

JACK: Everything is under control.

NATHAN: I want answers, Jack.

RODNEY: So do I.

Everyone starts arguing again, each either defensive or horrified at all that has happened. Only MARSHEL *stands silent, still holding his bow.*

MIKENZIE: They started it by kidnapping Mikal'—

LUKE: You kidnapped Sarah!

MIKAL': You tied me up!

DEBRA: They kidnapped my son?

NATHAN (*to* JACK): You had to know this was happening.

JACK: It wasn't supposed to happen until later and the Heritage fest was going and . . .

The fighting grows, threatening to get out of control again. MARSHEL *jumps into the center of the melee and shoves everyone apart forcefully.*

MARSHEL: Shut up! Stop it. That's enough! (*Surprised, the group falls into a silent semicircle.*) Look at what we're doing to each other. For what? To get stuff? To win? I don't even know what that means anymore.

MARSHEL *sees his bow and holds it up.*

MARSHEL: But I do know that this isn't what being a warrior is about. *(He breaks the bow and tosses it in the pond.)* A warrior used to be about helping people and respect. Mikenzie has been trying to tell me that, but I didn't listen. If it wasn't for her . . . I don't know what would have happened. *(He puts his arm around her shoulders.)* I'm so proud of you.

MIKENZIE *is touched.* MARSHEL *forces himself to look at* SARAH. *He crosses to her carefully.*

MARSHEL: Sarah, all I can say is . . . I'm sorry.

RODNEY *steps in front of her protectively.* MARSHEL *steps back, ashamed.* SARAH *puts her hand on her dad's arm and moves past him.* RODNEY *starts to pull her back, but she waves him away gently.* SARAH *walks up to* MARSHEL *and touches his hand.*

SARAH: It's OK. You were scared for Mikal'.

MARSHEL *is amazed by her forgiveness. He kneels down to her level, emotional.*

MARSHEL: Thank you. I'll make it up to you somehow.

SARAH *nods. Everyone is moved.* RODNEY, JONATHAN, *and* LUKE *stand behind* SARAH, *proudly. The silence is broken by enthusiastic clapping from one set of hands.* JACK *steps forward.*

JACK *(still clapping)*: That was great! I mean really, it was amazing. What brave little girls. But could you do it again? I can't be in the shot. The lederhosen ruins the era. Is there another bow you could break? Maybe we could get the one out of the pond or—
NATHAN *(ignoring* JACK*)*: Come on, kids, we're going home, to Minneapolis.
JACK: Never mind, that was so incredible it won't matter.

NATHAN: My kids could have been killed today. I'll send you a check somehow. We're done.

NATHAN *and* DEBRA *gather their family;* JACK *steps in his way.*

JACK: I don't care about the money. After this, you're what people will want to watch! You're way more than *(half-hearted finger quotes)* average. Please, this could be a huge break for all of us.

NATHAN: That's not why I signed up for this.

JACK: Isn't it?

NATHAN: No. I signed us up because . . . I don't know. I have tried everything I know to be a husband and a father, but I've failed. I thought if I had the time out here, things would be different, but it's all the same.

NATHAN *turns away from everyone, defeated. No one knows what to say.*

MIKENZIE: You can't quit on us now. We need a dad.

NATHAN: I've been right here.

MIKENZIE: No. It's just like home. You're off doing your job thing, Mom's doing whatever she does, Marshel's the big jock, and I'm still . . . me.

MIKAL': What do I do?

MIKENZIE: You pretty much follow Marshel.

MIKAL': Oh, right.

MIKENZIE: But being a family is more than that. It's like we read in my book, right, Mom?

MIKENZIE *pulls her book out of her bag.* DEBRA *is cautious.*

DEBRA: You mean . . . mitakuya?

MIKENZIE: Yeah, mitakuya. It's how our ancestors lived. It's like a plan.

DEBRA *(realizing this could work)*: For how to be a family.

MIKENZIE *(opens her book)*: It's all right here. *(Reading.)* "Kinship: A way of living in respect for each other and how we are connected." I didn't really get this before, but we need parents and you need us.

MARSHEL: So this could work, right now?

MIKENZIE *looks to* DEBRA.

DEBRA: I feel like the crazy one, after all of this, but, Nathan, if we leave now, nothing has changed. Mitakuya is worth a try.

MARSHEL: Dad, you've got my word, no more fighting.

MIKAL': Yeah. It's no fun.

MARSHEL: We can't give up now. Not like this.

MIKENZIE: We want to do this, Dad.

NATHAN: But out here?

DEBRA *takes in the beauty around them.*

DEBRA: Yes. I can't think of a better place to start. *(Smiles.)* Come on, Nate, are you with me?

NATHAN *(smiles back)*: I'm going to need a lot of help.

NATHAN *pulls his family into a hug.*

NATHAN: Thank you. *(To* RODNEY.*)* Rodney, I'm sorry this got so out of hand.

RODNEY: Yeah. *(Puts his hands on* SARAH's *shoulders.)* It won't happen again. You have my word. *(*NATHAN *and* RODNEY *exchange a nod.)* Well . . . back to the competition.

NATHAN: I guess so. See you at the finish.

RODNEY: Come on, kids. We've got work to do.

RODNEY *ushers his clan offstage.*

Scene 8

Confession cam comes on the screen. MIKENZIE *sits alone looking like a different girl. Her edginess is gone, but she's still a girl with depth.*

MIKENZIE: I can't believe it's almost over. We've figured out so
   much. Like Mom thinks of something, then Dad adds to it, then
   me or the boys, and soon we really are the Rockin' Roubidouxs.
   (She becomes a little sad.) But we never see the Monroes anymore.
   It's like they're not even here. It'll be weird going back to the
   real world. I mean, I'll probably still be Freak Face, but it's like
   I don't care. It's just a stupid name. *(Thinks.)* OK, I'll care, but at
   least I know that's not all I am. I'm a sister and a daughter, and
   that's cool. And I even almost had a friend.

*The screens go dark. Stage lights come up on a beautiful late-summer day
in the glen. The screens show waving, amber grass. Strips of fish dry on
poles around a fire pit. The* ROUBIDOUX *family adds the last bundles of
food and goods to a large pile in the middle. Everyone is excited.* DEBRA
*carries a rough woven basket. She gathers the drying food and adds the
basket to the pile.*

MARSHEL: I think this is everything.

High fives all around. The family is proud of their accomplishment.

DEBRA: I can't believe it's so much.
MIKAL': We're going to win for sure.
NATHAN: When Jack counts up the goods tomorrow, he's going to be
   impressed.
MARSHEL: Do you really think we've won?
NATHAN: I took a walk by the Monroes' today, and I'd say it's almost
   for sure.
MIKAL': We get an RV!
DEBRA: I'm proud of all of you.
NATHAN: But the important thing is what we've become as a family.
DEBRA: I'm so grateful your crazy idea helped us find our way.

DEBRA *and* NATHAN *kiss.* MIKENZIE *studies her happy family.*

MIKENZIE: Are you really grateful?

DEBRA: Yes, of course.

MIKENZIE: Then shouldn't we show it? I mean what did we come here for? To win or to learn something?

MARSHEL: Well, the winning doesn't hurt.

MIKENZIE: But it's like we read in the book. If our ancestors were grateful for something, they showed it.

NATHAN (*concerned*): You don't mean—

MIKAL': What?

MARSHEL (*realizes*): Oh, man. I don't know if I can.

MIKAL': Man, what?

DEBRA (*hesitant*): It is the traditional way.

NATHAN: Yes, but . . .

MIKAL': But what?!

The lights go dark.

Scene 9

The lights come up on the glen. Two piles are in the middle of the stage with JACK and his podium between. Even the tepee is pulled down and stacked neatly on the pile. The families stand by their piles. The ROUBIDOUXS' is larger. RODNEY isn't happy.

JACK: What a summer, but we made it to the finish line! All that's left is determining our winner!

RODNEY: If they get to count their tepee, I want credit for the wood that the cabin's made out of. We cut that ourselves.

JONATHAN: This isn't fair.

MIKAL': Just wait, you'll like it.

JACK: Can we get on with it?

NATHAN: We have gotten so much on this journey.

JACK: That's nice.

DEBRA: We have one more thing to do before this game is over.

NATHAN *takes out a handmade drum and starts to beat it slowly.*

Sarah (Elaine Patterson) is given a dress by Mikenzie (Raven Bellefleur) as a token of honor. Photograph by Rob Levine.

MIKENZIE: The Dakota have a ceremony called a giveaway.

DEBRA *hands a beautiful dress to* MARSHEL.

MARSHEL: We use it to honor someone we are grateful for.

MARSHEL *hands it to* MIKAL' *who hands it to* MIKENZIE.

MIKENZIE: Sarah Monroe, we want to thank you for showing us how to be better people and a normal family. And for being a good friend.

MIKENZIE *hands the dress to* SARAH. *She is stunned.* MIKAL' *picks up a stack of dried fish and hands it to* RODNEY. *He takes it, confused.*

RODNEY: These are gifts?

MARSHEL *hands a bow and arrow to* JONATHAN.

MARSHEL: All of it. We show how much we have gotten by how much we give away.

MIKAL' *hands a basket to* JACK.

JACK: That doesn't make any sense.
MIKAL': I felt the same way, but once you do it, it feels better.
SARAH: If you give everything away, you won't win.

MARSHEL *picks up a small drum and hits it in double time to* NATHAN'S *beat.*

MIKENZIE (*smiles*): Trust me, we've won already.

She looks to her family. DEBRA *puts her arm around* MIKENZIE *reassuringly. Suddenly* MARSHEL *bursts into Dakota song.* NATHAN *sings counter to his son.* MIKENZIE, DEBRA, *and* MIKAL' *continue to distribute all of their items. From around the auditorium more drums join the beat. Voices join and counter* MARSHEL'S *song from all corners, flooding the auditorium with sound as the* ROUBIDOUXS *continue their giveaway until there is nothing left. Finally the* ROUBIDOUXS *come together in a family hug. Everyone joins in the singing until the final beat of the drums reverberates through the theatre and the lights go black. After the applause we hear* RODNEY'S *voice from the darkness.*

RODNEY: Wait, so we get the RV, right?

THE END

Marshel (Noah Kol Balfour), Nathan (Steven Monés), Mikal' (Jack Wyatt Jue), and Mikenzie Roubidoux (Raven Bellefleur) play the drums in a Dakota giveaway ceremony. Photograph by Rob Levine.

BROOKLYN BRIDGE

Melissa James Gibson

Directed by Daniel Aukin
Featuring the song "Wire Wings" by Barbara Brousal

The world premier of *Brooklyn Bridge* opened on January 21, 2005, at Children's Theatre Company, Minneapolis, Minnesota. *Brooklyn Bridge* was developed through a collaboration with New Dramatists funded by the Jerome Foundation and produced in association with AT&T: Onstage administered by Theatre Communications Group.

CREATIVE TEAM
Scenic design: Louisa Thompson
Costume design: Maiko Matsushima
Lighting design: Matt Frey
Sound design: Victor Zupanc and Chris Heagle
Dramaturgy: Elissa Adams
Ensemble codirector: Matthew Howe
Stage manager: Kathryn Sam Loftin
Assistant stage manager: Erin Tatge

CAST

SASHA	Emily Zimmer
SAM	Neil Dawson
TRUDI and VOICE OF TEACHER	Angela Timberman
JOHN	Steve Hendrickson
TALIDIA	Susanna Guzman
SINGER/SONGWRITER	Barbara Brousal
MUSICIAN and WORKER	Robert Beahen
MUSICIAN, MAIL CARRIER, and WORKER	Jen Scott
SHADOWY FIGURE	Hillary Bertran-Harris
OTHER SHADOWY FIGURE	Rebecca Lord
PIZZA DELIVERY MAN, WORKER, and CIVILIAN	Damian Robinson

WASHINGTON ROEBLING and WORKER Benjamin Hanna
EMILY ROEBLING and WORKER Emily Van Siclen
WORKER and CIVILIAN ENSEMBLE Celeste J. Busa, Erin
Nicole Hampe, Theo
Langason, Jessie Slagle,
Katie Weber, Jessica
Miano, and Anna
Richert

CHARACTERS

SASHA

SAM

TRUDI

JOHN

TALIDIA

SINGER/SONGWRITER

MAN WITH BASS

MAN WITH DRUMS

MAIL CARRIER

PIZZA DELIVERY MAN

WASHINGTON ROEBLING

EMILY ROEBLING

Scene 1

The Brooklyn Bridge, floating in space. Then, hallways, apartment doors, stairs, windows, a front stoop, a fire escape, a roof, and an elevator stuck between floors become visible in the foreground, thereby placing the bridge in perspective. As with an Advent calendar, five tenants of the building are suddenly visible standing in their respective windows. Just as suddenly, the tenants and the bridge are gone. (The building [and the bridge as its elements are gradually introduced] should probably be represented through architectural bare bones—steel and pipes and cables—as much as possible.)

Scene 2

Offstage sound of the bell ringing at the end of class and of kids leaving the classroom.

TEACHER (*voice-over, over the noise*):

> Don't forget your New York City research papers
> > are due *tomorrow*
> No excuses
> No twenty-four hour flus
> No dogs ingesting homework

The noise starts to die down as most of the kids have left the classroom.

TEACHER (*voice-over*): Sasha, I *will* have a completed New York City research paper from you tomorrow, riiiight (*Slight pause.*) Does that not noncommittal movement of the head mean yes
SASHA (*tiny voice-over*): Mmhmm
TEACHER (*voice-over*): Good

SASHA *starts to leave the room.*

TEACHER (*voice-over*): Oh, and Sasha, remind me of the subject of your New York City research paper
SASHA (*tiny voice-over*): The Brooklyn Bridge.
TEACHER (*voice-over*): Pardon
SASHA (*slightly less tiny voice-over*): The Brooklyn Bridge.
TEACHER (*voice-over*): Pardon
SASHA (*slightly too loud voice-over*): The Brooklyn Bridge.

Scene 3

SASHA, *a girl of ten, appears. She walks in a tilted-forward fashion, propelled by the weight of the enormous book bag she carries on her back. Throughout the following, as* SASHA *moves through the building its sounds are amplified (not in a fee-fi-fo-fum way; rather, the amplification should reflect what happens when one focuses on the sounds that surround us at all times). We watch as she ascends the steps to her apartment building's stoop. She inserts one of the keys hanging from her neck into the outside door's lock, checks the mail—it hasn't arrived— and trudges to the elevator. She presses the button, realizes the elevator is out of order* AGAIN, *and trudges up two flights of stairs. She walks to her apartment door, inserts another of the keys hanging from her neck into the lock, and then another and another into the other two locks, and enters her apartment. After she has crossed the threshold, she turns around three times and then falls backward onto the floor from the weight of her book bag. The phone rings.* SASHA *checks the clock. She extricates herself from the clutches of her book bag and picks up the phone; she speaks into it immediately, without waiting to hear the caller identify herself, as she knows who's calling. During the above, the* SINGER/SONGWRITER *begins to work on a song in her apartment. During the following,* SASHA *looks around for a writing implement.*

SASHA: Hi mom

Sorry

Hi *mamochka*

Yes

I came straight home

Yes

I turned three times

Yes

I locked the door

No

I won't go out

Yes

I'll eat what's there

No

there wasn't mail

Yes

I spent it all

Yes

of course it's done

Yes

I'm sure I'm sure I'm sure I'm sure I'm sure I'm sure

Do you know what happened to all our pens

Pens

Pens as in

No I looked there

No I looked there

No I looked there

Nevermind

I'll talk to you later

Bye *mamochka*

SASHA *hangs up the phone. Slight pause.*

SASHA: Uh-oh

SASHA *goes to her book bag and begins to look for a pen. As she does so,*
she removes book after book after book after book after book. Finally,
she reaches the bottom of her book bag and comes up with a . . . fuchsia
crayon, which she casts aside. She turns over her book bag and shakes
it. Nothing. She riffles through various as yet unchecked piles in her
disorganized foyer—clearly, both she and her mother are bibliophiles, as
their apartment is jammed with books and newspapers in both English
and Russian. Underneath a particularly thick volume she comes up with
a . . . huge thick permanent green marker. She tosses the marker aside, too.
Then, from across the room she spies, resting on a shelf—could it be?—a
pen! She rushes over and grabs the pen, tests it on a nearby newspaper and
discovers that it is out of ink. She throws the pen over her shoulder.

SASHA: Uh-oh

For this next section, SASHA *engages in a dance of sorts, comprised of*
the actions listed below, but whose engine is a deep ambivalence made
up of equal parts of fear of the unknown and fear of the known: mom.
SASHA *thinks,* SASHA *paces,* SASHA *thinks and paces.* SASHA *moves to*

the door, SASHA *moves away from the door.* SASHA *unlocks all the locks.*
SASHA *opens the door,* SASHA *closes the door.* SASHA *opens the door, steps
into the hall, and then runs back into her apartment and locks all the
locks.* SASHA *unlocks the door again, moves into the hall, walks up to
a neighbor's door and raises her hand to knock.* SASHA *moves her hand
away and then up again, away and then up again, away and then up
again. The above is unwittingly scored by another section of the* SINGER/
SONGWRITER'S *song in progress.* SASHA *knocks on the neighbor's door,
and all sound stops. Silence, then we hear footsteps approach the door.
The door opens quickly and all the way. Standing in the doorway is a
tall West Indian man with long dreads—*SAM. SAM *speaks with a thick
Caribbean accent.*

SASHA: Hi
SAM: Hi
SASHA: Hi
SAM: Hi
SASHA: Hi
SAM: Hi
SASHA: Hi
SAM: Are we going to be doing this for a long time, because I could
    get us some chairs
SASHA: I'm Sasha I live over there
SAM: I'm Sam I live here
SASHA: Hi
SAM: Hi
SASHA: Hi
SAM: Hi
SASHA: Hi
SAM: Is this a local custom I'm just now finding out about
SASHA: I'm looking for a pen but I'm not supposed to
SAM: You're not supposed to look for a pen
SASHA: I'm not supposed to leave the apartment
SAM (*hmmm*): Hmmm
SASHA (*what does hmmm mean*): Hmmm

SAM (*hmmm*): Hmmm

SASHA (*uh-oh*): Hmmm

SAM: This is what's known as a predicament

SASHA (*is it*): It is

SAM (*it is*): It is

SASHA (*I knew it*): It is (*what's a predicament*) What's a predicament

SAM: Well, you're not supposed to leave your apartment

SASHA: No

SAM: But you did leave your apartment

SASHA: Yes

SAM: And you do need a pen

SASHA: Yes

SAM: And if you were to turn around right now and go back into your apartment you will have both broken a rule *and* failed to find a pen

SASHA: Yes

SAM: So I think the only way for us to address this predicament is to make your behavior Bad But Successful

SASHA (*a new thought*): Bad But Successful

SAM: So let me go see if I have a pen

SASHA: Okay

As SAM *goes off in search of a pen,* SASHA *holds the door open with her foot. Suddenly a cat escapes from* SAM'S *apartment.*

SASHA: Uh-oh. (*To* SAM.) Uh, Sam . . .

SAM: She's Red

SASHA: Excuse me

SAM: My cat's name is Red

SASHA: She's gray

SAM *retrieves the cat and pets her for a moment before putting her down inside the apartment.*

SAM: She wishes she were red

SASHA: Oh. Did you find a pen

SAM: I had a pen

SASHA: Had

SAM: Last night at school

SASHA: You go to school

SAM: I'm studying to be a dentist

SASHA *instinctively recoils.*

SAM: Don't worry, I'm not a dentist *yet*. I drive a cab

SASHA: I never get to take cabs

SAM: The subway's significantly safer, believe me

SAM'S *cat escapes from the apartment again.* SAM *retrieves her and pets her for a moment before putting her down inside the apartment.*

SASHA: Why do you want to be a dentist

SAM: Ah I can tell you view dentistry in a negative light and you are not alone There's no question the profession has a PR problem of major proportions Major proportions I keep trying to enlist my classmates in my cause I want to change people's philosophy and get them to view the dentist/patient relationship this way (*Gestures as if reading a large sign.*) Together We Are Building A Smile

SASHA (*Together We Are Building A What*): Together We Are Building A Smile

SAM: I'm having T-shirts made up

SASHA: So Sam it seems you're saying that you don't have a pen

SAM: Last night I was taking a test on the typical progression of molar decay

SASHA: What's that

SAM: Do you like horror stories

SASHA: No

SAM: Then you don't want to know It was a hard test and I chewed on the end of my pen until it began to leak and I was forced to throw it out

SASHA: Oh

SAM: And of course at my school they knock off a whole letter grade if they catch you chewing on your pen

SASHA: That's terrible

SAM: Not as terrible as the damage chewing on your pen does to your upper central cuspids

SASHA: Upper central cuspids

SAM: Your front teeth

SAM: Sasha

SASHA: Yes

SAM: Why do you need a pen

SASHA: My fifth-grade research paper is due tomorrow

SAM: What's a fifth-grade research paper

SASHA: It's a lower-middle-school assignment of milestone proportions

SAM: So it's like a comprehensive exam on periodontal tissue graft

SASHA: I guess

SAM: That's major What's the subject of your research paper

SASHA: The Brooklyn Bridge

SAM: That one over there

SASHA: There's only one as far as I know

SAM: Someone tried to sell it to me when I first came to this country

SASHA: For how much

SAM: Three million

SASHA: That's a lot of money

SAM: On the contrary in my country three million is equivalent to roughly ninety-five dollars so I thought it was a pretty good deal What have you written about the Brooklyn Bridge

SASHA: You mean so far

SAM: Yes

SASHA: Nothing

SAM: Nothing

SASHA: Nothing

SAM: But I thought you said your middle-school assignment of milestone proportions was due tomorrow

SASHA: I HAVEN'T BEEN ABLE TO FIND A PEN HAVE I I'm sorry I yelled I don't yell

SAM: This subject seems to be for you what we call in my profession
a tender region

SASHA: It's not that I haven't done research

I've read every book there is

I know everything there is to know about the Brooklyn
Bridge

SAM: So what's the problem

SASHA: I don't know where to begin

I don't know where to end

I don't know where to middle

SASHA *looks as if she is about to cry. At this moment the woman we will later know as* TRUDI *exits her apartment, checks her watch, then reenters her apartment. At the same time the* SINGER/SONGWRITER *composes the first two lines of her song, writing down the lyrics after she sings each line.*

SINGER/SONGWRITER *(sung)*:

Sheltered by its wire wings

They come with offerings

SINGER/SONGWRITER *(said)*: Hmmm

SAM *(please don't cry)*: I bet I know something you don't know about
the Brooklyn Bridge

SASHA *(it's not as if I want to cry)*: Well excuse me if this sounds
egotistical Sam but I very much doubt that

SAM: Okay What's the best way to drive across the Brooklyn Bridge

SASHA: In a car of course

SAM: Yes but how

SASHA: I don't understand the question

SAM *acts out the following.*

SAM: At the bottom of the ramp on the Manhattan side there's a
pothole the size of Montana so you need to stay left but then
you immediately encounter a buckling steel road cable that
necessitates a veer to the right which brings you to the center lane

which is fine for all of three seconds when you hit a pave-ment
dip that makes you have to swerve left again and then without even
time to remove a hand from the steering wheel you encounter
some deadly serious roadway rutting so that you're forced to go
left right left right center left right left which brings you to the
Brooklyn ramp where you are greeted with no option but to take
the first exit if you want to avoid replacing your shock absorbers
directly after driving off the Bridge Did you know that Sasha

SASHA: No

SAM: Maybe you could put that in your research paper

SASHA: I don't think it would go

SAM: What's the paper about

SASHA: I told you the Brooklyn Bridge

SAM: Yes but what *about* the Brooklyn Bridge

SASHA: Just stuff

SAM: Stuff

SASHA: THINGS
          DETAILS
          STUFF LIKE THAT
          JUST STUFF
          I'm sorry I yelled I don't yell

SAM: So you said Can your parents help you with your paper

SASHA: My mother works nights

SAM: What about your dad

SASHA: He's not here

SAM: Oh

SASHA: He's away on Business

Slight pause in which SASHA *regards* SAM *regarding* SASHA *with
compassion.*

          I can take care of myself
          I can take care of myself
SAM: Okay
          Okay

Slight pause.

> How long have you lived here

SASHA: In New York or this building

SAM: Both

SASHA: All my life

SAM: How long is all your life

SASHA: Ten years six months and seventeen hours

A plaintive meow.

SAM: I'm coming, Red. She's hungry

SASHA: How long is all your life

SAM: I've stopped counting in hours put it that way

SASHA: Wow

SAM: How long has it been since you've seen a dentist

SASHA *covers her teeth tightly with her lips.*

SAM: I was only going to offer to clean your teeth

SASHA: Thanks but my mom would notice right away if my teeth
looked cleaner and I'm pretty sure I'm not allowed to get my
teeth cleaned when she's not at home

An impatient meow.

SAM: Good luck with your pen and paper

SASHA: Enjoy your dinner Red

SAM: Bye

SASHA: Bye

SAM: Bye

SAM *starts to close his door.*

SASHA: Bye

SAM: Bye

SAM'S *door is closed.* SASHA *stands there for a moment looking at it, looking very alone.*

SASHA: Bye
           I can take care of myself

She heads back toward her door just as the silence is filled once more with the sound of the SINGER/SONGWRITER *working on her song.* SASHA *listens.*

SINGER/SONGWRITER *(sung)*:
           A long list of wishes and dreams
           Is left here by the sea

The SINGER/SONGWRITER *writes down these new lyrics.*

   Meanwhile, the doors to the elevator (which has been stuck between the basement and first floor) suddenly open, and inside we see the interior of a caisson, an airtight chamber employed in the construction of the underwater portions of the bridge's towers. Several men dig with shovels and pickaxes. The mud on the bottom is thick and the rock beneath it hard. The only light source is a calcium lamp. The only sounds are of the implements in use and the men's exertion.

   The flashback ends abruptly, and SASHA *still hears the music from the floor above. She crosses to the stairwell and starts up stairs. By the time she is about to put her foot on the landing,* SAM *enters from his apartment. The music stops, and* SASHA'S *trance is broken.* SASHA *regards her foot, which is still hanging midair.*

SAM: Going upstairs to look for a pen
SASHA *(putting her foot down)*: I don't go upstairs
SAM: Why not
SASHA: I don't wish to discuss it
SAM: Why not
SASHA: Where are you going
SAM: Red is blue
SASHA: Red is gray actually

SAM: No Red is blue
               by which I mean
               she's sad

Meow of sorrow.

               We've run out of cat food so
               I'm going to get more
               Are you afraid to go upstairs
SASHA: I told you
               I don't discuss it
SAM: Red's afraid to go up those stairs
SASHA (*great relief*): She is (*amended to*) I mean (*clinical interest*)
    She is
SAM: Makes it easier to catch her when she slips out the door (*Loud
    whisper.*) Don't tell her I told you but she's an archetypal 'fraidy cat

Meow of protest.

SASHA (*guard down*): Maybe there's something scary on the fourth
    floor (*guard up*) to her
SAM: The fourth floor is exactly like the third floor is exactly like the
    second floor
SASHA: The tenants aren't all the same Maybe a larger-than-fairy-
    tale giant lives on the fourth floor
SAM: You think a larger-than-fairy-tale giant lives on the fourth floor
SASHA: I DON'T BUT IT SOUNDS LIKE YOUR CAT DOES
               I'm sorry I yelled I never used to yell
SAM: You think a giant lives up there
SASHA: Ten-year-six-month-and-seventeen-and-a-half-hour-
    year-olds do not believe in giants
SAM: But cats do
SASHA: Red probably hears footsteps
               Early in the morning and late at night Red probably
               hears footsteps that are *so* incredibly heavy *so* incredibly

> textbook mythical they could *only* be the footsteps of a
> fourth-floor larger-than-fairy-tale giant

SAM: Do you hear footsteps like that Sasha

SASHA: That's a second thing I don't discuss

Mournful meow.

SAM: I'd better get to the store
          Need anything

SASHA *(rote)*: I'm fine

*SASHA walks into her apartment as SAM walks down the stairs. A few
seconds after SASHA closes her door, she reopens it, runs to the stairwell
and yells.*

SASHA: I mean YES
            I NEED A PEN

*Alas, we are watching SAM exit the building as SASHA calls; he doesn't
hear. SASHA turns to reenter her apartment just as the music starts once
more, the SINGER/SONGWRITER trying another variation. SASHA is again
entranced, and this time slowly walks up the flight of stairs to the floor*

**The Singer/Songwriter
(Barbara Brousal) in
the apartment above
works on her song
during the world
premiere of *Brooklyn
Bridge* by Melissa
James Gibson in 2005.
Photograph by Rob
Levine.**

above. She follows the sound down the hall, trying to figure out from which specific apartment the music is emanating. After approaching several doors, SASHA *finally identifies the right one.*

SINGER/SONGWRITER (*sung*):
>   Take a moment

The SINGER/SONGWRITER *writes down this new lyric, taking a moment to figure out the rest of it.*

SINGER/SONGWRITER (*sung*):
>   there's a perfect view
>   *(A different note.)*
>   view
>   *(A third note—the right one.)*
>   view

Just then, thunderous footsteps are heard approaching the door next to where SASHA *stands.* SASHA *gasps, as she realizes she has unwittingly brought herself to the floor on which the giant resides.* SASHA *starts to take a step in the direction of the stairway, but suddenly the giant's apartment door swings open, and standing in the doorway is, in fact, the giant, except it turns out the giant is a very tiny and impeccably dressed businesswoman.*

SASHA: (*gasp*)

*The tiny giant woman (*TRUDI*) assumes from* SASHA'S *reaction that an ax murderer is standing behind her, so she, too, emits a*

TRUDI: (*gasp*)

which causes SASHA *to run partway down the hall, only to stop in a there's-nowhere-to-run pose, punctuated by another*

SASHA: *(gasp)*

which causes TRUDI *to do the same, also punctuated by a*

TRUDI: *(gasp)*

which causes SASHA *to make yet another Jackson Five movement accompanied by a*

SASHA: *(gasp)*

which causes TRUDI *to once again do what* SASHA *did, accompanied by a*

TRUDI: *(gasp)*

only to recall her identity as the grown-up of the situation, which inspires her to ask a grown-up question.

TRUDI: Wait
           Why are we doing this

SASHA *is staring at* TRUDI'S *feet.*

SASHA: You're not a giant
TRUDI: You're not so tall yourself
SASHA: I meant it as a compliment
TRUDI: I'll take you at your word for you are young
           Why are you staring at my feet
SASHA: No reason
           Do you um live alone
TRUDI: Yes why do you ask
SASHA: No reason *(Sasha looks up suddenly.)* Do you um have a pen
TRUDI *(makes a writing gesture)*: A pen
SASHA: Yes
TRUDI: I'm in a hurry

SASHA: You don't carry pens when you're in a hurry

TRUDI: Is that slightly veiled sarcasm

SASHA: What's slightly veiled sarcasm

TRUDI: It's when you say something snotty while pretending it's the
farthest thing from snotty

SASHA: You mean like teenager language

TRUDI: Grown-ups speak it fluently too

SASHA (*trying not to get upset again*): I wasn't trying to be unsnottily
snotty I just really Really REALLY need a pen and anyway I
shouldn't even be asking you because I'm not supposed to have
any strange talk

TRUDI (*What the heck is*): Strange Talk

SASHA: My mother's English isn't so great That's how she says

SASHA and TRUDI: Don't Talk to Strangers

TRUDI: Well I'm sorry about your troubles but
           I have troubles of my own
           For instance I can't be late
           I'm on probation as it is

SASHA: Late for what

TRUDI *suddenly makes another there-must-be-an-ax-murderer-
standing-right-behind-me gesture.*

TRUDI: OH-NO-AM-I-LATE

Sasha responds with an in-kind gesture.

SASHA: I don't know
           When are you supposed to be where you're supposed to be

Trudi consults her wristwatch.

TRUDI: I have a board meeting
           and I purposely walked out my door forty-five minutes
           early because of my recently diagnosed condition

SASHA: What's your recently diagnosed condition

TRUDI: It's called *Sensus Lackus Ofus Timus,* which means I have a
tendency to lose track of time

SASHA: But we've only been standing here for a minute or two

TRUDI *consults the wristwatch on her other arm.*

TRUDI: Of course we have
That's *quite right*
You needed a pen

TRUDI *begins looking through her purse.*

SASHA: What's your job
TRUDI: I move money
SASHA: You mean with a van or something
TRUDI: Oh no I don't *touch* the money
I just move it

*(Trudi empties out her purse onto the floor, still looking for a pen.
We should notice several timepieces among her purse's contents.)*

SASHA: Sounds confusing
TRUDI: No
boring
SASHA: Is that why they call it a board meeting
No wonder you're running late

TRUDI *is once again terribly alarmed.*

TRUDI: WHAT TIME IS IT
SASHA: About a minute after the last time you checked
TRUDI: That's right and I left my apartment seventeen minutes
early so let's all just try to stay calm shall we
Why do you need a pen
SASHA: I have a research paper due
TRUDI: What's it about

SASHA: Do you really want to know or are you just making
    conversation
TRUDI: Both
          I'm a New Yorker
SASHA: The Brooklyn Bridge
TRUDI: The Brooklyn Bridge
          I love the Brooklyn Bridge
          I jog across it every morning

For the first time since she initially left her apartment TRUDI *lifts a foot
to take a step.* SASHA *experiences this moment in slow motion; as* TRUDI
raises her foot, SASHA *covers her ears in preparation for the explosive
footstep. When* TRUDI *lowers her foot to the ground, however, there is no
noticeable thump.*

SASHA: Do you um wear wooden clogs when you're at home
TRUDI: No why
SASHA: No reason
TRUDI: So you're writing a paper about the Brooklyn Bridge
          What *about* the Brooklyn Bridge
SASHA: I
          DON'T
          KNOW
          I'm sorry I yelled I've recently turned into a yeller
          For me this is what's known among students of dentistry
              as a tender region
TRUDI: Oh
          Well
          is your paper about the Brooklyn Bridge's construction
          Is it about that father-son team who designed and built it
          What was their name
TRUDI and SASHA: Roebling
SASHA: Kind of
TRUDI: Is it about how it forever changed the lives of the inhabitants
    of the boroughs of Manhattan and Brooklyn

SASHA: In a way

TRUDI: You haven't started have you

SASHA (*suddenly upset*): No

TRUDI (*you mean*): Nothing nada nyet zippo

SASHA: Well I've done the research part
           I just need to do the paper part

TRUDI: When's it due

SASHA: Soonish

TRUDI: Tomorrowish

SASHA: Yesish

TRUDI: We've got to find you a pen before it's too late

TRUDI *suffers another panic attack.*

TRUDI: WAIT A SECOND

SASHA *is drawn into* TRUDI'S *panic attack.*

SASHA: What

TRUDI: It's not tomorrow yet is it

SASHA: No and as long as it's today I'm quite sure it will not be
    tomorrow

TRUDI: Right you are So
           tell me about the Brooklyn Bridge

SASHA: Why

TRUDI: Practice
           It'll be like a verbal rough draft

SASHA: Aren't you in a hurry

TRUDI: Yes but I left my house an hour and a half early so I still have
    time to hear you speak about the Brooklyn Bridge *and* make it
    to my board meeting on time

SASHA *clears her throat. She opens her mouth as if to speak but nothing
comes out. She paces. She stops.*

SASHA (*a very long sentence for four words*): The Brooklyn Bridge is

SASHA *paces some more. She stops.*

SASHA (*a very short sentence for six words*):
> a third thing I don't discuss
> plus
> my mother would be very upset if she knew we were
> having
> this
> strange talk
> plus
> I'm not allowed to leave the apartment this late

Meanwhile, TRUDI *has fallen asleep;* TRUDI *snores loudly and wakes herself up.*

TRUDI: UH-OH-WHAT-TIME-IS-IT-AM-I-LATE
SASHA: I'm not wearing a watch
TRUDI: And all of mine seem to have stopped
> What's your name
SASHA: Sasha
TRUDI: That's Russian
SASHA: That's right
TRUDI: Sasha
SASHA: Yes
TRUDI: We need to go up to the roof
SASHA: We do
TRUDI: We do
> We need to check the time on the clock of the
> Williamsburgh Savings Bank
SASHA: We do
TRUDI: I have to be on time for my board meeting Sasha
> Did I mention that I'm already on
TRUDI and SASHA: probation

SASHA *and* TRUDI *climb the flights of stairs to the roof. They converse as they climb.*

TRUDI: And after we check the time on the clock of the Williamsburgh
      Savings Bank you need to go buy yourself a pen
SASHA: I can't
TRUDI: Why not
SASHA: My mother doesn't give me Leeway Money
TRUDI: Leeway Money
SASHA: Just In Case Money
TRUDI: Oh Just In Case Money
SASHA: Every spare cent goes to my college fund
TRUDI: But what if something comes up
SASHA: You mean like an Unforeseen Crisis
TRUDI: Yes
SASHA: I'm not allowed to have Unforeseen Crises

At the same time, SAM *reenters the building and climbs the stairs to the third floor with cat food. At the same time, the man we will come to know as* JOHN *wheels out into the hallway in his wheelchair and leaves an empty pizza box. He reenters his apartment. At the same time, the* SINGER/SONGWRITER *da-da-das to an upbeat riff on her theme.* TRUDI *takes* SASHA'S *arm and leads her over to the side of the building from which the Williamsburgh Savings Bank building is visible.*

TRUDI: What time is it
           in your opinion
SASHA: It's five after six
TRUDI: In your opinion
SASHA: I would say it's five after six
           in most people's opinion
           unless you live in Australia or something
TRUDI: Okay
           Phew
SASHA *(you're going to be late, aren't you)*: You'll still be on time

TRUDI: I have lots and lots of time

SASHA: Would you like to say hi to my mom

TRUDI: Does she live on the roof

SASHA: Of course not
          She lives with me in an apartment below a fourth-floor
          larger-than-fairy-tale-gian'
          (but that would be impolite)
          below
          You

TRUDI: In that case I'll meet her when she gets home

SASHA: She works very hard and very *(starts to say)* la—(te) *(amends it to)* long hours

TRUDI: What about your father

SASHA: My mom says he's out of town

TRUDI *(on business)*: Oh

SASHA: permanently

TRUDI *(Uh-)*: Oh

SASHA: But we can say hi to my mom right now

TRUDI: Are you asking to borrow my cell phone

SASHA: We don't need a cell phone
          See that building two buildings east of the one with the
          flashing red light on top

TRUDI: No

SASHA: Squint

TRUDI: Okay I see it

SASHA: Start on the right-hand side

TRUDI: Okay

SASHA: Count seventeen windows down from the top

TRUDI: Okay

SASHA: Count three over

TRUDI: Okay

SASHA *waves.*

SASHA: Hi mom

The mom in her head corrects her.

> Sorry
> Hi *mamochka*

SASHA *nudges* TRUDI.

SASHA: Say hi

TRUDI (*waving*): Hi Sasha's mother

SASHA: *Mi mamochka* says
        hi yourself
        Mom's always trying to use American ideams

TRUDI: You mean idioms

SASHA: No kidding

TRUDI: Who takes care of you at night

SASHA: What do you mean

TRUDI: Who makes your dinner

SASHA: Lots of people

TRUDI: Like who

SASHA: Aunt Jemima Chef Boyardee and the Swanson family pretty
    much

TRUDI: You eat dinner alone every night

SASHA: No
        My mom and I eat dinner together every night

TRUDI: I'm confused

SASHA: My mom goes on break at eight
        I bring my dinner up here at eight
        We have dinner together every night at eight

TRUDI: Does your mother know you have dinner together every
    night at eight

SASHA: How could she not know We have long conversations

TRUDI: When will your mother be home

SASHA *squints at her mother's building.*

SASHA: *Mi mamochka* says what's it to you

TRUDI *addresses* SASHA'S *mother's building.*

TRUDI: I'm worried about your daughter's research paper
SASHA: *Mi mamochka* says don't be
           Mi mamochka says she calls me every three hours to
           check in
           and besides
           Mom's not there
TRUDI: Excuse me
SASHA: You're looking in the wrong office
TRUDI: You said seventeen windows down and three over
SASHA: That was several minutes ago
TRUDI: Your mother has more than one office
SASHA: My mom has between twenty-one and twenty-three
               offices
           depending upon the day
TRUDI: I don't understand
SASHA: My mom cleans
TRUDI: Offices
SASHA: My mom's four windows over now
           My mom's got to work fast
           No more than nineteen minutes per office
TRUDI: Oh
SASHA: And my mom's supervisor really watches the clock
           None of the maintenance crew is allowed to run late

TRUDI *gasps.*

TRUDI: WHAT TIME IS IT
SASHA: In my opinion it's six fifteen
TRUDI: Oh no
SASHA: What
TRUDI: I'm late for my board meeting

TRUDI *rushes to exit from the roof, and* SASHA *follows. They continue to converse as they rush. At the same time, the* SINGER/SONGWRITER *takes another stab at the upbeat music, her da-da-das punctuating the dialogue between* SASHA *and* TRUDI.

SASHA: What time did it start
TRUDI: It started at six
SASHA: In your opinion
TRUDI: In fact
SASHA: But at five after six you said you had plenty of time
TRUDI: My *Sensus Lackus Ofus Timus* must have been in an acute phase

When she reaches the third landing, TRUDI *rushes over to the elevator and presses the button, but then remembers that:*

TRUDI and SASHA: It's out of order
                      again

TRUDI *returns to the stairs and continues to rush down them.* SASHA *remains on the third floor and simply leans over the banister to continue the conversation.*

TRUDI (*calling up the stairs*): Tell your *mamochka* it was nice to meet
    her but not to be offended if I don't recognize her in a crowd
SASHA (*calling down the stairs*): Are you going to take a cab
TRUDI (*calling up the stairs*): Of course
SASHA (*calling down the stairs*): Lucky

SASHA *starts to straighten up and then suddenly leans over the banister once again.*

SASHA (*calling down the stairs*): Do you um wear steel-toed slippers
    around the apartment
TRUDI (*calling up the stairs*): No why do you ask
SASHA (*calling down the stairs*): No reason

TRUDI *exits the building;* SASHA *hears the sound of the front door closing.*

SASHA: Bye

Flashback begins as SASHA *slowly makes her way center stage. Workers on all three levels appear and pull on ropes, lifting a piece of the bridge.*

WORKER 1: Ready! Pull!
WORKER 1: Ready! Pull!
WORKER 1: Ready! Pull!
WORKER 1: Ready! Pull!
WORKER 1: Ready! Pull!

As Sasha (Emily Zimmer) works on her report, we see the construction of the Brooklyn Bridge. Photograph by Rob Levine.

Flashback ends. Sasha realizes the phone is ringing. Sasha rushes to the
phone.

SASHA: Hi *mamochka*
               No
               I was in the other room
               Yes
               the door's still locked
               Yes
               I ate what's there
               Yes
               of course it's done
               Yes
               I'll tuck myself in
               Yes
               I'll give myself a goodnight *pozeluy*
               Yes
               I'm sure I'm sure I'm sure I'm sure I'm sure I'm sure
SASHA *(Help, please)*:
               mamochka
               Could You Come Home Early
               (Okay, forget it.)
               Uh huh
               Uh huh
               Uh huh
               I know
               Never mind mom
               I'll see you later
               Bye mom

SASHA *hangs up the phone and lets out a half-plaintive, half-angry*
sound of distress. She heads out into the hallway once more; the
potted plant catches her attention. She crosses over to it and picks off a
dead leaf. The door right next to the plant is suddenly unlocked, and,
feeling somehow that she's been caught doing something wrong, SASHA

instinctively hides behind the potted plant. The door is pushed open
slowly, and an old, but not frail, man in a wheelchair emerges: JOHN.
He closes his door and wheels himself over to the elevator. He presses the
button. SASHA *speaks before she thinks.*

SASHA: It's out of order
SASHA and JOHN: again

The old man spins his wheelchair around.

JOHN: Who's there
SASHA *(from behind the potted plant)*: Nobody
JOHN: Nobody who
SASHA *(from behind the potted plant)*: Just plain nobody
JOHN: Do you make a habit of hiding behind potted plants and
    informing tenants as to the status of the elevator Just Plain
    Nobody
SASHA *(from behind the potted plant)*: This is my first time
JOHN: I'm honored
SASHA *(from behind the potted plant)*: I'm Sasha
JOHN: No
           I'm not
           honored
SASHA *(from behind the potted plant)*: You said you were
JOHN: It's an expression It means
           Lucky Me
SASHA *(from behind the potted plant)*: Then why didn't you say Lucky Me
JOHN: It wasn't what came to mind
           and that's all one has at one's disposal
           after all
SASHA *(from behind the potted plant)*: Oh
JOHN: I'm John
SASHA: I'm in trouble
JOHN: I thought you were Sasha
SASHA: I'm both

JOHN: If I were you I'd keep the former and drop the latter When did
the elevator break down

SASHA (*from behind the potted plant*): It was working this morning

JOHN: Drat

SASHA (*giggling from behind the potted plant*): Did you say drat

JOHN: Did I say something amusing

SASHA (*from behind the potted plant*): My father used to say drat
My mom told me it was the first word of English he
learned

JOHN: It's a handy one all right

SASHA (*from behind the potted plant*): My mom says it's out-of-date

JOHN: Each generation has a right to its own words of frustration It's
how we tell each other apart

SASHA (*from behind the potted plant*): What's a generation again

JOHN: People of your grandparents' age make up one generation
People of your parents' age make up another
People of your age make up another

SASHA: I don't know what my generation's words of frustration are

JOHN: That's because you're too young to feel frustration

SASHA (*from behind the potted plant*): HOW WOULD YOU KNOW
WHAT I FEEL

JOHN *is taken aback.*

JOHN: You're right that was presumptuous of me

SASHA (*from behind the potted plant*): Is presumptuous another one of
your generation's words

JOHN: It means I thought I knew more about you than I do
Would you mind coming out from behind there It's a bit
disconcerting

SASHA (*from behind the potted plant*): I'm not supposed to have
strange talk

JOHN: Excuse me

SASHA (*from behind potted plant*): I'm not supposed to talk to
strangers

JOHN: Well I'm not supposed to talk to plants

SASHA *emerges from behind the potted plant.*

SASHA: We've never met have we

JOHN: No

SASHA: That's what I thought
        But you never know when some adult is going to tell you
        they've known you all your life when as far as you know
        you've never seen them before

JOHN: Ah yes My mother used to make me kiss all sorts of strangers
    who claimed to be close relations

SASHA: Ugh

JOHN: There you go
        That's a good one

SASHA: Good what

JOHN: Expression of frustration

SASHA: Ugh

JOHN: Ugh is simply a modern translation of drat Could I ask a favor
    of you

SASHA: Does it involve breaking the rules

JOHN: It involves going to the mailboxes
        I'm expecting an important piece of mail and
        it doesn't look as though I'll be getting downstairs today

SASHA: I'm not even supposed to be outside of my apartment this late

JOHN: In that case never mind
        Rules are rules

SASHA: But you need a favor

JOHN: Rules overrule needs

JOHN *turns to wheel himself into his apartment.*

SASHA *(a genuine question)*: They do

JOHN *(a genuine realization)*:   Truthfully I'm not sure
                        I just said that

SASHA *(a genuine question/realization)*: What do you do when rules
    stop working

JOHN: You rewrite them but
           I'm not recommending that you rewrite this particular
               rule
SASHA: What's your apartment number
JOHN *(backtracking is in order here)*: Now hold on a minute

SASHA *suddenly grabs the mail key out of* JOHN'S *hand as the* SINGER/
SONGWRITER *gets up and stretches.*

SASHA *(looking at his door)*: 3E
JOHN: as in
           Egalitarianism
SASHA: What's egalitarianism
JOHN: A dying art I'm afraid

SASHA *runs down the two flights of stairs to the mailboxes, checks* JOHN'S
mail and runs back upstairs, empty-handed. At the same time, the
SINGER/SONGWRITER *sings some scales.*

SASHA: There was no mail
JOHN: The mailman's awfully late today
SASHA: She's a mailwoman
JOHN: Yes but she's still a mailman
           That's what you say
SASHA: She's a letter carrier
           That's what you say
JOHN: All right I will
SASHA: Do you have a pen
JOHN: Of course I have a pen
SASHA *(at last)*: You do
JOHN: Of course I have a pen
SASHA: Could I borrow it
JOHN: Of course you may borrow it but every child should have a pen
    of her own
SASHA: Of course every child should but this child lost hers

JOHN: Where did you lose it

SASHA: Why do people ask that question
I just told you I lost my pen
If I knew where I lost it my pen would be found

JOHN: Yes but sometimes it helps to identify the general
location of the loss
For instance
In the living room
In the store
In the park
In the

JOHN *gestures for* SASHA *to finish the sentence.*

SASHA: middle of a really bad day
JOHN: Why do you need a pen
SASHA: I've already explained this twice today
JOHN: I apologize for my absence from your previous explanations
SASHA: Was that slightly veiled sarcasm
JOHN: Absolutely not

SASHA *steals a look at* JOHN'S *watch.*

SASHA: I'm losing valuable time
JOHN: I'm ninety-nine years old
Imagine how I feel

SASHA *sighs.*

SASHA (*getting upset again*):
It's a research paper on the Brooklyn Bridge
It's very important
I haven't started
JOHN: Why haven't you started
SASHA: I can't find a pen

JOHN: What's the real reason

SASHA: I can't find a pen

JOHN: What's the real reason

SASHA: I can't find a pen

JOHN: What's the real reason

SASHA: I don't know
Yes I do
I am in awe

JOHN: You are in awe
of what

SASHA: That
bridge

JOHN: Ahh

SASHA: Awe

JOHN: Yes
I see

SASHA: Yes
Whatever I write will not live up to what I see
That's the problem
Does that sound silly

JOHN: It sounds precocious

SASHA: That sounds bad

JOHN: It's not
in the long run
How old are you

SASHA: I am ten years six months and close to nineteen hours old

JOHN: And able to articulate awe
Awe is complex

SASHA: Awe is simple
Haven't you ever felt awe

JOHN: Not since I lacked a word for it

SASHA: All I know is
I have read too much and
I can't figure out what matters
except
graduating to the sixth grade

JOHN: Is your graduation to the sixth grade in doubt

SASHA: Sorta

JOHN: What does sorta mean

SASHA: Sorta means yes

JOHN: I see

SASHA: I owe a lot of assignments
but they had a meeting and
decided I could graduate to
the sixth grade if I did a really good
job on my New York City research paper

JOHN: Why didn't you do your assignments Sasha

SASHA: John
I did all my assignments
(Pointing to her head.)
I did all my assignments John
The problem was I did them all up here
the problem was I
didn't
write
them
down
(Getting upset again.)
and at my school they really hold that against you

JOHN *(hitting the arms of his wheelchair)*: You have a serious condition

SASHA *(alarmed)*: Is it as serious as *Sensus Lackus Ofus Timus*

JOHN: What's that

SASHA: Hard to explain
You think I have a serious condition

JOHN: Clearly
you can't commit

SASHA: I can't commit to what

JOHN: paper
I remember when you were born

SASHA *(taken aback)*: You do

JOHN: Your parents brought you home in a cab

TALIDIA *exits her apartment on the floor below and walks out the front door of the building and goes down into the subway.*

SASHA (*excited*):   I took a cab
                     (*Back to being taken aback.*)
                     Wait
                     How do you know
JOHN: I look out the window
                     a lot
SASHA (*question before thought*): Did my parents look happy

Slight pause.

JOHN (*not at all*):   Very

Slight pause.

                     Let me go see about your pen

JOHN *opens his door and wheels into his apartment, and as he does the* SINGER/SONGWRITER *plays a few bars.*

SINGER/SONGWRITER (*sung*):
                     We're not waiting for anything

SASHA *returns the plant to its place by the elevator. Flashback begins as the elevators on the third floor open, and workers ascend from the subway. Ropes are dropped down from the third level to the deck and attached.*

WORKER 2: Clear!
ALL WORKERS: Clear!

Workers exit the stage. SASHA, *awaiting* JOHN'S *return, has been oblivious to the preceding event.* SAM *emerges from his apartment and crosses to the elevator.*

SAM: Still no pen

SASHA: Trudi didn't have one so now John's looking

SAM: Who

SASHA: Trudi lives upstairs She moves money
   John lives there He moves on wheels

SAM: Oh I know her
   She's always in a hurry

SASHA: She has a recently diagnosed condition

SAM: And he's always recycling pizza boxes
   He must eat pizza every single day

SASHA: I wish I could eat pizza every single day

SAM: It's not good to do anything every single day
   except brush your teeth of course

SASHA: I don't have time to build a smile with you Sam so
   please don't ask

SAM: I don't have time to build smiles right now either
   I've got to get to school
   We have another test tonight

SASHA: What's the test on

SAM: Gum Disease
   Yesterday Today Tomorrow

SASHA: Yuck

SAM: I'll show you pictures
   You'll never forget to floss again

A pathetic meow emanates from SAM'S *apartment.*

SAM: Feline separation anxiety

SASHA: What's that

SAM: She don't want me to go

SASHA: Don't be blue Red

SAM: Bye Red
   Bye Sasha

SASHA: Bye Sam

SASHA and SAM: Good luck

SAM (*at elevator*): What am I doing

SASHA and SAM: It's out of order

                  again

SAM disappears down the stairs. At the same time the MAIL CARRIER enters the building and begins depositing mail in the mailboxes. At the same time there is another disconsolate meow from SAM's apartment.

SASHA (*whispers through the door*):

          Red

          Here's what I'd recommend

          One

          Avoid waiting by the door

          A watched door never opens

          Two

          Take advantage of your time alone to do

          something a bit bad

          For instance go jump on the bed for a really

          long time

          Three

          Curl up with a good book

          or perhaps in your case you could

          Curl up *on* a good book

          Most of all

          Don't worry

          He'll be back

As SASHA awaits JOHN's return with a pen, she becomes conscious of the sound of the MAIL CARRIER closing the mailboxes. She then notices that she still holds JOHN's mail key. SASHA arrives at the mailboxes and retrieves JOHN's mail. She also removes the keys from around her neck and checks her own mail. She stops short when she sees the handwriting on a certain letter; she removes just that letter and leaves her keys as she rushes to the front door and exits the building. Waving the letter, she calls to the MAIL CARRIER, who is still within sight.

SASHA (*to* MAIL CARRIER):   'SCUSE ME
                        I NEED TO RETURN TO SENDER

But the MAIL CARRIER *doesn't hear her. Slowly,* SASHA *sinks down onto the stoop. Meanwhile, there has been the sound, emanating through the window, of the* SINGER/SONGWRITER *trying out another version of her song.*

SINGER/SONGWRITER (*sung*):
> *Just when you thought you were alone in the room*
> *Rises the platinum arc of the moon*
> *Suspended patiently*
> *Waiting for*
> (*said*) What

A moment later JOHN *emerges from his apartment, only to discover that* SASHA *is gone.*

JOHN: Drat

JOHN *lingers for a minute before reentering his apartment and closing the door as a Puerto Rican woman with a tremendous cart full of laundry,* TALIDIA, *arrives at the front of the building. If all times out as it should,* TALIDIA'S *appearance should coincide with the end of the song and* JOHN'S *entry into his apartment.*

TALIDIA (*Puerto Rican/Brooklyn accent*): Coming through

SASHA, *in a daze, doesn't move.* TALIDIA *is struggling under the weight of her cart.*

TALIDIA: *Ay*
            Hello
            Chica
            Coming through
SASHA: Sorry

SASHA *moves to the right, one hand still clutching the letter.* TALIDIA *searches through her pockets for her keys while balancing the cart.*

TALIDIA: *Ay*
                    Ay
                    Ay

Slight pause.

SASHA: Is *Ay* your generation's expression of frustration
TALIDIA: It's my culture's expression of frustration
                    We say it every single time we go to the laundry and
                        forget our keys
                    Would you mind unlocking the door for me *chica*
SASHA: I'm not allowed to let strangers into the building
TALIDIA: That's not a problem since I'm not a stranger
                    I live in 2C
                    I've lived in 2C since before you were a single cell
                    awaiting division
SASHA (*a single what awaiting what*):   Excuse me
TALIDIA: I was helping my kid with his biology homework last night
SASHA: You do look familiar but
                    I don't think I know you
TALIDIA: You don't
                    But we haven't known each other for a Very Long Time
                    That should count for something

SASHA (*too tired to argue, reaching for her keys that habitually hang from around her neck*):

                    If you say so
                    uh-oh
                    (*to* TALIDIA)
                    I forgot my keys too
TALIDIA: *Ay*
SASHA: Ugh

TALIDIA *pulls back her cart so that it rests on solid ground.*

SASHA (*getting upset*): I'm dead
TALIDIA: Don't say that
SASHA: But it's true
                I'm dead
TALIDIA: Don't say that
SASHA: But it's true
                I'm dead
TALIDIA: I don't like that kind of talk
SASHA: BUT YOU DON'T UNDERSTAND MY PREDICAMENT
TALIDIA: *Cálmete cálmete*
                Okay let's think
                Anyone you can buzz on the inside
SASHA (*I'm telling you It's True I'm Dead*): My mother's at work
                You
TALIDIA: Frida has band practice
                Freddie's at the library
                Frankie's at the bowling alley
                Frannie's visiting her cousin
                Felix is doing his paper route
                Flora's riding her bike
                Fidelia's playing basketball
                My husband left eight years ago and
                the Super and I aren't speaking
SASHA: So what do we do
TALIDIA: We wait
                We fold

TALIDIA *takes out a clean sheet from her pile and silently coaxes* SASHA *to accept two corners of it. They fold the sheet and then another and another, but* SASHA *manages to hold on to the letter all the while.*

SASHA: Where did your husband go
TALIDIA: That's a funny question
SASHA: It's a simple question

TALIDIA: It's a simple question if it's a geography question but
             I don't think it's a geography question

SASHA: I don't think I know what you mean

TALIDIA: I mean it's a history question disguised as a geography
                question
             I mean I can tell you that my husband went to Pittsburgh
             but that's not what you're asking
             You're asking why he went to Pittsburgh
             You're asking why he went

SASHA: Why did he

TALIDIA: Ask him

SASHA: He's not here

TALIDIA: Exactly
             Here's a towel for you

SASHA: It's still damp

TALIDIA: *Ay*
             Those dryers drive me crazy
             I'll have to hang it on the clothesline

SASHA: You have a lot of laundry

TALIDIA: I have a lot of children

SASHA: I see them sometimes

TALIDIA: They're hard to miss

Slight pause.

SASHA: You've lived in this building a long time

TALIDIA: I've lived in this building forever

SASHA: Did you know my father

TALIDIA: That's a strange question

SASHA: Do you call every question names before you answer it

TALIDIA: My mother used to do the same thing
             It buys you time to formulate your response

SASHA: It's a simple question

TALIDIA: It's a simple question if it's a yes-or-no question but
             I don't think it's a yes-or-no question

SASHA: Yes it is

TALIDIA: No it's not

It's a complicated question disguised as a yes-or-no
question

I can tell you that I knew your father

But that's not what you're asking

You're asking me what your father was like

SASHA: What was he like

TALIDIA: I hardly remember him

SASHA: I don't remember him

TALIDIA: I knew him only
to say hello to

SASHA: He said hello to you

TALIDIA: It's an expression

When you know someone to say hello to it means
you know them hardly at all

SASHA: So he didn't say hello to you

TALIDIA: Maybe he did
I don't remember

They fold.

TALIDIA: How long has he been gone

SASHA: Seven years five months three days and seven hours

SASHA *registers* TALIDIA'S *surprise at her precision.*

SASHA: Ish

They fold.

TALIDIA: How's school

SASHA: Ugh

TALIDIA: What

SASHA: People only say how's school when they don't know what else
to say

They fold.

TALIDIA: If a person's not allowed to say how's school how does a
    person find out how school is

SASHA: UGH

TALIDIA: *AY*

SASHA (*said very quickly and with increasing upset*):
        School is terrible
        I'm supposed to be writing a very important paper on
            the Brooklyn Bridge and I don't have a pen because
            Sam and Trudi didn't have one and even though John
            says he does have one that does me no good because
            I'm locked out of the building and I'm destined
            to remain in the fifth grade for the rest of my life
            expectancy which for people my age is twenty-nine
            thousand seven hundred and seventy-three more
            days but for me will probably be more like another
            couple of hours because I've somehow managed to
            lie to my mother about seven thousand times today
            and she doesn't find that sort of behavior charming
        but anyway I don't care what my mother thinks because
        My Mother's Never Here
        That's how school is

Slightest pause.

TALIDIA: Don't tell me you're trying to tell me that you haven't
        written your very important paper because you can't
        find a pen
        Don't tell me you're trying to tell me that

SASHA: It's the truth

TALIDIA: Listen *chica*
        I have seven children okay
        Four with my husband two adopted one foster
        I know when I'm being fed a preadolescent line
        and for preadolescent lines I'm not hungry

SASHA: It's the truth

TALIDIA: No

It's an avoidance technique disguised as the truth

You might think you haven't written your very important

paper

because you can't find a pen

but that's not the real reason

So what's the real reason

They fold.

SASHA: That's the real reason

TALIDIA: So what's the real reason

SASHA: That's the real reason

TALIDIA: So what's the real reason

SASHA: That's the real reason well

okay that's Not the real reason but

I've already been through this with John I just

get overwhelmed when it comes to

Writing Things Down

TALIDIA: Why

SASHA: Because it makes me think about everything I'm

not writing down

TALIDIA: But you can always erase what you write down and

write something else down

SASHA: I could

but that looks messy

TALIDIA: But you can get another piece of paper

SASHA: I could

but that's a waste of paper

TALIDIA: But you can use a computer

SASHA: I could

but I don't have a computer

TALIDIA: But you can go to the library

SASHA: I could

but the library's closed

TALIDIA: *Ay*
           It's like talking to one of my kids
           Enough already
           Let's get to work

TALIDIA *digs around in her pocket and produces:*

TALIDIA: Fidelia's chalk
           I confiscated it this morning
SASHA: You want me to write my research paper on the sidewalk
TALIDIA: You recite
           I'll write

SASHA *is cleaned out of excuses, so she paces.*

SASHA: The Brooklyn Bridge

SASHA *paces the other way.*

               by Alexandra Trusotsky

SASHA *paces the other way, notices what* TALIDIA *has written and corrects her.*

               "s" not "z"

SASHA *paces the other way.*

               May 24, 2001

SASHA *paces the other way.*

               Ms. Cohen's class

SASHA *paces the other way.*

P.S. 121

SASHA *paces the other way.*

Copyright 2001

SASHA *paces the other way.*

Brooklyn
Comma

TALIDIA *shoots her a look.* SASHA *paces the other way.*

SASHA: New York

SASHA *paces the other way.*

US

SASHA *starts to pace the other way before turning to add:*

of A

SASHA *paces the other way.*

Northern Hemisphere

TALIDIA really *shoots* SASHA *a look and is about to reprimand her but then notices:*

TALIDIA: *AY*
¿Que voy a hacer contigo?

Slightest pause.

TALIDIA: *(genuine curiosity)*: What's that paper you're clutching for
  dear life

SASHA: It's a letter
           from my father

TALIDIA: What does it say

SASHA: I haven't read it

TALIDIA: Why not

SASHA: He sends a letter
           every year
           For my birthday
           every year
           but the letters always arrive six months
           late

Slight pause.

SASHA: You don't have a problem with the word *late*
           do you

TALIDIA: No

SASHA: Good

TALIDIA: So you haven't read the letter because it's
           late

SASHA: I'm not allowed to read the letters

TALIDIA: Does your mother read the letters

SASHA: In my mother's family when someone leaves they no
               longer exist
           My mother no longer exists for her mother
           My father no longer exists for my mother
           My father's not supposed to exist for me

They are quiet.

TALIDIA: The problem with people who no longer exist is that they
  show up all the time

Slight pause.

SASHA: I'm not allowed to read the letters but I
           read one once It was sitting on top of the trash
TALIDIA: What did it say
SASHA: I don't remember I just
           remember lots and lots of
           words

SASHA *carefully folds up the letter and puts it in her pocket.*

TALIDIA: Are you going to read it
SASHA: I don't know
TALIDIA: Does he ever try to see you

Talidia (Susanna
Guzman) chats with
Sasha (Emily Zimmer)
about their life in the
apartment building.
Photograph by Rob
Levine.

SASHA: I don't know but
how hard could it be He knows where I
live
TALIDIA: Listen
I don't know your father
I don't know your mother
I don't know you
But I do know that the other thing about people who
aren't here
is that they lose their shape
Some become huge
Some become tiny
None resemble what they really are
What I'm saying is you can't trust what people's absences
turn them into
One funny-but-not-so-funny thing is that your
mother's not here
because she's working so *you* can be here
in this apartment building
in this country
in this other life that she wants you to have
Another funny-but-not-so-funny thing is that your
father's not here
but his words are
thousands and thousands of them
because for whatever reason they are all he has to give
you right now
Does it matter what those words are
I don't know
You have to decide
But I do know
that parents are exactly who they are
and even if they are not enough
they are what you have
You're not supposed to have to deal with such a fact at

your age
But for whatever reason life constantly asks us to deal
with all sorts
of age-inappropriate things

Slight pause.

TALIDIA: Wait
There's one last thing I know
whatever your mother and father aren't able to do or be
whatever it is that you need that they can't give you
you must find it somewhere else
because it exists somewhere else
because everything we need exists somewhere
We just have to find where

Slight pause.

SASHA: My mother's a very sad person
TALIDIA: Why is that
SASHA: Because she's a very tired person
because she works very hard
And she's a very sad person
because she's a very smart person
who was a professor in Russia
who everybody listened to
But here nobody listens to her
because her English is broken
and she traded in a good life in a hard place
for a hard life in a good place
And she wonders why she did that
though she wants me to have a great life in a good place
And she wants me to be Russian
but she wants me to be American
but she wants me to be Russian

And she has no family around except me
and nothing feels truly familiar except me
except sometimes I think even I am becoming
unfamiliar

Slightest pause.

My mother's a very sad person

Slightest pause.

And my father is
I Don't Know Who My Father Is
And I'm not sure I want to anymore
And I'm not sure I feel bad about that
Although I do feel sad about it

They sit quietly for a long moment until SASHA *remembers.*

SASHA: John
TALIDIA: Who
SASHA: John can buzz us in

SASHA *walks over to the intercom and buzzes* JOHN'S *apartment.*

JOHN *(through intercom)*: Who's there
SASHA: Just Plain Nobody
JOHN *(through intercom)*: What are you doing out there
SASHA: I stepped outside and left my keys inside
JOHN *(through intercom)*: That was silly but
        you're in luck
        I've been expecting Just Plain Nobody

The door buzzer sounds, unlocking the entryway. SASHA *holds the door
for* TALIDIA, *and they both enter the building.* SASHA *helps* TALIDIA

haul her cart up the steps. TALIDIA *and* SASHA *reach the landing outside* TALIDIA'S *apartment door.* JOHN *exits his apartment into the hallway.*

TALIDIA: *Ay*
SASHA: Ugh

TALIDIA *extends her hand.*

TALIDIA: Talidia
SASHA: Sasha
TALIDIA: Wait right here

TALIDIA *retreats into her apartment, leaving the cart of laundry in the hallway.* SASHA *suddenly remembers that she left* JOHN'S *mail out on the front stoop.*

SASHA: Oops

SASHA *runs downstairs, props open the door, grabs the mail, and runs back up the stairs all the way to the third floor.* JOHN *is waiting for her in the hallway.*

JOHN: I'm afraid I have good news and bad news
           Which would you like to hear first
SASHA (*out of breath*): The bad news
JOHN: My pen's run out of ink
SASHA: That's bad
JOHN: Yes I thought I named the news aptly
SASHA: What's the good news
JOHN: The good news is
           I have other pens
SASHA: That's good
JOHN: I'm just not exactly sure where they are at the moment
SASHA: That's bad
JOHN: I know I used at least three different pens yesterday
SASHA: That's good

JOHN: They just all seem to have evaporated

SASHA: That's bad

JOHN: However I am hopeful they will soon turn up

SASHA: That's good

JOHN: Although I'm unsure they will turn up tonight

SASHA: That's disastrous

JOHN: But the thing is
          (said simultaneously with SASHA*)*
          the pen's not your problem

SASHA *(said simultaneously with* JOHN*)*: the pen's not my problem

JOHN: You knew that

Slight pause.

SASHA: I don't know what to do

JOHN: That's easy
          Write your paper

SASHA: I can't

JOHN: You can

SASHA: I can't

JOHN: You can

SASHA: Can't

JOHN: Can

SASHA: Can't

JOHN: Can

SASHA: Can't

JOHN: Can

SASHA: Can't

JOHN: Can

SASHA: CAN'T CAN'T CAN'T CAN'T CAN'T
           keep yelling like this

Slight pause.

JOHN: Step into my office

JOHN *starts to wheel himself into his apartment, and* SASHA *starts to follow but then stops.*

SASHA: At what point is a person no longer a stranger

JOHN: That's an excellent question

SASHA: At what point does a stranger become a neighbor

JOHN: When your mother says so

SASHA: My mother insists that I turn around three times whenever I
    enter our apartment

JOHN: Why is that

SASHA: It's an old Russian superstition
        It's supposed to shake off any evil spirits that attached
        themselves to you while you were outside

JOHN: I'll have to try that

SASHA *moves behind* JOHN'S *wheelchair, runs around him in a circle three times, then pushes him into his apartment. Just then,* TALIDIA *emerges from her apartment.*

TALIDIA: So listen

TALIDIA *finds that* SASHA *is gone.*

TALIDIA: *Ay*

TALIDIA *hangs the damp towel on the fire escape and then pushes her cart full of laundry into her apartment as* JOHN *and* SASHA *become visible again; we see the wall open and* SASHA *following* JOHN *onto the fire escape.*

SASHA: Nice office

JOHN: It's a little drafty in the winter months but
        you can't beat the view

JOHN *produces two sets of binoculars. He passes one set to* SASHA; *they both look through the binoculars. Slight pause.*

JOHN (*through binoculars, to* SASHA): I must tell you something
           Binocular to Binocular
           I am a Brooklyn Bridge Buff
SASHA (*through binoculars, to* JOHN): I had no idea you were a
    Brooklyn Bridge Buff
JOHN (*through binoculars, to* SASHA): I am a Brooklyn Bridge Buff
SASHA (*through binoculars, to* JOHN): I also have no idea what a Buff is
JOHN (*through binoculars, to* SASHA): A Buff is an enthusiast
           a fan
           one who is fascinated by a certain subject
SASHA (*through binoculars, to* JOHN): Then we are Both Brooklyn
    Bridge Buffs

JOHN *now turns his binoculars in the "direction" of the Brooklyn Bridge, out to the audience, even though the Bridge actually appears at this moment to be diagonally bisected by the apartment building.* SASHA, *too, gazes through her binoculars at the Bridge; the two remain oriented this way through the entire following conversation, but lower their binoculars.*

JOHN: It's time for a quiz
           What were the main phases of the Bridge's construction
SASHA: In order
JOHN: In order
SASHA: The sinking of the caissons
JOHN: And then
SASHA: The construction of the towers above them
JOHN: And then
SASHA: The building of the anchorages that would support the great
    cables
JOHN: And then
SASHA: The spinning of the great cables that would support the
    suspenders
JOHN: And then
SASHA: The hanging of the suspenders that would support the
    roadway

JOHN: And then

SASHA: The construction of the road and walkways that would support the traffic

JOHN: And then

SASHA: The placing of the diagonal stays that would support the support

JOHN: And then

SASHA: And then

Slight pause.

Opening Day

Slight pause as the two gaze at the magnificent bridge in silence.

JOHN: Full length of the Bridge

SASHA: 5,989 feet

JOHN: Weight of the Bridge

SASHA: 14,680 tons

JOHN: Number of cables

SASHA: Four

JOHN: Number of suspenders

SASHA: 294

JOHN: Diameter of each cable

SASHA: Just under a foot and a quarter

JOHN: Length of wire in each cable

SASHA: 3,515 miles

JOHN: Did you say miles

SASHA: Miles

JOHN: Good
                Height of towers

SASHA: Above the roadway or above the water

JOHN: Water

SASHA: 276 feet 6 inches

JOHN: Length of time it took to build the Bridge

SASHA: 14 years

JOHN: First person to travel across the Bridge

SASHA: Before there was a road or after

JOHN: Both

A change occurs from now on, as SASHA *increasingly takes the reins of the Bridge narrative. As she does so,* JOHN *laughs and nods his head and perhaps even vocalizes concurrence—basically, he delights in watching* SASHA'S *knowledge insist on expression.*

SASHA: Before there was a road
             and to the great thrill of thousands of onlookers
             Master Mechanic E. F. Harrington traveled across on a
             sort of swing that was suspended by a wire rope that was
             strung between the towers

JOHN (*said simultaneously with* SASHA): And after there was a roadway

SASHA (*said simultaneously with* JOHN): And after there was a roadway

SASHA: The honor of the first official crossing was given to
                 Emily Roebling
             wife of the Bridge's Chief Engineer
             who traveled by carriage across the Bridge in the
             company
             of a rooster
             signifying victory

JOHN: The Bridge's Chief Engineer

SASHA (*finishing his thought*):
             was plagued by a mysterious medical condition
             Washington Roebling suffered from Caisson disease
             later known as the bends
             caused by a too rapid return to normal air pressure
             from the underwater environment of the caissons

JOHN (*said simultaneously with* SASHA): And as a result

SASHA (*said simultaneously with* JOHN):
             And as a result he was forced to oversee the majority
             of the Bridge's construction from the window

of his Brooklyn Heights bedroom
which luckily had an excellent view of the Bridge
and where he would sit sometimes for hours
gazing out the window through old-fashioned binoculars
which of course weren't old-fashioned at the time

JOHN (*said simultaneously with* SASHA): And as a result

SASHA (*said simultaneously with John*): And as a result Washington
  Roebling's
wife Emily became instrumental in the Bridge's progress
acting as her husband's spokesperson at the work site
and providing full updates on the Bridge's progress at
  home
Emily in short became Washington's right-hand man
except of course she was a woman

JOHN (*said simultaneously with* SASHA): And as a result

SASHA (*said simultaneously with* JOHN): And as a result it was good
for Washington Roebling
good for feminism
and especially good for those who were awaiting an
easier means of crossing the East River

JOHN (*said simultaneously with* SASHA): The Bridge's official name

SASHA (*said simultaneously with* JOHN): The Bridge's official name
is The New York and Brooklyn Bridge

JOHN (*said simultaneously with* SASHA): The Bridge's nickname

SASHA (*said simultaneously with* JOHN): The Bridge's nickname
is The Eighth Wonder of the World

JOHN (*said simultaneously with* SASHA):
The Bridge's Opening Day date

SASHA (*said simultaneously with* JOHN):
The Bridge's Opening Day date
was May 24, 1883
(*said as a question to* JOHN)
The time
(*but* JOHN *is visibly stumped*)
was two o'clock p.m.

Highlights of the Bridge's Opening Day festivities
included the following
(becoming more animated than we've ever seen her)
President Chester A. Arthur accompanied by other state
and local officials crossed the Bridge by foot
In the pictures it looks like a sea of top hats
The crowd roared and military guns saluted
Then when night fell there was the grandest festival of
fireworks anyone had ever seen
But the best thing of all happened when light of a
different sort
filled the sky
In a time when nobody had electricity in their homes
imagine the feeling as they watched the Brooklyn Bridge
become illuminated
light by light along the promenade
as if by scientific miracle

JOHN: I believe you have accomplished something I thought
          not possible
    I believe I am in awe

Slight pause.

SASHA: But why
    Those are just a bunch of facts
    Facts are only part of the assignment
    The other part is having a point of view
    Taking a stand
    Deciding what's important
    The other part is what I'm missing

Slight pause.

JOHN: Then it's high time for you to determine what you are left with
SASHA: Left with

JOHN: You've done your research
          You've gathered
          as you say
          your facts
          What are you left with
SASHA: What do you mean Left With
JOHN: There are facts and there is what matters
          and what matters is what you are left with
          So
          Sasha
          when you think about the Brooklyn Bridge what are you
          left with

SASHA *paces in the limited area of the fire escape.*

JOHN: What are you doing
SASHA: Pacing
JOHN: Oh
          In that case carry on

SASHA *continues to "pace."*

SASHA: When I think about the Brooklyn Bridge
           I am left with what it cost
JOHN: $15,211,982.92
SASHA: I don't mean what it cost I mean what it
           Cost
           Besides money
JOHN: Besides money
SASHA: My mother says that *some* things cost money but *everything*
        costs something *besides* money
JOHN: Such as
SASHA: Whole neighborhoods were demolished to make room
           for the Bridge's anchorages

Dozens of men lost their lives
Others lost their health

JOHN: All worthwhile endeavor costs
and even though we know this
it is human nature to hope the price that's paid won't be
personal

The two of them gaze at the Bridge without their binoculars.

SASHA: But the price *was* personal

JOHN: Yes

SASHA: And yet people stayed
Almost all of them
who worked on the Bridge
They stayed

JOHN: Yes

SASHA: Even though it was very hard

JOHN: Yes

SASHA: Even though it would have been easier not to stay

JOHN: Yes

SASHA: Staying costs

JOHN: Yes yes yes
and
I would argue that
considering Cost is another way of considering Worth
and trust me on this one
Worth is infinitely more satisfying to consider

SASHA: You think I should write about the Bridge's worth

JOHN: I think you should write about what you are left with

SASHA: That sounds like a riddle

JOHN: For some perhaps
but you're a girl whose awe is informed

SASHA: UGH
DRAT
AY

SASHA *paces some more.* TALIDIA *enters hallway to retrieve her towel and exits again.*

SASHA: THE WORTH OF THE BRIDGE IS THAT IT WAS A
                FEAT OF
            UNPARALLELED ENGINEERING
            THE WORTH OF THE BRIDGE IS THAT IT WAS
            THOUGHT NOT POSSIBLE
            THE WORTH OF THE BRIDGE IS ITS ITS ITS
            what's that word your generation uses for pretty in an
            important way

JOHN: Magnificence

SASHA: THE WORTH OF THE BRIDGE IS ITS MAGNIFICENCE
            THE WORTH OF THE BRIDGE IS THAT IT LINKS
            GEOGRAPHIES
            THE WORTH OF THE BRIDGE IS THAT IT LINKS
            POPULATIONS
            THE WORTH OF THE BRIDGE IS THAT IT'S A BRIDGE
            (Pause.)

JOHN: YES

SASHA: THE BRIDGE IS A BRIDGE

JOHN: YES

SASHA: IT'S A BRIDGE JOHN
            AND BRIDGES CONNECT THINGS
            AND WHEN THINGS AREN'T ENOUGH IN ONE PLACE
            ALL YOU HAVE TO DO IS CROSS A BRIDGE
            TO ANOTHER PLACE TO FIND THE THING THAT
            WILL BE ENOUGH
            THE BRIDGE IS A BRIDGE JOHN
            AND BRIDGES ARE NECESSARY THINGS

Slight pause.

JOHN: A simple and elegant truth Sasha
          Thank you for pointing it out

Slight pause. SASHA *is a bit exhausted.*

SASHA: Okay
          but does *anybody* in this universe have a pen

At this moment a musician carrying a very large bass is buzzed in downstairs. Over the next few minutes we will watch as he guides it over to the elevator, discovers that it's not working

MAN WITH BASS: Aargh

and begins the extremely arduous task of carrying the bass up the stairs, stops, and plays on third landing. The SINGER/SONGWRITER *also begins to play with the* MAN WITH BASS'S *line. Meanwhile,* JOHN *spins on his wheelchair and heads back into his apartment.* SASHA *follows. We see them disappear and then reappear in the hall. Wordlessly, they split up.* SASHA *heads first to the floor below, while John wheels himself down the hall. They each begin knocking on doors. Each time a door opens we won't be able to see the face of the tenant, only the door itself and the disappointed faces of* JOHN *and* SASHA, *as each of their queries is apparently responded to in the negative. The language of their repeated questions is as follows:*

JOHN: I'm terribly sorry to bother you at this late hour
          but I wonder if I might trouble you for the temporary
          loan of a pen
SASHA: Do you have a pen I could borrow

After a few minutes JOHN *has knocked on every door on his floor.* SASHA *ascends the steps and encounters the* MAN WITH BASS. SASHA *impulsively grabs the* MAN WITH BASS'S *collar.*

SASHA: GIMME YOUR PEN

MAN WITH BASS: Uh okay

With his bass leaning against him, the MAN WITH BASS *searches through his pockets and produces a pen, which he hands over to* SASHA, *whose mood, momentarily, becomes positively positive.*

SASHA: Thanks

SASHA *runs off to join* JOHN, *holding her pen triumphantly as the* MAN WITH BASS *continues on his way up to the floor above. At the same time,* TRUDI *arrives at the front stoop, enters the building, and begins climbing the stairs.*

JOHN: I'll get you some paper

Sasha (Emily Zimmer) contemplates her New York City research paper among her fellow apartment dwellers. Photograph by Rob Levine.

JOHN *disappears into his apartment.* TRUDI *emerges from the stairwell just as* SAM *arrives at the front stoop.* SAM *enters the building and begins climbing the stairs through the following.*

SASHA: I thought you had a board meeting
TRUDI: I did
           but get this
           All the other board members
           got mixed up and showed up for the meeting two hours
           before it was scheduled to start
           Can you imagine
SASHA: Are you in trouble
TRUDI: Trouble
           I can't help it if all eleven of them are compulsively early
           people
           Anyway
           I grabbed the president of the board's pen on my way out
SASHA: You did
TRUDI: I just have to find it

TRUDI *begins riffling through her purse as* SAM *emerges from the stairwell.*

SASHA: I thought you had an exam on
           Gum Disease
           Yesterday Today Tomorrow
TRUDI: Yuck
SAM: I did but the proctor had food poisoning so I had to drive
           him in my cab to the Emergency Room
           (*to* TRUDI)
           I'll show you pictures
           You'll never forget to floss again
SASHA: I never get to take cabs
SAM: Anyway
           I grabbed the Emergency Room doctor's pen on my
           way out

SASHA: You did

SAM: But what did I do with it

SAM *searches his person for the pen.* TALIDIA *exits her apartment and walks up a flight of stairs to join the others.*

TALIDIA: There you are
        I grabbed a pen out of Felix's book bag
        It's got green ink is that all right
        Ay I just had it
        What did I do with it

TALIDIA *searches her person for the pen.*

SASHA: It's okay
        I don't need a pen

SAM, TRUDI, *and* TALIDIA *halt their searches.*

SAM and TRUDI and TALIDIA (*vague disappointment*): Oh

JOHN *emerges from his apartment with a large stack of paper.*

JOHN: That ought to do it

All four grown-ups regard SASHA.

SAM: She'll need a place to work

The following four lines are said simultaneously and to each other.

TRUDI: She should come to my place
        My apartment's got wonderful cross ventilation

JOHN: She should come to my place
        I have a desk and a desk chair with a pillow

SAM: She should come to my place
           I'll move my orthodontia textbooks over to the side
TALIDIA: She should come to my place
           My kids will stay as quiet as proverbial church mice

SASHA *sits down in the hallway.*

SASHA: I'm perfectly comfortable right here
           Thank you though

The following four lines are said simultaneously and to each other.

TRUDI: She's fine right here
           Give the girl some space
JOHN: She's fine right here
           What she needs is time to collect her thoughts
TALIDIA: She's fine right here
           Can't you see she wants to work in peace
SAM: She's fine right here
           She doesn't need you breathing down her neck
SASHA: I'll let you know if I need anything

The following four lines are said simultaneously and to each other.

TRUDI: She'll let Me know if she needs anything
JOHN: She'll let Me know if she needs anything
TALIDIA: She'll let Me know if she needs anything
SAM: She'll let Me know if she needs anything

This last section is punctuated by a Saaaaaaaam meow. The four grown-ups sort of wait around for a moment or two, not wanting to be the first to leave. Then, each of them reluctantly sort of backs his or her way toward his or her apartment, enters, and closes the door.
SASHA *with pen and paper in hand writes:*

SASHA: The Eighth Wonder of the World
           by Alexandra Trusotsky

Suddenly the apartment doors of JOHN, TALIDIA, TRUDI, *and* SAM *open at once. All four look/listen to see how* SASHA *is faring, discern little, and then close their doors at once. A* PIZZA DELIVERY MAN *enters from House Right. At the front of the building the* PIZZA DELIVERY MAN *is buzzed in. He, too, goes through the routine of attempting to call the elevator before realizing it is broken.*

PIZZA DELIVERY MAN: Rats

The PIZZA DELIVERY MAN *embarks on the trip up the stairs and arrives at* JOHN'S *door.*

PIZZA DELIVERY MAN: Hello Mr. O'Hara
JOHN: SHHHHH
PIZZA DELIVERY MAN: What's the matter
JOHN *(can't you see)*: She's thinking

JOHN *hands the* PIZZA DELIVERY MAN *some cash, and the* PIZZA DELIVERY MAN *hands* JOHN *the pizza.*

PIZZA DELIVERY MAN: No kidding
           I used to do that all the time
           See you tomorrow Mr. O'Hara

The PIZZA DELIVERY MAN *leaves. As the* PIZZA DELIVERY MAN *exits the building, a guy trying, rather unsuccessfully, to simultaneously manage several containers that together make up his drum kit enters the building. As he goes through the comic motions of getting all his equipment inside the building, he sees immediately the elevator is out of order.* SASHA *paces and sees* JOHN'S *mail.*

SASHA: Oops

SASHA *crosses to* JOHN.

JOHN (*whispering*): I thought you were thinking
SASHA (*whispering*): I *was* thinking
              but then I thought of something
              Why are we whispering
JOHN (*whispering*): Because
              you're thinking
              (*normal voice*)
              What did you think of
SASHA: The mail

SASHA *passes* JOHN *his mail.* JOHN *riffles through it.*

JOHN: Aha

JOHN *has stopped at a particularly thick envelope, which he opens.*

SASHA: What is it
JOHN: For my collection
              An original Tiffany invitation to the
              New York and Brooklyn Bridge's Opening Day
              Ceremonies
SASHA: Can I see

JOHN *shows her the invitation very briefly.*

JOHN: Now resume thinking

JOHN *starts to wheel himself back into his apartment, but then changes his mind and gives* SASHA *the invitation before he goes inside and closes the door.* SASHA *goes back to her spot on the floor with the invitation. The* MAN WITH DRUMS *has by now made his way over to the stairwell.*
MAN WITH DRUMS: Yikes

The MAN WITH DRUMS embarks on a literally percussive and somewhat epic journey up the stairs. The SINGER/SONGWRITER and the MAN WITH BASS provide a bass line and counterpoint to the MAN WITH DRUMS'S journey upstairs. TALIDIA appears with a blanket and then disappears. JOHN appears, hands SASHA a piece of pizza, and then disappears. SAM appears, hands SASHA a toothbrush. TRUDI appears with an alarm clock and hands it down to SAM who puts it next to SASHA. SAM and TRUDI disappear. SASHA reaches for her pen and begins to write. Now the trio of musicians is all set up and stand in silhouette behind the blind in the SINGER/SONGWRITER'S apartment. And at last we hear the song—which up to now we've come to know only in bits and drafts as the SINGER/SONGWRITER labored over its composition—we hear the song in all its richness and glory. SASHA continues to scribble away.

MUSICIANS *(sung and played)*:

>Sheltered by its wire wings
>They come with offerings
>Steamboats sigh, tugboats sing
>A long list of wishes and dreams
>Is set here by the sea
>Take a moment there's a perfect view for free
>Just when you thought you were alone in the room
>Rises the platinum arc of the moon
>Suspended patiently
>Waiting for you to turn your head and see
>Here's the bridge, here's the water, here's the gift
>Here's my time, my words, here's my blanket
>Here's what you've been telling me along
>We're not waiting for anything
>Just lean back into the wind
>We're not missing anything
>If I lean
>If I lean
>If I lean
>You'll hold me

Throughout the song, we see a sea of MEN IN TOP HATS, *the* ROEBLINGS, *and families moving forward. As the* MEN IN TOP HATS *continue to cross, we see a projection of fireworks. And then* SASHA *has stopped writing. And then* SASHA *and the cast have picked up binoculars and joined the others in gazing at the Bridge. And the Bridge is lit up for the first time, light by light. As we and the characters gaze at the Bridge, we understand that naming it the Eighth Wonder of the World was no hyperbole, for it is a beautiful thing.*

THE END

ESPERANZA RISING

Lynne Alvarez

Based on the story by Pam Muñoz Ryan
Directed by Rebecca Lynn Brown

The world premier of *Esperanza Rising* opened on March 17, 2006, at Children's Theatre Company, Minneapolis, Minnesota. *Esperanza Rising* was funded in part by The Joyce Foundation and the National Endowment for the Arts.

CREATIVE TEAM

Music composition: Victor Zupanc
Scenic design: Riccardo Hernandez
Costume design: James Schuette
Lighting design: Matt Frey
Sound design: Victor Zupanc
Dramaturgy: Elissa Adams
Choreography: Joe Chvala
Stage manager: Chris Schweiger
Assistant stage manager: Jody Gavin

ORIGINAL CAST

ESPERANZA	Erin Nicole Hampe
HORTENSIA	Catalina Maynard
SIXTO and ALPHONSO	Raúl Ramos
MIGUEL	Desmin Borges
RAMONA and MODESTA	Melanie Rey
LUIS and MEXICAN BUREAUCRAT	Bob Davis
SERVANT GIRL and ISABEL	Maeve Moynihan
MARIELENA	Celeste J. Busa
MARTA	Amanda Granger
OKIE FATHER	Leif Jurgenson
OKIE MOTHER	Rebecca Lord
OKIE BOY	Albert Dudek

ENSEMBLE: Chelsea Bohmer, Tegan Carr, Jacob Duhon, Patric Faunillan, Kate Howell, Ryan Howell, Katie Moss, Natasha Roy, Gabrielle Silverman, and Kaliya Warren.

MUSICIANS: Roberto Rodriguez (vihuela and guitar), Joe Cruz (guitarrón and guitar), and Victor Zupanc (accordion and guitar).

CHARACTERS

ESPERANZA

HORTENSIA

Three MARIACHIS

DON SIXTO

RAMONA

SERVANT GIRL

MARIELENA

MIGUEL

LUIS

"OKIE" FAMILY: FATHER, MOTHER, and BOY

ISABEL

MODESTA

ALFONSO

MARTA

Three WOMEN WORKERS

All action takes place in 1929–30 at Rancho Linda Flor, at the Mexico–U.S. border crossing, and at various locations at the workers' camp in California.

ACT ONE

Scene 1

MARIACHI 1 *(shouts over music)*: ¡México!

MARIACHI 2: ¡Viva México!

MARIACHI 3: ¡Viva México!

ALL THREE:	Bonito es México entero
	Bella tierra nacional
	Donde Dios puso un letrero
	¡Como ésta no hay otra igual!
MARIACHI 1:	Yes. Yes. I love you Mexico!
MARIACHI 2:	¡México lindo!
MARIACHI 3:	¡Ahora en inglés!
ALL THREE:	All of Mexico is beautiful
	As seen with loving eyes
	Where God himself put up a sign
	This is paradise!
MARIACHI 1:	You tell them!
MARIACHI 2:	Okay!
MARIACHI 2:	La Virgen tendió su manto
	En la tierra de amor
	¡Y con eso hizo el rancho
	Que se llama Linda Flor!
MARIACHI 3:	Yes. Yes. El Rancho Linda Flor
MARIACHI 1:	In the state of Aguascalientes!
ALL THREE:	The Virgin spread her mantle
	Over a land that she adored
	And so created el rancho
	That we now call Linda Flor.

The stage is dark except for a splendid bed looking as if it is suspended in air. Among the white lace covers and many ruffled and beaded white pillows, we see movement. ESPERANZA *turns over in her sleep. Dressed in a white silk and lace nightgown, she at first looks like part of the bed. But we see her dark head move. She lifts her head, and suddenly a huge pile of colorfully wrapped birthday presents lights up at the foot of her bed, which we now see is on a platform. She sits up, and as she does,* HORTENSIA *in local dress rushes in with a silver tray with a brush and roses on it.*

HORTENSIA: They're coming. They're coming. Miss Esperanza. Quick into your dress.

ESPERANZA *gets up sleepily and holds out her arms.* HORTENSIA *slips on her white frilly dress and buttons it.*

ESPERANZA: You woke me up! I was having the best dream!

HORTENSIA: May the rest of your life be a beautiful dream, niña. But now—hurry! Let's brush your hair!

HORTENSIA *brushes out her hair.*

ESPERANZA: I want the red satin ribbon.

HORTENSIA: The white one is just as pretty.

ESPERANZA: You didn't iron the red one, did you!

HORTENSIA: I've been busy with your birthday.

ESPERANZA: Fine then. The white one will do. Ouch—you're pulling my hair!

HORTENSIA: ¡Que latosa es Usted!

We hear the beginning of "Cielito lindo" as HORTENSIA *ties the ribbon in* ESPERANZA'S *hair.*

ESPERANZA: They're here! Hurry up!

She runs to throw open the large doors to the patio; light streams in. The three MARIACHIS, *their black suits studded with silver, start playing and singing the traditional birthday song "Las mañanitas." Two* CAMPESINOS *are holding poles with a banner saying "Rancho las tres rosas" with three large beautiful roses painted on it. Behind them is a crowd of* CAMPESINOS *in work clothes and a little* SERVANT GIRL. *Friends and family are there too, decked out in European style.* ESPERANZA'S *father,* SIXTO, *is holding twelve roses.* MIGUEL *beside him is holding a large brightly wrapped box. They all sing.*

ALL: *Éstas son las mañanitas*
       Que cantaba el rey David
       A las muchachas bonitas

Se las cantaba así:
Despierta, mi bien, despierta
Que ya se amaneció
Y los pájaros ya cantan
La luna ya se metió.

They end with cheers of "happy birthday" (¡Feliz cumpleaños!), and some chant "Esperan-za! Esperan-za!" And they clap. They all come forward with little gifts or offerings of fruit.

ESPERANZA: Mama, Papa—what a beautiful fiesta! You've made me very happy.

RAMONA: Then I'm happy, too.

SIXTO (*approaches with* MIGUEL *behind him*): ¡M'hija adorada! What a sad birthday it would be without a gift of roses! Twelve roses— one perfect rose for each precious year of your life!

ESPERANZA: Mmmmmmm. Huele a dulce. They smell so delicious.

The little SERVANT GIRL *comes up and stands on tiptoe to smell them. First she looks at* SIXTO *to make sure it's all right. He nods to* ESPERANZA, *who holds them out to the girl.*

SERVANT GIRL: Mmmmmmm. Huele a dulce.

She runs away.

ESPERANZA: ¡Ay!

SIXTO: What is it?

ESPERANZA: My finger. Look, Mama.

HORTENSIA (*crosses herself*): That means bad luck!

SIXTO: No, Hortensia, that's life. No hay rosas sin espinas. You can't have roses without thorns.

RAMONA (*rubs her finger*): Sana, sana
Colita de rana
Si no sana hoy
¡Sanará mañana!

SIXTO (*he kisses her finger*): Now all better! Yes?

ESPERANZA: Yes, Papa.

SIXTO: Miguel. Ven.

MIGUEL *steps forward with the package.*

SIXTO: As I have every year since you were born: a beautiful doll for my own muñequita.

ESPERANZA: Yes! Yes!

MARIELENA *approaches to see.*

SIXTO: This year's doll comes right from Spain—Sevilla, con mantilla. Olé!

ESPERANZA: Oooooooo.

SIXTO: This doll is the most special of any I have given you before. Do you know why?

ESPERANZA: It's the most beautiful! Its eyes open and close!

SIXTO: No. This doll is special because it is the last doll I will ever give you.

ESPERANZA: But Papa—

SIXTO: Next year you'll be thirteen, on your way to being a young woman. You won't want dolls anymore.

ESPERANZA: I'll always want dolls!

SIXTO: I'm afraid not. You'll want dresses and purses and shawls and even more ribbons for your hair. So treasure this doll, and keep it always to remember what it was like to be twelve and how much your papa loved you! Now—todos—¡a divertirse! Today is a fiesta. Dance, eat, drink, ándale, mi gente. You too, Miguelín, Doña Hortensia!

Some campesinos come up and kiss SIXTO's *hand or* RAMONA's *and say, "Gracias, patrón," "Gracias, seño'," "Gracias, patrona," "Gracias, señora." They say "Felicidades, señ'ito" to* ESPERANZA. SIXTO *goes to* RAMONA *and presents her with a single rose.*

SIXTO: And you, mi amor, as I said since the first day I met you— I give you my life in this rose!

RAMONA: You have such good taste.

SIXTO: Yes. Of course, the good taste to fall in love forever! Shall we dance?

Huge platters of food are brought out. The little SERVANT GIRL *carries a very heavy one that makes her stagger.* MIGUEL *helps her. The* MARIACHIS *play and some people dance.*

ESPERANZA: ¡Hortensia!

HORTENSIA: Yes, mi reina . . .

ESPERANZA: Buckle my shoes, please. My hands are shaking. I'm too excited. My papa's brought me a doll from Sevilla!

Esperanza (Erin Nicole Hampe) dances with her father (Raúl Ramos), mother (Melanie Rey), and guests at her birthday party during the world premiere of *Esperanza Rising* by Lynne Alvarez in 2006. Photograph by Rob Levine.

HORTENSIA *shakes her head. As soon as the shoes are buckled,*
ESPERANZA *runs for the door, where a well-dressed girl,* MARIELENA,
approaches her, and the little SERVANT GIRL *follows.*

MARIELENA: Felicidades, Esperanza, felicidades. I love your dress.
   So much lace. Almost like mine—oooo, and a mountain of
   presents. You are so lucky. Let's open some!
ESPERANZA: Let's look at the doll!

The little SERVANT GIRL *follows hesitantly. But she isn't noticed until they*
arrive at the stack of presents. MARIELENA *turns to the girl.*

MARIELENA: Yes? What do you want?
SERVANT GIRL: To see all the pretty things.
MARIELENA: Don't they need you in the kitchen?

ESPERANZA *unwraps her father's present. It is a traveling chest with a*
beautiful doll inside.

MARIELENA: Ooooo, look, an itty bitty comb with pearls . . . and a
   white mantilla and gloves. Mine doesn't have gloves.
ESPERANZA: And look at all these clothes!

She takes out dress after dress.

MARIELENA: What are you going to name her?
ESPERANZA: I don't know yet . . . I have to think of a very special
   name.
MARIELENA: She has real lashes on her eyes. Ooooooooo. I'm so
   jealous!

The SERVANT GIRL *reaches out to touch the dresses.*

SERVANT GIRL: Ayyyy, mona . . . qué mona . . .

ESPERANZA *jerks the doll away from her.* MARIELENA *slaps her hand.*

MARIELENA: India prieta—¡anda! I . . . I told you to go to the kitchen!

The SERVANT GIRL *starts to cry.* RAMONA *and* HORTENSIA *enter.*

HORTENSIA: Escuincla, ¿qué haces aquí?

SERVANT GIRL: Quise ver los regalos, no más.

RAMONA: Girls! Shame on you. I don't think it would hurt to let her
    hold the doll for a few moments!

ESPERANZA: Mama. This doll is special! Besides, she's poor and
    dirty . . .

HORTENSIA: Con permiso, Señora.

She exits with the doll.

RAMONA: Esperanza!

ESPERANZA: What?

RAMONA: When you scorn these people, you scorn Miguel and
    Hortensia. And you embarrass yourself. Now, come in and
    receive the rest of your gifts from our gente, with a smile.

ESPERANZA: Ay, Mama, they only bring fruit. Let them put it in a bowl.

RAMONA: People give what they can. At the very least, you owe them
    respect in return. This life we enjoy rests on their shoulders!

ESPERANZA: No. Their life rests on ours! Papa made this life for
    us. He cleared this land with his own machete. He brought the
    grapes from Spain and the cattle from Brazil. He dug the roses
    from Sevilla and planted them here! Without us, our gente would
    have no work!

TÍO LUIS *enters with one* PISTOLERO.

ESPERANZA: Isn't that true, Tío Luis?

She laughs and starts to run off. One of LUIS'S PISTOLEROS *stops her and_
points to her uncle.*

LUIS: Don't forget your manners, young lady.

ESPERANZA: Yes, Tío. Hello, Tío.

LUIS: Muchacho—

A PISTOLERO *brings over a large papaya.*

LUIS: I brought you this papaya from Veracruz.

ESPERANZA: Oh, fruit! Thank you, Tío.

LUIS: Happy birthday.

ESPERANZA *exits.*

LUIS: Ramona, qué hermosa te ves. Como siempre.

RAMONA: You're too kind.

LUIS: My brother is a very, very fortunate man. I may have the money in the family—but he . . . he has the treasure! ¿Verdad, muchacho?

The two PISTOLEROS *chuckle and smile in agreement.*

RAMONA: Must you always bring your pistolero, Luis? Certainly you have no enemies here.

LUIS: Yes—I apologize for this vermin. But these are dangerous times. There are bandits in the hills, and—¡caray! as president of the bank, one must always show one is a very serious man. In my position it is better to be feared than loved, don't you think?

RAMONA: I think you've accomplished exactly what you wish.

LUIS: Good. Good. Stay as lovely as you are, cuñada.

He bows. RAMONA *hurries away.* LUIS *and his men go mix with the other guests. On the way to her father* ESPERANZA *takes off her shoes, and she runs weaving through the crowd past* MIGUEL *with his mother.*

ESPERANZA: Look, Miguel, I'm a gypsy. I have no shoes!

MIGUEL (*pulls out her ribbon*): Gypsies don't wear ribbons. They put flowers in their hair!

ESPERANZA: Hortensia, look what he did!

HORTENSIA: Here, I'll tie it for you.

ESPERANZA (to MIGUEL): Did you bring me a present?

MIGUEL: No.

ESPERANZA: Yes, you did. Let me see!

She tugs at his arm.

MIGUEL (*pulls something out of his pocket and hides it behind his back*):
    Pepe Ven. One, two—mangos de Manila, ¡suave y dulce como un
    meringue! Your favorite!

ESPERANZA: Oh, fruit! Thank you. Would you put them in a bowl,
    Miguelín? I can't carry them around with me right now!

She runs off to join her father.

MIGUEL: She's spoiled!

HORTENSIA: She's only twelve.

MIGUEL: You were selling tortillas in the street at twelve.

HORTENSIA: Otro mundo. And it's time you understood it.

MIGUEL: What do you mean?

HORTENSIA: You can't go around pulling her hair anymore.

MIGUEL: So what if I pull her hair?! We always kid around.

HORTENSIA: "Always" no longer exists. You're older now. So is she.
    You can't be friends in the same way.

MIGUEL: Are you telling me to know my place?!

HORTENSIA: Yes. You are the housekeeper's son. Esperanza is the
    ranch owner's daughter.

MIGUEL: And?

HORTENSIA: And a deep river runs between you, Miguel. Esperanza
    stands on one side of this river and you on the other—and this
    river can never be crossed. ¿Me entiendes?

MIGUEL: Claro que sí.

Three VAQUEROS *in dusty clothes rush in and over to* SIXTO. *They pull him
away excitedly. He listens and becomes very serious.*

SIXTO: Ándale, pues.

They hurry away.

SIXTO: ¡Miguel! ¡Ven!
MIGUEL: A sus órdenes.
ESPERANZA: What's wrong, Papa?
SIXTO: Nothing, mi muñequita. Just some trouble with the cattle.
    Saddle our horses. There's trouble near the six hills!
MIGUEL: Right away, patrón.

He runs off.

ESPERANZA: What do you mean, trouble?
SIXTO: Nothing you should worry about!
ESPERANZA: I want to go with you, Papa.
SIXTO: No. Not now.
ESPERANZA: I can ride a horse, too. Why does Miguel get to go,
    not me?
SIXTO: Because Miguel knows how to fix things and he's learning his
    job! Now, enjoy your party. Don't eat too many mangos. Leave
    some for me. You promise?
ESPERANZA: Yes, Papa.

She runs after MIGUEL *and watches as he straps on a gun and kisses his
mother.* SIXTO *hurries out. He stops and whispers something to* RAMONA.

RAMONA: ¡Ay no! So close?!
SIXTO: No le hagas. ¡Soy hombre de acero, mi amor!
RAMONA: Be careful!

Scene 2
It is night. The patio has been cleared. There is a huge moon. We see
RAMONA *silhouetted against it. The* MARIACHIS *are playing softly, but
they are invisible to the people onstage.* RAMONA *is singing the song the*

MARIACHIS *are playing while she searches the horizon. As she sings,* ESPERANZA *opens her window. She hasn't been able to sleep either.* HORTENSIA *enters and starts placing lit candles everywhere.*

RAMONA: 　　　　　*Ay si la ra la ra la*
　　　　　　　　Ay, la, la, la
　　　　　　　　Vuela, vuela jilguerillo
　　　　　　　　Rayo brillante del sol
　　　　　　　　Llévate este papelito
　　　　　　　　Al dueño de mi amor.
　　　　　　　　Ay si la ra la ra la
　　　　　　　　Ay, la, la, la

ESPERANZA *opens her window. She sings the second verse.* RAMONA *is startled.*

ESPERANZA: 　　　*Vuela, vuela jilguerillo*
　　　　　　　　Donde tú puedes volar
　　　　　　　　A buscar mis amores
　　　　　　　　Que no los puedo olvidar
　　　　　　　　Ay si la ra la ra la
　　　　　　　　Ay, la, la, la
　　　　　　　　Ay si la ra la ra la
　　　　　　　　Ay, la, la, la

RAMONA: Did my singing wake you?

ESPERANZA: No. I couldn't sleep.

RAMONA: I know. Ven, mi amor.

ESPERANZA *in her nightgown climbs out the window and runs to her mother. They embrace.*

ESPERANZA: Did Papa come home?

RAMONA: No.

ESPERANZA: Ay.

RAMONA: He's just a little late.

ESPERANZA: I know. But, Mama?

RAMONA: What, m'hija?

ESPERANZA: I saw Miguel take a rifle.

RAMONA: Yes.

ESPERANZA: Papa, too?

RAMONA: Yes.

ESPERANZA: I heard Hortensia warn Miguel about the bandits. Who are the bandits?

RAMONA: They're desperate men.

ESPERANZA: Why are they desperate?

RAMONA: They have no land. They're very angry.

ESPERANZA: Are they angry with us?

RAMONA: Yes.

ESPERANZA: But they don't even know us.

RAMONA: They don't see us as people—they only see our land. They see cattle grazing on acres and acres as far as the eye can see, while some of them are forced to eat cats. Imagine. Many of these bandits hate all people who own a lot of land. They try to . . . to hurt them and make them leave. People say these bandits steal from the rich and give to the poor. But these men don't always give to the poor, and they kill innocent people.

ESPERANZA: Papa says we own a lot of land.

RAMONA: Yes, we do. But your papa is a good and generous man. Our workers eat for free. And your papa has given them land of their own and houses. The people know that.

ESPERANZA: But do the bandits know that?

RAMONA: I hope so.

HORTENSIA (*enters with some candles*): Señ'ra, is there something I can get for you?

RAMONA: No, thank you.

HORTENSIA: Some candles. Surely Our Lady will see our little lights of hope.

They light them. HORTENSIA *kneels near one of the candles and prays quietly.*

ESPERANZA: Mama?

RAMONA: Yes.

ESPERANZA: Will we lose our land?

RAMONA: No. This is our home.

ESPERANZA *lies down on the ground.*

RAMONA: Esperanza! What are you doing?

ESPERANZA: I'm afraid. I need to feel the land.

She lies down.

ESPERANZA: You lie down, too, Mama.

RAMONA: Not now, mi amor.

ESPERANZA: Please.

RAMONA: Why?

ESPERANZA: Because the land will speak to you. If you are very, very still and very patient, you can hear its big heart beat, and if you wait even longer, you can feel it breathe. Papa always says if you are connected to the land, you are connected to life! Lie down, Mama! I hear something! Listen!

RAMONA: Now is not the time. I think you need a quiet heart to hear the earth. Now, I would hear only my own heart beating.

The MARIACHIS *get up and shrug their shoulders. They didn't hear anything. It starts to get darker. One of the* MARIACHIS *taps another on his shoulder and points excitedly in the distance.*

RAMONA *(jumping to her feet)*: Horses! M'hija! Horses!

ESPERANZA: Oh. Someone's coming! Papa! Papa!

RAMONA *sinks to her knees and prays silently.* ESPERANZA *joins her. A silhouette appears against the moon, walking toward them, followed by some men. They are carrying something heavy between them. The* MARIACHIS *go quickly to see them.*

RAMONA: Sixto? Is that you?

MIGUEL *steps forward into the light.*

MIGUEL: It's me, Doña. Miguel.
RAMONA: And Sixto? . . .
ESPERANZA: Where is Papa?!
MIGUEL: Over there.
RAMONA: ¡Dios mío! Sixto, Sixto. ¡Mi amor, mi vida! . . .

She runs to the men and embraces the form they are carrying. We see this only in silhouette. MIGUEL *and* ESPERANZA *are the only two standing in the light.*

MIGUEL: I'm sorry.
ESPERANZA: What?
MIGUEL: I'm so sorry. He's dead, mi reina.

ESPERANZA *takes her father's belt and hat, covers them with kisses, and starts crying.*

ESPERANZA: Liar!
MIGUEL: It's true.
ESPERANZA: No!
MIGUEL: Yes.
ESPERANZA: Then it's your fault.
MIGUEL: I didn't kill him!
ESPERANZA: How dare you come back here alive when he's dead. How dare you show your face. You let him die. ¡Bestia! ¡Cobarde!
MIGUEL: No, mi reina. I didn't leave him. I loved him like a father. I would have given my life for him, but he went off on his own . . . and they shot him.
ESPERANZA: Shot him.
MIGUEL: Yes.
ESPERANZA: Was it the bandits, Miguel? Tell me.

MIGUEL: Yes. I'm sorry.

ESPERANZA: He lied then! Papa lied! How can land mean life—if they killed my papa for land?!!

She cries.

Scene 3

The MARIACHIS *sing as a long line of workers, neighbors, and the family follows* ESPERANZA *and* RAMONA *to a grassy spot near the house.* DON LUIS *has his two* PISTOLEROS *place a heavy headstone among the roses. The* WORKERS *are in their work clothes. The family is dressed very formally in black.* RAMONA *and* ESPERANZA *wear heavy black mantillas. A* PRIEST *sprinkles holy water on the grave. All kneel and cross themselves. The* SERVANT GIRL *cuts roses and gives them to each person so they can place them on the grave.*

(In the rhythm of a corrido, every other verse has the accent on the first syllable. The remainder of the verses are accented on the second.)

> Corrido of El Rancho Linda Flor
> *Here fell Don Sixto Ortega*
> *In the dust of his ranch Linda Flor.*
> *Shot in the back by bandidos*
> *Who kill the rich and rob the poor!*
> *Ramona his widow is crying*
> *His daughter distraught and in tears*
> *His ranch Linda Flor in disorder*
> *His brother Luis much too near.*

SERVANT GIRL *sings Ave María.* RAMONA *almost faints at one moment.* DON LUIS *helps her to stand. She pulls away from him.* ESPERANZA *is kneeling, smelling the roses.* MIGUEL *approaches.*

ESPERANZA: Do you remember, Miguel? When Papa planted these roses for us?

MIGUEL: I can never forget.

ESPERANZA: The pink ones. Like dawn, for me?

MIGUEL: The red ones

ESPERANZA: Like sunset, for you.

MIGUEL: We were such small children then.

ESPERANZA: Papa loved you like a son.

MIGUEL: But I'm not his son. See? *(He places his arm next to* ESPERANZA*.)* Soy raza de bronce, reinita, and you—white as the best Spanish lace.

ESPERANZA: So?

MIGUEL: White is the color of money. Brown is the color of work.

ESPERANZA: But Papa loved you—

MIGUEL: Your father was a good man. He gave us a cabin and land. Perhaps I was almost a son. But your uncle would take it all away and treat us like animals.

ESPERANZA: No! That will never happen. My mama will talk to him. He listens to my mother.

MIGUEL: Ojalá.

They join the crowd at the grave.

LUIS: Are you all right?

RAMONA: As you see.

LUIS: You look so sad and pale. Grieving does not suit you. I hope you won't wear black all year.

RAMONA: Black will be my favorite color, Luis.

LUIS: It doesn't need to be. I said, it doesn't need to be.

RAMONA: What do you mean?

LUIS: Ramona, I want you to know . . . to know . . .

RAMONA: What, Luis?

LUIS: You don't have to be alone. I'm here for you. In all ways. In any way that would bring you happiness.

RAMONA: Be careful what you say!

LUIS: I have always loved you.

RAMONA: You're grieving. You don't know what you're saying.

LUIS: I do. I have always longed for you. You knew that. You knew that!

RAMONA: ¡Buitre! You offend me! How dare you propose with the earth still fresh over your brother's grave!

LUIS: I'm concerned for you. I love you. I'm no beast. We would wait the appropriate amount of time out of respect for my brother. One year is customary, is it not?

RAMONA: I have no desire to marry you, Luis. Now or ever.

LUIS: I see. I am wounded to the core by your words. But emotions aside, I hope you will consider my proposal from another perspective.

RAMONA: There is no other perspective.

LUIS: Actually, there is. Your husband, Sixto Ortega, left this house and all its contents to you and your daughter. You will also receive a yearly income from the grapes.

RAMONA: I'm aware of that, Luis.

LUIS: Are you aware that women cannot inherit land! Sixto left the land to me. So, if you wish to be free of the burden of my continued presence—I will purchase the house for this amount.

He hands her some papers.

RAMONA: Are you mad?! This is our home. My husband meant for us to live here. And the house . . . is worth twenty times this much!

LUIS: Not really. I own the land the house is on. No one would dare buy it from you.

RAMONA: I would never sell it. We have nowhere else to live.

LUIS: I will give you a place to live.

RAMONA: The answer is still no.

LUIS: You will regret your decision, Ramona. Keep in mind that this house and those grapes are on my property. I can make things difficult for you. Very difficult. I will let you sleep on your decision: marry me, or sell. Both offers are more than generous!

He exits. RAMONA *cries.* ESPERANZA *goes to her.*

ESPERANZA: Don't cry, Mama. Everything will be all right.

MARIACHIS:	*Here lies Don Sixto Ortega.*
	Shot like a dog in the back.
	Red roses grow on his gravestone
	His wife and his daughter in black.
	Who will take care of his cattle?
	Who will harvest his fields of grapes?
	Who will water his red Spanish roses?
	Who will be tending his grave?

It grows dark. A blood-red quarter moon comes out. Everyone places their flowers, kisses the headstone, and leaves. ESPERANZA *and* RAMONA *retire.*

Scene 4

We hear night noises. The MARIACHIS *are keeping watch, perhaps carrying rifles.*

> *Night drops down like a black curtain*
> *The moon is bright red in the skies*
> *A flame leaps from torches to rooftops*
> *Don Luis smiles as everyone cries—*
> *"Fire! Fire! Fire!"*

This cry blends into everyone crying out "Fire! Fire!" We hear horses and shouts. We see smoke and then flames.

ESPERANZA: Mama—where are you?

RAMONA: Here. Take my hand.

ESPERANZA: Mama, what's happening?

RAMONA *(offstage)*: The house is on fire! We must get out!

HORTENSIA *runs in as* ESPERANZA *and* RAMONA *climb out the window.* RAMONA *trips and falls.*

HORTENSIA: ¡Señora Ortega! ¡Esperanza!

RAMONA: Here! We're here!

HORTENSIA: ¡Jesús, María, José!

ESPERANZA: Wait! Wait! I forgot something!

She runs back in.

RAMONA: No! Esperanza. No!

She tries to get up and cannot.

RAMONA: Miguel! Esperanza's in the fire!
MIGUEL: Where? Esperanza!
ESPERANZA: Up here!
MIGUEL: ¡Escalera! ¡Escalera!
HORTENSIA: Hurry! Ai, ¡Dios todopoderoso!
RAMONA: I have to get in there!

She tries to walk and can't.

HORTENSIA: Can you get up?
RAMONA: No. Please God, I can't lose my daughter, too!

RAMONA *and* HORTENSIA *hold each other.* MIGUEL *comes out with*
ESPERANZA, *who clasps her doll in its case. They are both coughing and*
covered with ash.

RAMONA: Esperanza, why did you do something so silly! I thought I
    lost you, too!
ESPERANZA: I'm sorry. I'm sorry. I had to get Papa's doll. I couldn't
    let her burn. It's all I have of him.
RAMONA: I understand. I know.
HORTENSIA: Ay look, the stairs are beginning to burn!
MIGUEL: The stables caught fire! Ay, the horses! ¡Vámanos,
    muchachos!

He runs offstage.

CHORUS: ¡Claro! ¡Pronto!

We hear more horses. DON LUIS *enters.*

HORTENSIA: The vines! Oh, the vines! Look, the whole hillside's on
    fire! The rose garden is gone! It's the end of the world!

RAMONA: We've lost everything.

LUIS: Ramona! I was out fixing fences, I saw the smoke! Are you all
    right?

RAMONA: I'm fine.

ESPERANZA: Mama, Mama. What will we do? Where will we go?

LUIS: Don't be afraid. I will take care of you both. Come. I will help
    you. Now you must stay with me.

RAMONA: Thank you, Luis. But I can't leave here. My husband is
    here. My life is here.

LUIS: But there's nowhere to stay. Come home with me.

RAMONA: No, Luis. We will stay in the servants' quarters. With
    Hortensia and Miguel.

LUIS: Of course. If you prefer.

RAMONA: I prefer.

LUIS: But . . . how long can you live with the servants?

RAMONA: Until I rebuild.

LUIS: You expect to rebuild?

RAMONA: Yes. Of course.

LUIS: But, cuñada—where will you get the money to rebuild? The
    house is gone. The vineyards have burned to the ground. You
    are destitute. You have nothing. I will not pressure you to marry
    me, but I must beg you to consider it. Right now you are thinking
    only of yourself, which is understandable. But you must think
    of others. Think of your gente, who depend on you for their
    livelihood. Think of your darling daughter. Sixto worked so
    very hard . . . you might say he gave his life so you two would be
    cherished and protected. Do you think he would want anything
    less now when you need it most?

ESPERANZA: Mama?!

RAMONA: Quiet. Let me think.

LUIS: A word from you can make everyone's life easier . . . or not.

RAMONA: I see. Yes, Luis, I will consider your proposal.

ESPERANZA: Mama, no!

LUIS: I have no doubt that you will make the right decision. Although you don't love me, my heart is yours! I will be back in the morning for your answer.

He starts to leave.

ESPERANZA *(to LUIS)*: I hate you!

LUIS: And Ramona, if Esperanza is to be my daughter, she must learn better manners. In fact, today I will look into boarding schools where they can teach her to act like a young lady.

He exits.

ESPERANZA: Mama, why? Why did you tell him that?

RAMONA: I know what I'm doing. I will never marry that man. I have money in the bank.

HORTENSIA: His bank.

RAMONA: Friends will help.

HORTENSIA: And pay with their lives.

RAMONA: You are right. You are right.

HORTENSIA: Ay, señora. The truth is—if you stay here, you will be destitute. You will have to marry Don Luis.

RAMONA: I don't know what to do.

She tries to walk and can't.

RAMONA: I think my ankle is broken.

ESPERANZA: I'll help you, Mama. Sana, sana colita de rana . . .

RAMONA: My ankle is the least of our problems. The bone can be fixed by a doctor. This situation can only be fixed by me. Our lives and the lives of everyone around us are depending on my decision.

HORTENSIA: Doña Ramona. There's something you should know.

RAMONA: Yes?

HORTENSIA: Don't sacrifice yourself for us. Miguel and I have decided to go to the United States. My brother Alfonso has been writing to us about the big farm in California where he works now. He can arrange jobs and a cabin for us.

ESPERANZA: You're deserting us, too?!

MIGUEL: We have his letter. Proof of work will allow us to cross the border.

RAMONA: When are you leaving?

HORTENSIA: Tonight, si Dios quiere.

RAMONA: What if Esperanza and I went with you to the United States?

ESPERANZA: Mama—we can't just leave!

RAMONA: What should we do, Esperanza? Do you want me to marry Tío Luis and let him send you far away from me?

ESPERANZA: No.

RAMONA: Hortensia, what do you think?

HORTENSIA: Doña, I don't know.

MIGUEL: There's only field work there. Hard, dirty work.

RAMONA: I'm not afraid of work.

MIGUEL: Doña, with all due respect, you can't travel with a broken ankle. You can't work, and worse, they might stop us at the border because of you.

RAMONA: I have thought of that, Miguel. Let me speak to Esperanza for a moment. Anza, come here. Are you feeling strong?

ESPERANZA: Yes. I feel fine.

RAMONA: You are strong! ¡Conste!

ESPERANZA: Sí, Mama.

RAMONA: Good. You're only twelve. But twelve will have to be old enough. We are going to be like that beautiful bird, the phoenix, that dives into the fire and rises, reborn from its ashes. We will rise again, with a new life ahead of us in California with Hortensia and Miguel.

ESPERANZA: All right.

RAMONA: Good. Because you will go first.

ESPERANZA: What do you mean, me? What about you?

RAMONA: My ankle is broken. I can't travel. You must go without me for now.

ESPERANZA: No, no, no, no, no, no, no! Don't send me away, Mama. Please, please don't. I'll be good. I promise. I swear. I'll be nice to Tío Luis. Whatever you want. I promise.

RAMONA: You will go first. The nuns at La Gloriosa will care for me until my ankle heals. Then I'll come find you with enough money so we all can live well.

HORTENSIA: Don Luis is muy macho. He'll never let you leave.

RAMONA: He won't find me. He'll believe I fled with you.

ESPERANZA: No, no, no, no, no! I'll stay at the convent with you!

RAMONA: Hiding one is difficult enough. Hiding two is impossible! Hortensia, you know my life is my beautiful daughter. Can I trust you with my life?

HORTENSIA: Always. Que Dios nos bendiga.

MIGUEL: Mama, Esperanza has never worked a day in her life. She can't even braid her own hair. She'll be nothing but trouble.

HORTENSIA: Miguel!

MIGUEL: If she goes, I will not be her servant. Remember that!

He stomps off and goes to SIXTO'S *grave. He takes out a knife and viciously stabs the earth again and again.*

ESPERANZA: Mama, how can I live without you?

RAMONA: Are you living without Papa? . . .

ESPERANZA: Yes. But I carry him in my heart and in my head.

RAMONA: And I will think of you, and I will pray for you every minute of every day and every night until we are together again.

ESPERANZA: How will I know when you're coming?

RAMONA: I will be there before you know it! I will write you whenever I can.

ESPERANZA: Please get well. Please come to me soon.

RAMONA: I promise.

HORTENSIA: Doña, the cart is ready. Miguel! Miguelín!

MIGUEL *is still furiously cutting the earth.*

MARIACHIS *(singing the folk song "La Rosita"):*
>   Cuando se mueren las rosas
>   Queda muy triste el jardín
>   Queda muy triste el jardín
>   Cuando se mueren las flores
>   Mueren las horas dichosas
>   Y ya no huele a jazmín
>   Y ya no huele a jazmín
>   Ni vuelan las mariposas.
>
>   When the roses die
>   The garden seems so sad
>   The garden seems so sad
>   When the flowers die.
>   The joy-filled hours die
>   And the scent of jasmine fades
>   And the scent of roses fades
>   And I can only cry.
>
>   Y ya no huele a jazmín
>   Ni vuelan las mariposas.

Scene 5

Two SOLDIERS *in uniform, one Mexican, one American, march in carrying a huge banner that reads "*THE BORDER.*" They stop center stage and secure it. Two* BUREAUCRATS *carrying flags enter: one Mexican, one American. As they enter, we hear each country's national anthem. They set up small desks and secure the flags. They salute each other, take out a huge pestle to stamp with, and sit down. Two of the* MARIACHIS *run in, out of breath; the other one is half in and half out of a "costal." He gets out and bows to a pretty young woman and hands her the costal. The three tiptoe with much fanfare past the bureaucrats—of course no one sees them. They are free to move back and forth at will. Throughout the scene,* *they watch all the people passing, tip their hats at pretty ladies, steal from the vendors, peek at the bureaucrats' papers, etc. A long line forms on the Mexican side, waiting to cross the border. A few people on the American side are waiting to cross into Mexico. There are vendors on both sides, people looking for relatives, etc. An obviously poor family, a* MOTHER, *a* FATHER, *and a little* BOY, *enter on the American side. They are displaced "Okies." The* FATHER *begins to play a harmonica or a violin, and the* BOY *does an awkward dance and sings. The* MOTHER *passes a hat. "Norteamericanos—bienvenidos a México. Pasen, pasen Uds. Ándale, pues." One of the* MARIACHIS *does a sort of riff on his trumpet when someone passes into Mexico. The other two pull him along.*

AMERICAN BUREAUCRAT: American nationals! Let 'em pass! Welcome home! [etc.]

ESPERANZA: Hortensia, I'm soooo hot.

HORTENSIA: We can take some of this off now, I think.

MIGUEL: Híjole. ¡Qué montón de gente! Mama, we have to be careful. Any little thing you do wrong up there and they throw you back. We have to do something about Esperanza. The papers say she is my sister but she looks nothing like us. They'll stop us. They won't let us cross!

HORTENSIA: I know what to do!

She braids ESPERANZA'S *hair.*

ESPERANZA: Stop that. I hate braids!

MIGUEL: Shhhhhh.

HORTENSIA: I'm sorry, niña—I have to do this.

MIGUEL: Mama, her dress is too nice.

HORTENSIA (*rips off the hem of* ESPERANZA'S *dress so it is too short*): Your dress is too new and too pretty. I have to make it look like you borrowed it.

ESPERANZA: Why? Why?

MIGUEL: Reinita. You must calm down. If the guards see you cry, they may stop us and ask too many questions.

HORTENSIA: Talk to no one. Pretend you are mute!

MIGUEL: And whatever you do, don't cry and call attention to yourself! We are trusting you with our lives, ¿entiendes?

ESPERANZA: Yes.

MIGUEL: She still doesn't look like my sister.

HORTENSIA: Wait! I must do this.

She takes up a handful of dirt and rubs it on ESPERANZA'S *skin.*

ESPERANZA: No!

HORTENSIA: We have to!

ESPERANZA: I look like a beggar!

MIGUEL: Your skin is too white.

ESPERANZA: Papa would be ashamed of me!

HORTENSIA: Muchachita, it's a disguise. So you will be safe and come with us. Let's pretend this is the most beautiful powder for your face.

ESPERANZA: It's dirt. You and Miguel are clean.

She starts to cry.

MIGUEL: Don't cry. We've escaped before. Remember when the two bandits came and your parents weren't home?

ESPERANZA: Yes.

MIGUEL: We hid under your bed.

HORTENSIA: And we were saved by a mouse! One Miguel had hid in his shirt just to scare you.

MIGUEL: And you sneezed! And the barefoot man yelled, "Someone's here!" And you were so scared you let the mouse go.

HORTENSIA: Just in time.

MIGUEL: And they saw him, and the one with the black boots said, "There's no one here. It's just a *ratón.*"

ESPERANZA: And they left!

MIGUEL: We escaped!

ESPERANZA: Thank God.

HORTENSIA: So now, what do you say about your disguise? You'll wear it?

MIGUEL: ¿Juega?

He shakes her hand.

ESPERANZA: Okay. ¡Juega el pollo pelón!

They laugh and get in line. An obviously wealthy AMERICAN WOMAN *and her* DAUGHTER *come by. They are handing out candy to the poor children. The* MARIACHIS *notice them and run over to get a piece of candy, too. Then they get in line behind* ESPERANZA. *The American couple stops in front of* ESPERANZA.

AMERICAN WOMAN: Isn't she sweet? Poor unfortunate creature. You'd think they'd wash once in a while. Would you like a piece of candy, dear? I know your mama can't afford it. Here.

ESPERANZA *draws herself up to refuse, but* MIGUEL *grabs it and hands it to her.*

AMERICAN WOMAN: These people! They don't even say thank you. *(She walks off.)* Why do I bother?!
ESPERANZA *(handing the candy to* MIGUEL*)*: You keep the candy!
MIGUEL: Sure. What's wrong, Anza?
ESPERANZA: She felt sorry for me! She thought I was poor.
MIGUEL: Good. Your disguise is working perfectly!
AGENT: Next!

The AGENT *examines their papers. He looks them up and down.*

AGENT *(to* HORTENSIA*)*: What's in that bag?
HORTENSIA: Our papers, señor.
AGENT: I see you have papers. Empty your bag.

HORTENSIA *empties the bag. The* AGENT *looks over everything and points to the doll case.*

AGENT: And that?

HORTENSIA: It's . . . it's only a doll.

The AGENT *opens it.*

AGENT: Where did you get something like this!

HORTENSIA: It belongs to her. To my daughter.

MIGUEL: My sister.

ESPERANZA: Yes. Yes . . . the . . . the . . . lady of the house where we
worked didn't want it anymore. She said I could have it.

AGENT: She did?

ESPERANZA: Yes . . . She was very nice. It was my birthday.

AGENT *(losing interest)*: Good. Good. Good. Mexican nationals—let
'em pass!

They cross the border. The OKIE FAMILY *is still performing.* MIGUEL
hands the candy to the OKIE BOY, *who gobbles it down.*

ESPERANZA: Are we through?

HORTENSIA *(crossing herself)*: He didn't bother to look at our papers!

MIGUEL: The future is ours! ¡Arriba y adelante!

OKIE BOY *(singing, the* BOY *dances)*:

> Many days you have lingered all around my cabin door
>
> Oh, hard times come a-gain no more.
>
> Oh, hard times come a-gain no more.

The MARIACHIS . . . *strike up a welcome as* HORTENSIA, MIGUEL, *and*
ESPERANZA *pass to the other side.*

ESPERANZA: This is America?

Scene 1

The MARIACHIS, ESPERANZA *(holding her doll),* HORTENSIA, *and* MIGUEL *are on a bus center stage. We see a backdrop of countryside that moves quickly past them. They stay still.*

HORTENSIA: So this is the United States of America!

MARIACHI 1: The beautiful State of California!

MARIACHI 2: The valley of San Joaquín! Land of plenty.

MARIACHI 3: Plenty of work. Ahuuaaa!

ALL: We smell oranges from a nearby grove

                Flowers bloom on the trees

                Melons dot the open field

                Brown people on their knees.

ESPERANZA: Look at all of them working in that field. There must be a hundred people. Two hundred.

MIGUEL: At least three hundred. Four hundred!

MARIACHI 1: Not just brown people!

MARIACHI 2: Poor people. All of them.

MARIACHI 1: Es triste, ¿no? So this is California. Mexico is gone.

MARIACHI 3:   Esperanza, Esperanza

                Is it hard to be believed?

                Mexico is like water spilled

                It cannot be retrieved!

OKIES *wander through. They sing verses from "Going down the Road Feelin' Bad" or Woody Guthrie's "Dust Bowl Blues."*

                We smell oranges from a nearby grove

                Flowers bloom on trees

                Melons dot the open fields

                What will this mean to me?

Other OKIES *arrive and wander by. They also sing from one of the two songs. They arrive at the camp. People start to enter, some dropping from the sky, some walking on. As they sing, they assemble the camp or go about tasks like washing clothes in tubs, sweeping, etc. Men walk by with heavy baskets of peaches, the crop in season now. A little girl,* ISABEL, *dressed in a man's undershirt, runs in, trying to make a kite fly. She crashes into* ESPERANZA, *who drops her doll.* ISABEL *goes to help pick her up.*

ISABEL: I'm sorry. I'm sorry.

ESPERANZA: Don't you touch her!

ALFONSO *enters behind her.* ALFONSO *runs to* HORTENSIA *and hugs her.*

ALFONSO: ¡Hermana!

HORTENSIA: ¡Alfonso!

ALFONSO (*embraces* HORTENSIA): Oye, hermana—¡qué gordita estás!

HORTENSIA: Y tú, ¡qué palillo!

ALFONSO: ¿Miguelito? Hombre—you look like a grown man.

HORTENSIA: Esperanza. This is my brother, Alfonso. He worked for Señor Rodríguez.

ESPERANZA: Our neighbor Señor Rodríguez?

HORTENSIA: Yes. And this is the girl I wrote you about.

ESPERANZA: Did you know Señor Rodríguez's daughter, Marielena? She was my best friend!

ALFONSO: No, Esperanza. I was a field servant. I didn't know the family.

ESPERANZA: Oh.

HORTENSIA: And Modesta?

ALFONSO: With the new baby! Our tent is right way. Bienvenidos. Welcome home.

The adults shake hands and embrace. They talk among themselves.
ESPERANZA *is cool to* ISABEL, *but* ISABEL *shows her the camp. People comment as the girls pass.*

ESPERANZA: What is that shack?

ISABEL: That's where we live.

ESPERANZA: Our horses had better stalls than that!

ISABEL: Wow! You'll like this camp. It has good water. All the toilets are over there.

ESPERANZA: So far away?

ISABEL: In some camps we had to go in ditches! You'll love our fiestas! We have them every Saturday night. There is music and food and dancing. I can't wait! Can you dance?

ESPERANZA: Of course.

A man (one of the MARIACHIS) drags a large bag with mail in it. He rings a bell.

MAILMAN: Mail! Mail! ¡Paquetes y correo!

ESPERANZA: Do you get mail here?

ISABEL: Oh, yes! Tía Hortensia used to write all the time…about you!

MAILMAN *(as he calls names, people come running out)*:
Enrique Arellano.
Teófilo Balendrano
Josefina Cruz Valencia
Faustino García Flores
¡Cartas de tus amores!

He moves on, ringing his bell. They stop in front of one of the shacks.
MODESTA *comes out the door and greets everyone.*

MODESTA: Hello. You must be Esperanza. I'm Modesta, Isabel's mother. Bienvenida, niña. I hope you'll feel at home here. Isabel will show you where to put your things.

MIGUEL *enters.*

MIGUEL: Tía, do you have some of those big tomato cans?

MODESTA: Isabel, get one of the cans for Miguel.

A baby cries as ISABEL *exits, followed by* MIGUEL.

MIGUEL: I need two.

ISABEL: Mama, Carlitos is crying.

MODESTA: I'll change Carlitos. Isabel—bring Esperanza her box!

ISABEL reenters, lugging a big cardboard box.

ISABEL: I'm back. This is your box, for all your things. I have one of
my own. We keep them under the bed.

ESPERANZA: Where's my room?

ISABEL: Here. You sleep with me.

ESPERANZA: In one bed.

ISABEL: I sleep with my head on this end, and you sleep with your
head on the other.

ESPERANZA: We sleep in the same bed?

ISABEL: Don't tell me, you had your own bed?!

ESPERANZA takes out her clothes from the sack and puts them in the box.

ISABEL: Why didn't you bring any of your pretty dresses?

ESPERANZA: They burned.

ISABEL: Oh. But you did have pretty dresses?

ESPERANZA: Many.

ISABEL: Did you really always get your own way and have all the dolls
and fancy dresses you wanted?

ESPERANZA: What?

ISABEL: Aunt Hortensia and Miguel wrote all about you. I'm happy
you're my cousin. I've never had a rich cousin.

ESPERANZA: I'm not your cousin.

ISABEL: Yes. Now you are. My mama told me to call you cousin. Is
your doll all right?

ESPERANZA: Yes.

ISABEL: Can I see her?

ESPERANZA: No. She's sleeping.

ISABEL: Oh.

ESPERANZA (singing softly): A la ruru niña

Duérmaseme ya

Que si no el coco

Se le comera . . .

ISABEL reaches to open the box.

ESPERANZA: I told you not to touch her. No one can touch her but me.
¿Entiendes? It was my father's dying wish.

ISABEL: Okay.

ESPERANZA: . . . and, ummmm . . . little girl?

ISABEL: My name's Isabel.

ESPERANZA: Isabel, yes, look: I'm tying a ribbon around the box in a
special way, so if you untie it, I'll know!

HORTENSIA: Esperanza. It's your turn to take a bath!

ESPERANZA: At last! ¡Qué divino!

She stands up near HORTENSIA, turns around, puts her hands out from
her sides, and waits.

ISABEL: Esperanza, what are you doing?

ESPERANZA: Hortensia helps me with my bath. Don't you,
Hortensia?

ISABEL: Tía—you really help Esperanza take a bath like I do with itty-
bitty Carlitos? ¡Ay ay ay!

ISABEL (holds out her arms): Tía, help me with my bath, too!

HORTENSIA: No. No. No more helping. Don't you think that you both
are old enough to take a bath by yourselves?

ESPERANZA (quickly drops her arms): Yes. Of course.

HORTENSIA: Isabel—go and tell your mother we need more hot water.

ISABEL (tiptoes out): Okay! But I'll be back. Then you can tell me
stories about what it was like to be rich.

She exits to get MODESTA.

ESPERANZA (*yells after her*): I'm still rich. This is only temporary.
Hortensia!

HORTENSIA: What, mi amor?

ESPERANZA: Hortensia. Nothing is right here! I can't live here! It . . .
it's not clean . . . and the people don't look trustworthy. Papa
would never let us live here! Mama would never approve.

HORTENSIA: As difficult as it is to accept, our lives are different now.

ESPERANZA: Can't we have a house to ourselves?

HORTENSIA: This is a family camp. We must have a male head of
household to live and work here. And that is Alfonso. He and his
family went to a lot of trouble to make sure we had this cabin!

ESPERANZA: I don't care. I don't like it.

HORTENSIA: Do you know how lucky you are? Most people wait
months for a job and a roof over their heads. Please be grateful
for the favors bestowed on us.

ESPERANZA: How can I be grateful?! I don't even have a bed to call
my own! We're all crowded in here in one shack! We're living
like horses.

HORTENSIA: That's enough. Sit down.

ESPERANZA: What?

HORTENSIA: Sit down. Sit. Now listen carefully. If you had stayed
in Mexico and your mother had married Don Luis, you would
have had one choice—to be separated and to be miserable. Here
you have two choices: to be together and be miserable, or to be
together and be happy! Your mother will join us soon. We have
jobs, we have a roof over our heads. I choose to be happy! And
you?

ESPERANZA (*angrily*): Happy.

HORTENSIA: Good.

She exits. ESPERANZA *cries.* MIGUEL *enters.*

MIGUEL: What's the matter, Anza?

ESPERANZA: Nothing.

MIGUEL: Nothing, eh? Good. You can help me.

Esperanza (Erin Nicole Hampe) discovers the harsh reality of being a migrant worker with Miguel (Desmin Borges). Photograph by Rob Levine.

ESPERANZA: With what?

MIGUEL: Shhhh. I have a surprise.

ESPERANZA: I'm not helping unless I know what it is.

MIGUEL: Let me show you something.

He takes her by the hand and leads her to a little spot where there are three large cans that seem empty and a half-broken statue of the Madonna.

MIGUEL: I'm making a garden.

ESPERANZA: This is a poor garden.

MIGUEL: Look in the cans.

ESPERANZA: There's just dirt.

MIGUEL: There will be roses, lots and lots and lots of roses—and all of them from Linda Flor.

ESPERANZA: But our garden was burned.

MIGUEL: Just the top. I found the roots were alive. So I brought them. And planted them. Just for us.

ESPERANZA: Ay, Miguel.

MIGUEL: You think you are the only one missing home? I miss it, too. I miss the ranch and Mexico and your papa and your mama—everyone. So now you'll help me with the roses, no? If I have to work, help me keep them in the sun, but don't let them dry out.

ESPERANZA: I will help.

HORTENSIA *(offstage)*: ¡Miguel! ¡Ven acá!

MIGUEL: ¡Voy, mama!

He exits.

ESPERANZA: Ay, Mama, Mama.

Her mother appears at the convent. Perhaps there is a large cross behind her or a stained-glass window. They can't see each other. RAMONA *sings the song "Vuela, Vuela, Jiguerillo," and* ESPERANZA *joins in the last part of the verse.*

RAMONA: Vuela, vuela, jiguerillo
Tú puedes volar
A buscar mis amores
Que no los puedo olvidar.

ESPERANZA: Ay si la ra la la la
Ay la la la

Scene 2
Morning. The camp. People rushing around getting ready for work. MODESTA *is hanging wash. One* MARIACHI *passes carrying a heavy load of peaches. The other two* MARIACHIS *run in quickly with a banner that says "PEACH SEASON" with pictures of peaches in piles and peaches falling from a tree. They quickly set up the banner and then run offstage to get empty baskets and straw hats, etc. Women pass wearing aprons and bandanas.* MIGUEL *exits the cabin with* ALFONSO. *He is putting on a clean shirt and has combed his wet hair back.*

MIGUEL: Tío, how do I look?
ALFONSO: Handsome like me. ¿Verdad, Tensa?
HORTENSIA: Ay sí, ¡cómo no!

ESPERANZA *enters.*

MIGUEL: See you, mi reina!

He runs out, kissing HORTENSIA *as he exits.*

ESPERANZA: Where is Miguel going?

HORTENSIA: He's applying for a job as a mechanic at the railroad. A real job. My boy can fix anything with a motor. Your father would be so proud.

ESPERANZA: Where are you going?

HORTENSIA: To work. Modesta and I will be packing peaches in the shed.

ESPERANZA: What do I do?

HORTENSIA: You stay here and help Isabel with the baby.

ESPERANZA: I want to work with you!

HORTENSIA: You're not old enough to work in the shed, and Isabel isn't old enough to watch the baby by herself.

ESPERANZA: I never held a baby in my life.

HORTENSIA: Isabel will show you . . . and Esperanza.

ESPERANZA: Yes?

HORTENSIA: You have a camp job, too—sweeping the wooden platform. You'll get paid for this . . .

ESPERANZA: I'll earn money?

HORTENSIA: Bueno, instead of paying you directly, the owners will deduct some money from our rent each month . . .

MODESTA *enters, singing to her baby,* CARLITOS.

MODESTA: *Señora Santana,*
            ¿por qué llores el niño?
            Por una manzana
            ¡Que se le ha perdido!

A bell rings loudly.

MODESTA: Ay, we have to go . . . Mi gordito precioso . . . How I hate to leave you! I miss you so much!

She kisses him all over. ISABEL *comes to take him.* MODESTA *has trouble handing him over.*

MODESTA: Don't put a diaper on after his bath. He gets a rash. And make sure you mash the bananas so there's no chunks. And don't leave him to cry and cry. He only cries when he needs something. All right?

ISABEL: Yes, Mama! Don't worry.

One last kiss, and MODESTA *exits with* HORTENSIA.

ISABEL: *Señora Santana,*
               ¿por qué llores el niño?
Come on—sing to him, Esperanza. Make him smile.

ESPERANZA: No.

ISABEL: You sing to your doll.

ESPERANZA: I don't like babies. I'm scared of them.

ISABEL: Go mash half a banana for him. ¿Sí, Carlitos? How delicious—a ba-na-na!

ESPERANZA: Where's the banana?

ISABEL: On the table.

ESPERANZA: Where do you keep a bowl?

ISABEL: On the shelf.

ESPERANZA: What do I mash it with?

ISABEL: Ay, a fork!

ESPERANZA: What if I leave chunks and he chokes?

ISABEL: Don't you know how to mash a banana?

ESPERANZA *shrugs.*

ISABEL: All right. The diaper pail is over there. Get the soap bar and . . .

ESPERANZA: Where's the soap?

ISABEL: Esperanza, don't you know anything?

ESPERANZA: I know A LOT. I went to private school starting at four, so I have already passed through level eight. When my mother comes, I will go to high school!

ISABEL: I'm going to start school, too—but here we learn in English.

ESPERANZA: Oh.

ISABEL: And when I go to school next week, you will be alone with the baby. What will you do?

ESPERANZA: Maybe my Mama will be here to show me.

ISABEL: I better teach you—in case she doesn't come. Maybe today you should start with the platform. You can sweep the floor, can't you?

ESPERANZA: Of course. Get me the broom.

ISABEL: You get it. It's over there.

> *Señora Santana,*
> *¿por qué llores el niño?*
> *Por una manzaza*
> *Que se le ha perdido.*

She exits, singing to the baby. ESPERANZA *gets the broom. She goes to the platform and starts to sweep, but she doesn't know how, and dirt flies through the air. She tries different ways, and dust gets in her nose, and she starts coughing and sneezing.* MAILMAN *enters, ringing his bell.*

MAILMAN: Mail! Mail!
                ¡Paquetes y correo!
                Jesús Posadas.
                Nicolás Salmeron.
                Juanita Chávez Reynoso.
                Manuela . . . Manuela . . . Gutiérrez Orozco . . .

ESPERANZA: Do you have a letter for me?

MAILMAN: Did I call you out?

ESPERANZA: No.

MAILMAN: Then no.

He moves on.

MAILMAN: Mail! Mail!
             ¡Paquetes y correo!

MARTA *enters and goes to the cabin door.*

MARTA *(calls)*: Mode! Mode!

ISABEL *enters.*

ISABEL: Marta—shhhhhh. The baby is sleeping. Mama's at work.
MARTA: I brought your mama some flyers.
ESPERANZA *(sounding out a word)*: Str . . . rike. Strike!
MARTA: Shhh, quiet.
ISABEL: She's all right. She's from Aguascalientes, too! El Rancho
    Linda Flor.
MARTA: Is that a town?
ESPERANZA: No, it's a ranch.
ISABEL: Her father owned it and thousands and thousands of acres
    of land. Her name is Esperanza. This is my real cousin, Marta!
    Esperanza had lots of servants and beautiful dresses, and she
    went to private school. Our cousin Miguel and his mother
    worked for them.
MARTA: Ahh, I see—a princess come to be a peasant.
ISABEL: A fire burned her house and everything! Now she has to
    work like us. She's nice. Her papa died.
MARTA: So? My father died, too. Before he came to this country he
    fought in the Mexican Revolution against people like her father—
    people who owned all the land.
ESPERANZA: You know nothing about my Papa! He was a good, kind
    man!
MARTA: Well, just so you know—this isn't Mexico. No one will be
    waiting on you here, Cinderella! Are you learning the skills you
    need to be a good servant?
ESPERANZA: I don't need to learn them . . . I—
ISABEL: She was teaching me! Watch!

She is really teaching ESPERANZA *how to sweep.*

ISABEL: Now . . . I hold the broom like this. One hand here, the other hand . . . here. Then you . . . I mean, I . . . pull it. I use small strokes. All in one direction. If the dust flies around too much, I sprinkle it with water—not too much or you'll, I'll, make mud . . . Now I get all the dirt in a pile and hold the broom down here and push it onto this piece of cardboard. I find if you wet the edge, the dirt goes in better. Is that how you do it, too, Esperanza?

ESPERANZA *(taking the broom)*: Yes. All the time. You are doing very, very well. And Isabel . . .

ISABEL: What?

ESPERANZA: Gracias, prima. Thank you for your help.

MIGUEL *enters.*

ISABEL: Miguel! Miguel! Do you have a day off already?! Pick me up!

MIGUEL: Not now, Isabel.

ESPERANZA: What are you doing back so soon, Miguel? Didn't they have a job at the railroad?

MIGUEL: Sure . . . if I wanted to lay tracks and dig ditches! They don't want mexicanos as mechanics! I might as well work in the fields!

ESPERANZA: I'm so sorry.

MIGUEL: It's not your fault, mi reina.

ISABEL: Oooooooo, he called you "mi reina," my queen. I want to be a queen, too!

She runs around making queenly poses.

ISABEL: I'm a queen. I'm a queen. La reina hermosa . . . I'm a queen . . . Marta, Marta. I'm a queen . . . I'm a queen . . .

MARTA: ¿Mi reina? I didn't know servants in Mexico could talk like that to their patronas.

MIGUEL: What business is it of yours? Who are you?

MARTA: Hi. I'm Marta Carranza. Modesta's my aunt, too. You should read this flyer!

MIGUEL: Marta. Marta . . . Yes, you're the one organizing the
workers!

MARTA: Yes! Shhhhh.

MIGUEL: My uncle says you'll cause us trouble.

MARTA: Tío Alfonso is a frightened man.

MIGUEL: Frightened for his family. We didn't come here for trouble.
We came here to work.

MARTA: What good does it do to work, if you can't live on what you
make!

ESPERANZA: They have nothing. Even a little is better than nothing.

MARTA: They? They? It's "we" now, Cinderella. Thousands of
mexicanos. We can't wait here helpless like sheep standing in
line for the slaughter. We are thousands. We have power.

MIGUEL: What power? Hunger isn't power!

MARTA: Our work is power! Our hands, our backs, our minds! If
we strike, if we stop working—the bosses will have no one to
plant their food, clean their homes, dig their ditches, drive
their trucks, take care of their children—if we take all that away
from them, they'll have to pay us more, give us running water,
electricity, and decent homes!

We hear a truck pull up. Men, including the MARIACHIS, *dirty from the
fields, file through.*

ISABEL: Uh-oh, Marta, Papa is home.

MIGUEL: If we strike, we lose our jobs. It's that simple.

MARTA: You're new. You'll learn. Listen, I shouldn't be telling you
this, but the strikers are more organized than they appear. In
a little while things are going to happen all over the county.
We're going to shut down everything, the fields, the sheds, the
railroad!

MIGUEL: The railroad?

MARTA: Everything!

MIGUEL: And a lot of people are joining this strike?

MARTA: A multitude! If you have not joined us by then, be very careful!
If you're not with us, you're against us! That's how we think.

ISABEL: Uh-oh!

ALFONSO *enters.*

ALFONSO: Marta, qué milagro. What's up?

MARTA: Tío. Aren't you glad to see me?

ALFONSO: I don't want you preaching the strike to my family.

MARTA: It's a free country. I can say what I want.

ALFONSO: Say it somewhere else. We don't want to be sent back to Mexico with you when you're caught.

MARTA: They can't send me back! I was born here. I am 100 percent puritita Americana—whether they like it or not! I've never even been to Mexico.

ALFONSO: Then think of the rest of us! We need to work! If we cause trouble—we have nothing. If we work hard, we keep our jobs, we make a future!

MARTA: What future, Tío? Hundreds of truckloads of poor white people come every day. If we work for four cents, they'll work for three! What future do we have with people like that?

ALFONSO: I think it is time you went home, Marta. I will tell Mode you came by!

MARTA: You better watch out, Tío. The line is drawn. Strikers against those who do not support us. Be very careful. We can get violent with those who stand in our way! Watch your back. *(Calls out, as she leaves.)* ¡Venceremos! We will win!

ALFONSO: Marta will get us all into trouble.

MIGUEL: The strike may be a good thing.

ALFONSO: Don't you start.

MIGUEL: Tranquilo, Tío. It's not what you think if so many workers are joining the strikes. I might be able to get a job at the railroad after all.

ESPERANZA: But if there's a strike and the rest of us lose our jobs? How will we live?

MIGUEL: "We"? All of a sudden it's "we"?

ESPERANZA: Yes. "We." The family. Our . . . our people.

ISABEL: Will we be sent back to Mexico, Papa?

ALFONSO: Not on my watch!

He picks up ISABEL, *and they exit.*

ALFONSO: Ayyy—you weigh more than . . . a sack of peaches!

ISABEL: A sack of . . . of asparagus?

ALFONSO: Much, much more! A sack of potatoes!

ESPERANZA: I don't like Marta! Didn't you see how rude she was?

MIGUEL: Yes, she is angry.

ESPERANZA: How could you even talk to her!

MIGUEL: I respect her. Unlike you, Señorita, I understand her anger!

Scene 3

Morning. ALFONSO *and* HORTENSIA *drink coffee on the porch of their cabin.* ESPERANZA *enters. She gives them a plate of food.*

> *We sing now for Esperanza*
> *Waiting each day for the mail.*
> *Three weeks, now four weeks have gone by*
> *And there is no letter still.*
> *Each day she rises at sunrise*
> *Hope with the new light is born.*
> *But where is her mother? How is she?*
> *Why does she leave her alone?*
> *Ay, what pain is separation*
> *For a mother and child*
> *What pain and what desperation*
> *Not knowing how each will survive!*

HORTENSIA: Felicidades, Esperanza. Your first breakfast is delicious!

ALFONSO: Yes. Heaven must smell like this meal!

ESPERANZA: It's only frijoles.

ALFONSO: But what frijoles!

HORTENSIA: I'm so proud of you!

ESPERANZA: The ones on the bottom are burnt.

ALFONSO: But the ones on top—¡exquisitos! And you made the tortillas!

ESPERANZA: Yes.

MIGUEL *enters, with a tortilla.*

MIGUEL: This one looks more like a tostada than a tortilla.

ALFONSO *puts on his sombrero to go to work.*

ALFONSO: As luck would have it, I adore tostadas! Isabel! Apúrate!
  Your cousin is ready to take you to the school bus!
MIGUEL: Not today, Tío.
ALFONSO: No?
MIGUEL: I can't.
ALFONSO: Why? What's her name?
ESPERANZA: Who?
ALFONSO: His new girlfriend. The one who put that smile on his face
  and is keeping him from taking his adoring cousin to the school
  bus!
MIGUEL: What girlfriend?! I'm going to the railroad. They're hiring
  extra people in case there's a strike. I'll have a chance to work on
  the engines. I know it might be temporary, but if I do a good job,
  maybe they will keep me.
ALFONSO: That is right. You do good work. They will see it. They will
  keep you! You see. This is America.

ISABEL *comes running in and goes to* MIGUEL.

ISABEL: Take me to school. I command it!
MIGUEL: So you're a queen today, giving orders. Is that why you have
  little gold stars stuck all over your face?
ISABEL: My teacher gave me five gold stars on my English spelling
  test. I did the best in the whole class.
MIGUEL: And you put them on your face?
ISABEL: So everyone can see.
MIGUEL: ¡Qué sangrona eres! *(He gives her a kiss.)* ¡Adiós!
ISABEL: Miguel!

HORTENSIA *and* MODESTA *enter, dressed for work.* MODESTA *carries* CARLITOS.

ALFONSO: Forget Miguel! Today's your lucky day. I'm taking you to the bus!

The MAILMAN *enters.*

MAILMAN: Mail, mail!
¡Paquetes y correo!
Emiliano Toto Urbano.
Andrés Aguirre Chacha.
María Chuchena—una bella azucena.
Narciso Ochoa Ramón.
Five letters from your home!

ESPERANZA *approaches.*

MAILMAN: Sorry, niña, nothing for you. Mail, mail! ¡Paquetes y correo!

He exits. Two MARIACHIS *follow* ESPERANZA, *who walks slowly to the porch.* MARIACHIS *sing.* ESPERANZA *goes to the garden. Flowers are blooming in the cans. She waters them and smells them and kneels before the Virgin and prays silently.* HORTENSIA *enters.*

ESPERANZA: Hortensia!
HORTENSIA: You made a good breakfast today.
ESPERANZA: Hortensia, I haven't heard from my mother in three months!
HORTENSIA: I know. I know.
ESPERANZA: Do you think she's all right?
HORTENSIA: But if anything very bad had happened, we would know. Bad news travels fast.
ESPERANZA: I hope so.

HORTENSIA: She is a good mother. She loves you with a thousand hearts. She will come as soon as she can.

ESPERANZA: And if I am a good daughter, I should go and get her.

HORTENSIA: But how? With what money? I would gladly loan you, but we barely have enough for us all . . .

ESPERANZA: I would never ask you for money. I can work. I can work. I can work and save money to go back and bring Mama here.

HORTENSIA: Modesta can't afford to pay you, m'hija.

ESPERANZA: No, no, no. I will find work in the shed. With you.

HORTENSIA: You're too young.

ESPERANZA: I can look older. See?

She holds up her hair. MODESTA *enters.*

MODESTA: Hortensia. It's getting late!

ESPERANZA: I'll go with you and ask about a job.

MODESTA: What? Who will stay with Carlitos?

HORTENSIA: We cannot ask Isabel to miss school.

ESPERANZA: I know. I know.

MODESTA: There are no jobs open.

ESPERANZA: What shall I do?

MODESTA: About what?

ESPERANZA: I need to work! I must save money and go get my Mama and bring her here, or something terrible will happen. I know it!

HORTENSIA: We can't talk now. We'll talk later. We help each other. We'll think of something!

The bell rings.

MODESTA: Wait!

She undoes her apron and her bandana and gives them to ESPERANZA.

You! Take my job for a while.

ESPERANZA: No. Not your job.

MODESTA: The bosses won't know. We all look alike to them!

ESPERANZA: But the money?

MODESTA: Alfonso works. We have enough for now.

ESPERANZA: Enough? You have nothing!

MODESTA: If I had been rich, it might seem like we have nothing. But for us, it is enough to live on.

ESPERANZA: You would do that for me?

MODESTA: I do this for me and for Carlitos.

ESPERANZA: I know you miss him all day. But you are making a sacrifice. For me.

MODESTA: That too.

ESPERANZA: But why?

MODESTA: I am sick of seeing people who live without hope!

ESPERANZA: But . . .

MODESTA: No but. Go!

ESPERANZA: How can I ever thank you?

MODESTA: Work hard. Bring your mother soon.

ESPERANZA *and* MODESTA *embrace.*

Scene 4

On one side, in the shed, a line of women including HORTENSIA *are cutting up potatoes at a long table. Every two* WORKERS *share two large baskets. Some pieces are thrown into one basket, the leftovers into the other basket.* FIELD-WORKERS *enter now and then, bringing empty baskets and removing the full ones. Once in a while one of the* WOMEN *grabs a broom and sweeps the floor clean. The* WOMEN *wear sweaters and gloves, bandanas, and big aprons. To enter the shed,* WORKERS *must pass through a gauntlet of* STRIKERS. MARTA *is among them. The* STRIKERS *are chanting.*

THE CROWD (*chanting*):　　　Huelga, huelga
　　　　　　　　　　　　　Don't let our children starve!
　　　　　　　　　　　　　Unite with us, compadres!
　　　　　　　　　　　　　Huelga, huelga

> Strike, strike
> We won't starve without a fight!

A few STRIKERS *have loudspeakers and yell over the chanting:*

> Join us, compadres.
> Strike now. Help us feed our children.

As people pass the picket line, the STRIKERS *and the* WORKERS *yell back and forth.*

THE STRIKERS:	Cowards! Traitors!
WORKERS:	Leave us alone!
	Our children are hungry, too. We need to work.
	I must support my mother.
	I came here to work. You lazy bums!

ESPERANZA *fights through the* STRIKERS; *someone grabs her bandana, which she grabs back. She joins* HORTENSIA. *The* STRIKERS *move offstage, still chanting and yelling, and we are in the shed.*

WOMAN WORKER 1: All that shouting drives me crazy!

WOMAN WORKER 2: The strikers are making it worse.

WOMAN WORKER 3: How could things get worse?

WOMEN: Shhhhh.

ESPERANZA *(to* HORTENSIA*)*: What do I do?

HORTENSIA: Just do as I do. First cut the potato into pieces.

WOMAN WORKER 1 *(making a little dance out of it)*: Cut potatoes into pieces.

HORTENSIA: Cut around the eyes.

WOMAN WORKER 2 *(doing the same)*: Cut around the eyes.

ESPERANZA *(almost dropping hers)*: Potatoes have eyes?

HORTENSIA *(lifting and showing her)*: This is a potato eye.

ESPERANZA: Oh.

General laughter.

HORTENSIA: Drop this part in this basket. The men will come to take
   them away.
WOMEN: Ay, men!

Some laughter.

HORTENSIA: They plant the eyes in the field. And new potatoes grow
   from them.
ESPERANZA: So that's where potatoes come from!

The WOMEN, *along with* HORTENSIA *and* ESPERANZA, *continue their
task. Some make a rhythmic song.*

EVERYONE: First cut the potato into pieces.
               Cut around the eye . . . etc. . . . .

All of a sudden there is silence.

WOMAN WORKER 1: Do you hear that?
HORTENSIA: What? What do you hear?
WOMAN WORKER 1: The silence.
WOMEN: Ay, sí.

*They are all quiet for a moment. Then we hear sirens and buses and
yelling!*

WOMAN WORKER 3: Oh my God! La Migra!
ESPERANZA: What?
HORTENSIA: Immigration. It's a sweep!
WOMAN WORKER 2 *(desperately looking for a place to hide)*: My mother
   is sick! They can't take me!
HORTENSIA: Cálmate, m'hija. They won't take you. You're a worker.
   You have a job.

WOMAN WORKER 2: Ay Dios! I have no one to take care of her.

ESPERANZA: Will they send us back?

HORTENSIA: Keep working. They're not here for us. The growers need the workers. That's why we have guards.

WOMAN WORKER 2: You look Mexican. Boom boom—on the bus.

Two male WORKERS *enter, carrying a very heavy basket. They put it in the back of the shed with other baskets and leave. An immigration* AGENT *with gun drawn comes in and looks around. He walks between the* WORKERS *and looks each one in the eye.*

AGENT: Has anyone come in here?

WOMAN WORKER 1: No. Only us.

HORTENSIA: Can't you see, we're just working?!

WOMAN WORKER 1: Put your gun away.

HORTENSIA: ¡Sin vergüenza! You don't have to scare us!

WOMAN WORKER 1: We have mouths to feed.

HORTENSIA: We don't want any trouble.

AGENT: A girl was running this way. Did you see her?

GUARD 2 *walks among them. As he passes, each one says "no" in turn.* ESPERANZA *has trouble looking up.*

AGENT: If any of you hide a striker, we'll pack you on a bus and send you back to Mexico. Just like them! Do you hear?

WOMEN: Yes.

WOMAN WORKER 1: Basket!

ESPERANZA: I'll get it.

She gets one.

MARTA: Shhhhhhhhh.

ESPERANZA *says nothing and returns to the line of workers.*

WOMAN WORKER 3: Did you forget my basket, Cinderella?

ESPERANZA: Yes. Yes. I forgot!

She goes back to the baskets. She takes off her apron and quickly stuffs it into the basket MARTA *is in and brings another basket. Then she gets the broom to sweep. She goes to the basket* MARTA *is in.*

ESPERANZA *(whispers)*: Marta?!

MARTA: Yes?

ESPERANZA: When we leave, leave with us. Put on the apron and carry some potatoes so you look like a worker.

MARTA: You'll help me?

ESPERANZA: Yes.

MARTA: Thank you.

ESPERANZA *stops sweeping and returns to* HORTENSIA.

AGENT: The strikers aren't your friends, you know. They aren't protecting you. I hear they put glass among the potatoes so you cut your hands. I hear they put rattlesnakes in some of your work baskets to slow you down. Is that true?

No one answers; they all work. He continues to check the baskets.

AGENT: Has anyone checked those for snakes or rats?

No one answers. Frightened, ESPERANZA *looks back at the baskets where* MARTA *is hiding.*

AGENT *(to* ESPERANZA*)*: You like that basket?

ESPERANZA: No.

AGENT: I like those baskets.

He lifts the top of the basket where MARTA *is hiding.*

AGENT: Well, well, well . . . these strikers put snakes everywhere!

MARTA *scrambles out and tries to run. The* AGENT *catches her.*

MARTA: Let me go.

AGENT: Gotcha!

MARTA: I'm an American citizen. It's a free country.

AGENT *(as he drags her out)*: Yes, you're free to leave if you don't like it here.

MARTA: I'm American!

AGENT 1: Your papers?

MARTA: I don't need papers. I'm a citizen.

AGENT: Not with that face! You wanna make trouble? Make trouble in Mexico! Go back where you belong!

MARTA *(struggles)*: I belong here. I was born here!

The AGENT *wrestles her out.*

MARTA: ¡Huelga! Strike! Unite so our people can eat!

They exit struggling.

Esperanza (Erin Nicole Hampe) learns what work she needs to do from Hortensia (Catalina Maynard) and other migrant workers (Kaliya Warren). Photograph by Rob Levine.

MARTA: ¡Venceremos!

HORTENSIA (lets out a wail):

ESPERANZA: Oh no! No!

WOMAN WORKER 1: Hush.

WOMAN WORKER 2: Keep working.

ESPERANZA: I was afraid for her. I couldn't help looking! I'm sorry.

HORTENSIA: It's not fair. She was born here. She knows no one in
    Mexico.

WOMAN WORKER 2: Keep working!

WOMAN WORKER 1: Unite. ¡Unidos venceremos!

WOMAN WORKER 2: Shut up, or we'll all be on that bus!

ESPERANZA: I'm sorry.

Scene 5

*The fiesta: a fiesta at the camp is just beginning. Women carry plates of
food. Men are drinking. The* MARIACHIS *are there, too. One is dressed in
full mariachi regalia; one is in work clothes but wears his sombrero; the
other has on his mariachi trousers, a cowboy hat, and a Brooklyn Dodgers
shirt, which he shows off to his buddies and takes an umpire's stance
calling an "out" on someone sliding into home plate. When approached by
the others, he keeps saying "Yerrrrrr out!" The* OKIE FAMILY *we saw at the
border reappears, looking hungrily at all the food. Everyone ignores them
until they start to play and sing and pass the hat. The* OKIE BOY *dances. A
circle forms around them. People are clapping.*

On stage left, ESPERANZA *is stuffing a jar full of bills. She holds her
doll and talks to her.*

ESPERANZA: Ten more dollars. Ten more dollars—that's four more
    weeks!

ISABEL: Come to the dance!

ESPERANZA: Isabel!

ISABEL: Ooooooo. Look at all the money. You're rich again!

ESPERANZA: Shhhhh. I don't want the whole world to know. This is
    money to bring my mother! Now cállate!

ISABEL: Then ven. Come dance. Your doll wants to go. I can tell. *(To the doll.)* Hello, chiquitita bonita. Do you know how to dance? *(To* ESPERANZA.*)* Have you given her a name yet?

ESPERANZA: Not yet.

ISABEL: Call her Reina! I might be a reina soon, too. The best girl student in third grade is chosen every year to be Queen of the May. And guess what?

ESPERANZA: You're going to be Queen of the May?

ISABEL: My teacher said I'm the best student—girls and boys . . . So, I'm going to pray every day.

ESPERANZA: That's good. But I think other girls will be praying, too!

ISABEL: I'll pray hardest! I want so much to be queen. I want to wear a new dress and hold the maypole so everyone can dance around me with colored ribbons. Then there will be three "reinas": you, chiquitita, and me! Hooray! Aren't you going to the dance?

ESPERANZA: No.

ISABEL: I am. Can I take your doll?

ESPERANZA: NO!

ISABEL *looks out of the room. At the fiesta, the* OKIE BOY *starts to dance, and his parents sing.* HORTENSIA *enters.*

ISABEL: Oooo—look, the Okie family's here.

HORTENSIA: Now what's this "Okie" I hear all the time?

ISABEL: "Okie" is short for Oklahoma. It's a state. There was no rain, and all the land blew away in the wind—so the Okies had to come here like us. Only they're lucky. They have hot water, and they're going to have a swimming pool. They can use it everyday, but we can use it only on Fridays.

HORTENSIA: And why only Fridays?

ISABEL: Because they clean the pool right after we swim!

ESPERANZA: Why?! Do they think we're dirtier than other people?

ISABEL: I don't know. Look! Come on. The Okie boy is dancing!

ESPERANZA: You go ahead.

ISABEL: Okeydokey.

She skips out and joins the crowd watching the OKIES.

HORTENSIA: Go dance.

ESPERANZA: No.

HORTENSIA: Why not?

ESPERANZA: I can't face anyone. Not after Marta! I gave her to La Migra!

HORTENSIA: No one blames you. You didn't mean to.

ESPERANZA: I blame myself. I didn't know how bad things could be.

The crowd is clapping. The MARIACHIS *are playing along with the family, once in a while joining in a refrain. Everyone is happy.* ISABEL *watches and then begins to dance with the* OKIE BOY. *Soon other people begin to dance.* MIGUEL *enters, covered in mud, intent on going straight to his cabin. He catches sight of* ISABEL *and grabs her by the arm and hauls her into the bedroom.*

MIGUEL: ¡Ven acá! ¡Caray! What do you think you're doing?!

ISABEL: What?

MIGUEL: Making a spectacle of yourself with that . . . that Okie!!

ISABEL: He's just a boy dancing!

MIGUEL: Well, you can't dance with him!

ESPERANZA: Miguel!

MIGUEL: We're not friends with Okies.

ISABEL *(getting loose)*: He can be my friend.

MIGUEL: Okies are bad news for us! A group of men showed up from Oklahoma. They said they would work for half the money, and the railroad hired all of them! Some of them never even worked on a motor before. My boss said he wouldn't need me anymore! He was going to train the Okies.

ESPERANZA: Just because some Okies made you mad, it isn't all the Okies' fault! Isabel, you go dance with whom you want!

ISABEL *goes back to the dance but only watches.*

ESPERANZA: How did you get so dirty?!

MIGUEL: My boss said I could dig ditches and lay tracks if I wanted.

ESPERANZA: And what did you do?

MIGUEL: Can't you tell from my clothes? I dug ditches!

ESPERANZA: Miguel, how could you agree to such a thing?!

MIGUEL: What would you have me do? Walk away? With no paycheck?! Do you want us to starve?!

ESPERANZA: Why didn't your boss tell the others to dig ditches!

MIGUEL: Why do you think?

ESPERANZA: Because you're Mexican?! Did you say anything?

MIGUEL: What would be the use of that? Eh?

ESPERANZA: So you did nothing?

MIGUEL: I worked. Does that offend you?

ESPERANZA: How dare you say that to me.

MIGUEL: Then what? Maybe I should go up north to Oregon to work so seeing me won't offend you!

ESPERANZA: Stay here. Stand up for yourself!

MIGUEL: I'll do what I want. What's the matter with you?

ESPERANZA: The matter with me?! You wanted to come to the United States. So here we are. And what? Is this the better life you left Mexico for? Is it? Nothing is better here. Nothing is right! You can't work on engines because you're Mexican. We go to work through angry crowds of our own people who are so poor they throw rocks at us or they're kidnapped and thrown from a bus into Mexico. White camps get indoor toilets and hot water and swimming pools—but not us! Why is that, Miguel? Why not us? Is it because we're Mexicans and we'll always be Mexicans no matter how long we live here or how hard we work?! Tell me, is this life really better for you than life in Mexico?!

MIGUEL: Yes. It is. In Mexico, I was a second-class citizen. A peasant. I could never change that! I was born on the wrong side of a river—do you remember, reina? At least here I have a chance, however small, to become more than what I was. You obviously can never understand this because you were on the right side. You never lived without hope!

ESPERANZA: How can you say that now?! I've lost everything. Every single thing that meant anything to me: my Papa, my friends, my land, my education and all I was meant to be. I'm not even thirteen! I need my mother here—but for all I know I may never see her again! I think it's you who doesn't understand. You crossed the river, but you're still a second-class citizen. Why? Because you act like one. You let the bosses take advantage of you. They won't give Mexicans a chance. Why don't you go to your bosses and confront them? Why don't you speak up for yourself and your talents and your people?! Be a man!

MIGUEL (*grabs the doll and shoves it at her*): Why don't you go play with dolls!

ESPERANZA: Look at yourself. You still believe you're a peasant!

ESPERANZA exits and goes over to ISABEL to watch the people dancing.

MIGUEL: And you still think you're a queen!

He takes ESPERANZA'S doll, and money drops out. MIGUEL stuffs it in his pocket and exits.

Scene 6

The roses are blooming in their cans and all over the stage. ESPERANZA and HORTENSIA are pruning and watering them. ESPERANZA'S doll sits at the feet of the Madonna. Two MARIACHIS are playing. The third will enter with the MAILMAN.

MAILMAN: Mail! Mail!
            ¡Paquetes y correo!
            Rafael Gómez de Ochoa.
            Ángel Romano Pérez.
            Natalia Valdes Flores.

A woman runs up to get her letter.

¡Cartas de tus amores!

She slaps him playfully and he laughs.

Adolfo Hernández.
Inocencia Zavala.

He exits still calling names.

María Andrea Medina.
Here's your medicina . . .

Sees ESPERANZA.

Not for you, little one!
Mail! Mail!
¡Paquetes y correo!

ESPERANZA: Not a word from my Mama! I've been away from her for
so long! I don't think she will ever come. And now—I have no
money. It will take me months to save again. Maybe I'll never
see my Mama again! Miguel has spoiled everything! I almost
hate these roses—because Miguel brought them. Every day they
remind me that Miguel is a thief, a *buitre* just like my Tío Luis.

HORTENSIA: I understand how you feel about Miguel. I don't know
what got into him. I am very ashamed. But, ¿qué culpa tienen
las rosas? How can you hate roses? Look at them, how they have
opened and bloomed even ripped from Mexican soil like us.

ESPERANZA: I don't really hate them, and I don't really hate Miguel.
Part of what he did is my fault. I got angry and called him a
"peasant" and then he left.

HORTENSIA: So you hurt his pride, and he left to mend it. He needed
work. There was work up north. He paid for his ride. He will
come back soon. He's not one to stay away from his family for
long. I'm sure he will bring you back your money.

ESPERANZA (*picking up a can*): I think these roses are getting too big for the cans. Will they die?

HORTENSIA: If we don't plant them in the ground here so they put down roots, they'll die. They need the land to breathe, to live, to grow—even this strange land where no one speaks their language or knows their heart. If the roses don't make their home in this soil, they will die. Like us. We have no choice. We are not going to die, so we will also put our roots down here.

ESPERANZA *throws herself to the ground and lies still.*

HORTENSIA: Esperanza! Anza! What are you doing?

ESPERANZA: Listening.

HORTENSIA: For what?

ESPERANZA: For a heartbeat. For a breath. Anything!

ESPERANZA *gets back up.*

ESPERANZA: I hear nothing. Nothing. This land will never speak to me. Maybe, if I never open my eyes again, I will fall all the way back to Mexico.

ISABEL *rushes in with her schoolbooks and throws them on the ground.*

ISABEL: It's not fair! It's not fair. I didn't win Queen of the May. I had the best grades, but the teacher said she chose on more than just grades! The Queen has to be blonde!

ALFONSO: I'm sorry. I'm sorry, mi amorcita, they didn't choose you. Well, you will always be my queen! Who cares about Queen of the May?

ISABEL: I care! I tried so hard!

ESPERANZA: Ay, Isabel, come here. (*She hugs her.*) You would have made a beautiful May Queen—but that lasts only one day. A day goes by fast, and then it's over.

ISABEL: But I prayed and prayed and prayed to be Queen of the May!

ESPERANZA: I know you did . . . but Isabelita, do you know what I think?

ISABEL: What?!

ESPERANZA: I think Our Lady knew things you didn't know. I think Our Lady was very wise in not granting your prayers.

ISABEL: What do you mean?

ESPERANZA: She wanted you to have something that would last more than one day.

ISABEL: Like what?

ESPERANZA: Hmmmmmm. *(Giving her the doll.)* Like this. To keep as your own.

ISABEL: Ohh . . . no, Esperanza. Your papa gave this to you.

ESPERANZA: Do you think my Papa would want her buried inside a valise all the time with no one playing with her? Look at her— she'd be too lonely. And look at me—I'm almost thirteen. I'm much too old for dolls. You would be doing me and my Papa a favor if you would love her.

ISABEL: Really?

ESPERANZA: Yes. And you know what else?

ISABEL: What?

ESPERANZA: I think you should take her to school and show all your friends. I'm sure that not even the Queen of the May has a doll as beautiful as this!

ISABEL *takes the doll and jumps up and down.*

ISABEL: Thank you. Thank you. I'll call her "Reina." I think my heart is dancing!

She dances with the doll and stops suddenly.

ISABEL: Oh no!

ESPERANZA: What's the matter?

ISABEL: What will your Mama say?

MIGUEL *enters.*

MIGUEL: I think her Mama would say she's very, very proud of her daughter.

RAMONA: Esperanza!

ESPERANZA: Mama! Mama! Is it you? ¿De veras?

They rush to embrace each other.

RAMONA: M'hija. Aquí estoy. I'm here. I'm here. How I missed you!

ESPERANZA: Mama!

HORTENSIA *and* RAMONA *embrace.*

RAMONA: Hortensia!

HORTENSIA: Doña!

RAMONA: You must call me "Ramona" now. A thousand thanks can never repay you for taking in my daughter!

ESPERANZA (*to* MIGUEL): But how . . . ?

MIGUEL: I felt you were right. Marta was right. Our lives will not get better until we take action ourselves. I snuck to the convent in Aguascalientes. Your Tío still had his men at the train station, so your mother dressed as a nun, and we took the train back. Punto.

ISABEL: This is your mother?

ESPERANZA: This is my mother! Mama, this is our cousin, Isabel, and her papa, Alfonso.

ISABEL: Are you really a queen?

RAMONA: Thank you, Isabel. I think you and I are going to be good friends.

RAMONA: Look at you, how you've grown! And look at all these roses. So sweet. So beautiful.

ESPERANZA: They are home, Mama. Miguel brought them from our garden.

RAMONA: Our garden! Our beautiful garden! Here! God bless you, Miguel.

ESPERANZA: But the roots have outgrown their little pots. They may not last much longer.

RAMONA: Then we must transplant them. Today.

ESPERANZA: Do you think they'll grow here? The soil's not the same.

RAMONA: It's not the same, but it looks very rich. Why don't we plant them and see?

They all kneel and start to dig. The MARIACHIS *enter to sing "Adiós—bienvenida" ("Good-bye—hello").*

MARIACHI 1:   *If you look up at the sky*
                     What do you see?

Ramona (Melanie Rey) and her daughter Esperanza (Erin Nicole Hampe) reflect on how they will continue to grow and thrive like their roses did back in Mexico. Photograph by Rob Levine.

The same slivered moon
That always shined on me
The same silver clouds
The same whirling stars
Who would think that all below
Is so changed by where we are.
Adiós, adiós
Adiós, adiós
My love
How sad was my goodbye
Adiós, adiós, adiós . . .

MARIACHI 2: *But look around*
The earth smells sweet
The birds still fly
Mothers with their girls
Delight.
The world turns
The sun still warms
Seedlings stretch and are reborn
How beautiful this morning comes
Like wanderers we're welcomed home
Like wanderers we're welcomed home.

MARIACHI 3: *Bienvenidos, bienvenidas*
Welcome, welcome home
To see us.
Bienvenidos, bienvenidas
Con gusto y placer
Arrimas.
Bienvenidos, bienvenidas
Welcome, welcome home
To see us.
Bienvenidos, bienvenidas
Welcome, welcome home
To see us.
Bienvenidos, bienvenidas

Welcome, welcome home
To see us.
Bienvenidos, bienvenidas
Welcome, welcome home
To see us.

END

SNAPSHOT SILHOUETTE

Kia Corthron

Directed by Michael John Garcés

The world premier of *Snapshot Silhouette* opened on March 19, 2004, at Children's Theatre Company, Minneapolis, Minnesota. *Snapshot Silhouette* was written with support from Sundance Writers' Retreat at Ucross.

CREATIVE TEAM

Scenic design: Troy Hourie
Costume design: Christal Weatherly
Lighting design: Jane Cox
Music: Victor Zupanc
Sound design: Victor Zupanc and Chris Heagle
Dramaturgy: Elissa Adams
Stage manager: Stacy McIntosh
Assistant stage manager: Chris Schweiger

CAST

NAJMA	Sonja Parks
ENGLISH TEACHER	Kristina Mitchell
TAY C	Amanda Granger
LAINE	Marie-Françoise Theodore
ESL TEACHER	Tracey Maloney
MUHAMED	Daniel Curry
MANUEL	Sam Ackerberg
ALICIA	Erin Nicole Hampe
BAO	Madison Martin
ZEINAB	Rokia Moallim
QALIN	Andrea Flowers
CAM	Hadija Steen-Omari
DAMAC	Marvette Knight
ABDI	Darien Johnson

There are three main characters: NAJMA, TAY C, and LAINE. A company may double for the rest. The white ESL TEACHER may be played by a Latina or light black actress.

The stage directions (characters ascending and descending stairs, etc.) imply a two-story house. The first floor includes a kitchen with a door to the outside and a living room, and the upper floor is the girls' bedroom, but this layout is flexible. There is a piano in the living room. The bedroom has twin beds. On TAY C's side of the room there may be posters, a bulletin board, and regular middle school stuff, and on NAJMA'S side a prayer mat hangs. The remainder of the walls is bare except for a kaman (Somali lute), which rests against a wall. NAJMA dresses like any other middle school girl—top, jeans, sneakers—and wears a casual veil.

CHARACTERS

NAJMA

THE IMAM

THE PEOPLE

ENGLISH TEACHER

TAY C

MIDDLE SCHOOL STUDENTS

LAINE

ESL TEACHER

MUHAMED

MANUEL

ALICIA

BAO

ZEINAB

QALIN

CAM

DAMAC

ABDI

Scene 1

NAJMA *in light holding a notebook; darkness behind.*

NAJMA: Chapter 1: Home.

Lights up behind: The PEOPLE *bowed in prayer, facing upstage, foreheads touching the ground. The* IMAM *stands before the* PEOPLE, *facing stage left.*

IMAM: Allah hu akbar.
PEOPLE: Allah hu akbar.
IMAM: Allah hu akbar.
PEOPLE: Allah hu akbar.
IMAM: Ashahadu an la allah il Allah.
PEOPLE: Ashahadu an al Allah il Allah.

Continuing under NAJMA, *the* IMAM *calls and the* PEOPLE *repeat:*
Ashahadu Muhammad el rasool Allah.
Allah hu akbar.
La Allah il allah.
La Allah il Allah.

Now the IMAM *turns completely around to face stage right. He repeats the lines, just once this time, with the* PEOPLE *echoing him. If time permits, he then faces downstage for all the lines, and finally upstage.*

NAJMA: Everyone got religion with the wars but my family *always* practiced my mother told me, our family women wore their veils even before, answering the call of the Imam five times a day: Dawn. Noon. Midafternoon. Sunset. Nightfall. Muslims all one. Between prayers people conducted business, went to the market. Bustling. Foreign visitors. Refugees, Somali-Ethiopians from the war, we had plenty, take care of them *and* us. Ours is yours. Then: drought. Famine. The clans attacked the president, then the president came back. Hard. Then the clans attacked each other. And us.

Gunfire: The PEOPLE *panic, scream, scatter.*

NAJMA: Then America came. Then America left. Then nothing: no Somali government.

The PEOPLE *are all gone. The* ENGLISH TEACHER *is now visible at her desk. A few other* STUDENTS *are present, including* TAY C.

NAJMA: But before: pancakes for breakfast! Supper we have fish, rice with milk and ghee, beans, my mother told me—
TAY C: Her mother dumped her.

Some of the other STUDENTS *giggle.*

ENGLISH TEACHER: Tay C!

Silence.

ENGLISH TEACHER: Go on, Najma.

An uncomfortable pause. Then NAJMA *looks at her paper for the first time. Flips a few pages.*

NAJMA: Can I skip to chapter 5? I skip around when I write, last night I wrote chapter 1 and chapter 5.
ENGLISH TEACHER: *Two* chapters?! Very good! Go on.
NAJMA *(reads)*: Chapter 5: America. My big brother Abdi and I and my aunt and her kids came to America. Texas. I was ten, Abdi sixteen. My aunt and my cousins and Abdi stayed in Texas but it was crowded, I had to come here, stay with my cousin Damac. Damac's close to us and happy to send money back home to my mom so she can come, but in the interim Damac has two kids

her own and a shoebox apartment, too crowded again. Then we moved to a bigger place, and bigger was better but not ideal, still too crowded, two years too crowded. Then Tay C's mom invited me to come stay with them, so last week I pack again—

TAY C: *Scuze me* but her story's forever we ain't gettin' to mine she keep readin' and you said on accounta my not doin' the other papers I get a F I don't read today so I just wantchu to know—

ENGLISH TEACHER: We'll get to it tomorrow, Tay C.

TAY C: *Tomorrow?* I was up half the night—

ENGLISH TEACHER: We'll get to yours tomorrow.

TAY C: How come she gets to—?

NAJMA: It's okay. I was mostly finished.

ENGLISH TEACHER: No, Tay C needs to learn to wait her turn.

TAY C *(slams book, not too hard, and mutters)*: I was up half the night—

ENGLISH TEACHER: Do I have to see you in detention? again?

The ESL class works on their English: Zeinab (Rokia Moallim), Bao (Madison Martin), Alicia (Erin Nicole Hampe), Muhamed (Daniel Curry), Najma (Sonja Parks), Manuel (Sam Ackerberg), and their teacher (Tracey Maloney). From the world premiere of *Snapshot Silhouette* by Kia Corthron in 2004. Photograph by Rob Levine.

The bell rings. TAY C *and the other* STUDENTS *exit.* NAJMA *stays.*

ENGLISH TEACHER: Excellent, Najma.

NAJMA: Thank you.

ENGLISH TEACHER: I'm glad I asked everyone to start their autobiographies with "home." Very astute to incorporate so many of your mother's memories alongside your own.

NAJMA *smiles politely. As the* ENGLISH TEACHER *shuffles papers,* NAJMA *puts on coat, hat, etc. Now* NAJMA *stares at the* ENGLISH TEACHER, *her homework still in her (now mittened) hand. The* ENGLISH TEACHER *starts gathering her things, now notices* NAJMA *hasn't left.*

ENGLISH TEACHER: Don't you have lunch now?

NAJMA: Field trip, science museum. We packed our lunches.

ENGLISH TEACHER: Science museum?

NAJMA *nods.*

ENGLISH TEACHER: I love the science museum! Write a report, ten extra.

NAJMA: Okay.

They stare at each other. Finally:

ENGLISH TEACHER: Don't you have to catch the bus for the trip?

NAJMA: Quarter after.

ENGLISH TEACHER: Oh. *(Glances at clock or watch.)* Well. I have to get my lunch.

NAJMA: You mind I stay a second? Practice next part of my speech?

ENGLISH TEACHER: Don't miss your bus.

Exits.

NAJMA *(turns to audience)*: Chapter 2: Climate. Mogadishu, on the coast, could burn one thirteen easy during Jiiláal, while

December in hottest season. But once we went to the mountains: temperature must have dropped to forty! I'd never heard of a place so cold.

NAJMA *puts on her hood and exits through the outside door, into the treacherous winds and subzero temperatures.*

Scene 2
In the bedroom, NAJMA *doing her prayers.* TAY C *in the kitchen eating cereal.* LAINE *enters, just finished jogging.* TAY C *never looks up at* LAINE, *who busily clears the table, washes dishes, etc., while speaking. In the background, morning radio chatter at a very low volume.*

LAINE: Five miles! And I'm early so I'll have time to stop by the church and pick up those cases of food. NAJMA, YOU WANT OATMEAL? I CAN TURN ON THE KETTLE oh she's probably doing her prayers. I can get those boxes and cans to the shelter and organize them before I serve the breakfast shift. Then work at nine of course except twelve to one when I'll be at the gym: step aerobics. No, this is Wednesday. Is this Wednesday? Power Yoga. Five to six the library, number's on the fridge, ask for the literacy program. Mrs. Hallman is seventy-two, three months ago her signature was "X," now she's reading second grade! NAJMA! Oh forgot! her prayers. Six to seven I'll stay at the library, help arrange books for tomorrow's book sale. Tomorrow's Thursday, right? Make sure Najma gets her oatmeal she never eats enough, hear?
(No immediate answer.)
Hear?

TAY C *vaguely nods.*

LAINE: I want you to be good to her. Okay? I want you to be nice, think of what she's been through. Lost her father, her little sister, her brother in Texas, mother in Somalia, hasn't heard her mother's voice in years, you know what that's like?

TAY C: *No.*

LAINE: Not good! You think I'm a nag well just be thankful you've
got a mom close enough to nag, Najma sure misses hers. You
don't even know the meaning of the word, if I didn't have my
obligations I'd show you the definition of "nag," sit right here
march you to school, one more tardy and you're grounded, only
leave the house to walk to and from school no bike. Though it's
a vast improvement from the truancy in the fall, finally resolved
that thank God, now if I could just get you there on time. Speaking
of the bike, saw you flying by yesterday I know the cold broke
but you know it fluctuates, pneumonia weather, keep your coat on
and scarf and hat, if you get too hot you can open the coat—

*Around "you know it fluctuates" TAY C picks up the remote control beside her
and zips up the radio volume until LAINE is completely drowned out, then
casually goes back to eating cereal. LAINE walks over and turns the radio off.*

LAINE: You're not the only one's suffered. *(Grabs her coat.)* Finish
the dishes before you leave.

*LAINE exits. A few moments later NAJMA enters, drops her backpack on
a chair. Pours a tiny serving of cold cereal, milk. TAY C continues eating.
Silence. Then TAY C puts down spoon: done.*

TAY C: 'Dju do your English?

NAJMA, chewing, looks at TAY C, doesn't answer.

TAY C: Oh that's right Somalis can't eat and talk at the same time.
Well I didn't do it I hate that autobiography stuff I don't know
what to write. She can flunk me all she wants, think I care? 'Cept
then I'm grounded. Or worse.

*NAJMA takes her bowl and spoon to the sink to wash. She also washes
other dishes in the sink. During NAJMA's monologue TAY C puts her own*

dishes in the sink, then sits, tears out a piece of notebook paper, and quickly, expertly, cuts out a shape.

NAJMA: I wrote about changing schools. I wrote about when I first came here two years ago, I was ten, I went to the regular mainstream public school and they said first I had to take ESL there and I said "Wáa maxay, ESL?" and they said English as a Second Language so I took ESL in the mainstream school, and then we moved and I was near the alternative public school with the Ecuadoran kids and Ethiopian kids and Mexican kids and Somali kids and teachers from the same places and I went there and I learned a lot, it was harder than mainstream school, the work was harder the teachers were tougher, I liked it. Then I came to stay with you and now I'm back in easy peasy mainstream school.

TAY C: See? I always been to the same dumb school. I mean now I'm in middle, which is different, but so's everybody else, nothin' to write about.

NAJMA: There's that picture in the living room of you at the water park on the slide you could write about that. There's your mother's flower pots and how she talks to her plants and how you water her plants sometimes. *(Refers to the cutout.)* That's good.

It is good: a girl on a bike.

TAY C *(starts another cutout)*: Art. Always count on that A, but don't it feel lonely among the Cs and Ds and F science, why isn't iron "I"?

NAJMA: F-E. A-G.

TAY C: Why F me when the scientist made up the chart can't spell?

NAJMA: How about that day you were first to climb top of the ropes before start of gym? Everyone cheered. You could write about that.

TAY C: Matthews gave me a detention for usin' the equipment without a teacher around and threatened to give my science F a twin now how'm I s'posed to autobiographicize that? Self-incriminate.

TAY C *holds up her new cutout: Manhattan skyline, including the Twin Towers.* NAJMA *is impressed.*

NAJMA: New York.

TAY C *tears away the Twin Towers one at a time, making booming or crashing sounds.*

NAJMA: Write about how you're good at art. You know everything about art.

TAY C: "Write what you know." "Write what you know." Tell you what. I oughta essay on detention, there's my expertise.

NAJMA: Why not? Interesting to me I don't know what it's like. I'm not washing your bowl.

NAJMA *leaves the kitchen to get her coat and wraps from the closet.*

TAY C: 'Course you don't know what it's like, perfect behavior. Ms. Conduct.

TAY C *washes her bowl.* NAJMA, *drawn to the piano, sets her coat down and walks over, lifting the wooden covering over the keys.*

TAY C: Here's my other expertise: washin' dishes. Then the next excitin' chapter: dryin' 'em.

NAJMA *clinks a couple piano keys. A few more. She can't play but enjoys the feel, starts hitting the keys bolder, bolder. She is quite carried away when* TAY C *finally enters the living room and slams shut the covering, almost catching* NAJMA's *fingers.* TAY C *goes back to the dishes. Until indicated late in the scene* TAY C *does not look up from the bowl she's washing. When* NAJMA *recovers from the scare, she quietly enters the kitchen. Speaks cautiously.*

NAJMA (*trying to lighten*): Only had a bowl and spoon, how long's it take to wash that?

NAJMA *chuckles. Silence. Then* NAJMA *pulls out her autobiography notebook, flips to a page.*

NAJMA: She said to explain why I came to live with you. *(Reads.)*
"Then Tay C's mom invited me to come stay with them. Damac's
Tay C's mom's friend. Tay C's mom said, 'Hey. We have an extra
bed, a too-quiet house.' So last week I pack again." *(Looks at* TAY
C.*)* You think your mom mind I write that? Our business?
TAY C *(shrugs)*: She don't care what you do, go to school naked all
she care long's you bring home the As. With me she don't aim so
high. Just do her prayer mantra I pass the seventh grade.
NAJMA: *You* mind?

TAY C *shrugs.*

NAJMA: Cuz I won't do it if you—
TAY C: I said I don't care.

NAJMA *goes to get her coat.*

TAY C: How come your brother never writes?

NAJMA *looks at her.*

TAY C: Practically every day a letter from your mother, Somalia.
Nothin' from your brother and your brother right here. America.
NAJMA: I dunno. When we first came, Texas, him working all the
time, studying all the time, playing catch-up for the years
without school he still wanted to graduate eighteen. Save money.
And did. Saved and graduated early, December. He won't be
eighteen 'til next week.
TAY C: Savin' for what?
NAJMA: I dunno. Car.

Beat.

NAJMA: Why you have a piano?

No answer.

NAJMA: Your mother ever play it?

Silence.

TAY C: *She* played it.

NAJMA *confused a moment. Then:*

NAJMA: Your sister?

No answer.

NAJMA: You could write about your sister. You could write what she
      liked to play, music *and* games. You could write did you look
      alike, what you did together. You could write about your sister—
TAY C *(glares at* NAJMA*)*: You could write about *yours.*

NAJMA, *startled, stares at* TAY C *a few more seconds, then exits through
the outside door.* TAY C *goes back to washing the bowl.*

Scene 3
NAJMA: Chapter 7. E F L : English as a Fourth Language.

Classroom: The ESL TEACHER *and six* CHILDREN, *including* NAJMA.
*On the walls: maps of Africa, Latin America, the world, as well as ESL-
related posters. Chaos.* CHILDREN *chattering. Throughout the scene*
ALICIA *and* MUHAMED *are particularly hyper, hitting each other, tickling
each other, not hurting each other. Both are always giggling, squealing in
delight.*

ESL TEACHER: *Okay!*

CHILDREN *quieter.*

ESL TEACHER: I want Alicia here, Bao here, no you stay there, and Najma.

Other table:

ESL TEACHER: Manuel here, Zeinab there. Yes. Quiet please. Yes, Muhamed, and Marta you're there. *Quiet.* Okay. We have a new student. This is Zeinab and she's from Somalia. Who else is from Somalia?

MUHAMED, MANUEL, ALICIA, and BAO: Najma.

ESL TEACHER: Najma, very good. And they have something else in common. They're both ten years old.

NAJMA: Two years ago, I was ten.

Now Najma moves into the scene, taking her assigned seat.

MUHAMED: I'm ten!

MANUEL: I'm seven!

ALICIA: I'm six!

ESL TEACHER: Sh!

MANUEL: And they have something *else* in common.

ESL TEACHER: What's that, Manuel? and please raise your hand.

MANUEL: They're new.

ESL TEACHER: Najma is *pretty* new, isn't she. Najma *recently* moved to this country, she's been with us a month. Okay, let's introduce ourselves to—*Muhamed stop hitting Alicia with the ruler!* Let's tell Zeinab who we are. Bao. Why don't you start?

BAO *shakes her head no.*

ESL TEACHER: Bao, you know how to introduce yourself.

BAO *shakes her head no.*

ALICIA (*loud whisper*): I am Bao and I am from Laos.

ESL TEACHER: I'm speaking to Bao, Alicia.

BAO: I am Bao and I am from Laos.

ESL TEACHER: And how do you introduce Alicia?

BAO: He is Alicia and he is from Mexico.

ESL TEACHER: "He"?

BAO *confused.*

ESL TEACHER: Alicia is a girl, Bao. Do we say "he" for a girl?

Several hands shoot up.

MUHAMED (*hand not up*): She. She.

ESL TEACHER: We raise our hands when we want to answer, Muhamed.

MUHAMED (*hand not up*): She.

ESL TEACHER (*a look to* MUHAMED): Najma?

NAJMA: She is Alicia and she is from Mexico.

ESL TEACHER: Very good. Bao?

BAO: She is Alicia and she is from Mexico.

ESL TEACHER: Good. Alicia?

ALICIA: I am Alicia and I am from Mexico. She is Najma and she is from Somalia.

ESL TEACHER: And what can we say about Najma *and* Zeinab? Alicia.

ALICIA: They are Najma and Zeinab and they are from Somalia.

ESL TEACHER: Excellent, Najma and Zeinab *are* from Somalia. Najma?

NAJMA: I am Najma and I am from Somalia. He is Manuel and he is from Ecuador.

MANUEL: I am Manuel and I am from Ecuador. He is Muhamed and he is from Algeria.

MUHAMED: I am Muhamed and I am from Algeria. She is Zeinab and she is from Somalia.

ESL TEACHER: Very good. Now I have something for Zeinab.

Goes to her desk to get it.

MANUEL: ¿Y ella no tiene que contestar?

ESL TEACHER: Can you say that in English, Manuel?

ALICIA: He said: She don't have to do it?

ESL TEACHER: I know what he said, Alicia, I was asking *Manuel* to say it in *English*.

ALICIA (*loud whisper to* MANUEL): She don't—

ESL TEACHER: Alicia!

MANUEL: She don't have to do it?

ESL TEACHER: *Doesn't* she have to do it?

MANUEL: Doesn't she have to do it?

ESL TEACHER: No, not today. Zeinab cannot introduce herself because Zeinab doesn't know any English yet. (*Coloring picture.*) Do you want the tree or the fish?

ZEINAB *points. The* ESL TEACHER *gives* ZEINAB *colored pencils and shows her how to hold them.*

BAO: Kuv yuav ntses.

ESL TEACHER: Bao, nobody else understands Hmong, you'll have to say it in English.

BAO: Fish!

MANUEL: Why can't *we* color?

ALICIA *bonks* MUHAMED *on the head with her book. He giggles.*

ESL TEACHER: Alicia!

Snatches book out of ALICIA's *hand.*

MANUEL: I wanna draw!

BAO: Pourquoi je'n peux pas avoir le poisson?

MUHAMED: Elle laisse seulement les nouveaux déssines.

ESL TEACHER: Bao! Muhamed! No French! Zeinab is using the colored pencils because she needs to learn how to hold a pencil.

ALICIA: How come she can't hold a pencil?

ESL TEACHER: Zeinab's family lived in the desert. Her family rode camels, they didn't need pencils.

ALICIA *and* MANUEL *gasp.*

MANUEL: You rode a camel?

ZEINAB *stares at him, blank.*

ALICIA *(to* NAJMA*):* You rode a camel?

ESL TEACHER: No, Najma's family is from Mogadishu, the city.

MUHAMED: Could you hold a pencil?

ESL TEACHER: Of course, Najma went to school. *(Beat. Unsure.)* Didn't you?

NAJMA *nods.*

ZEINAB: Ule juya Kiingereza kabla ya kuja hapa?

ESL TEACHER: Najma, could you please tell Zeinab that we only speak English in this class?

NAJMA *starts to.*

ESL TEACHER: That until she can speak it she should just listen quietly. We need a common language to communicate, no one else understands Somali.

NAJMA *(cuts her off):* That wasn't Somali.

ESL TEACHER: What?

NAJMA: She said, "Ule juya Kiingereza kabla ya kuja hapa" that wasn't Somali.

ESL TEACHER: Well, no one else understands Arabic.

NAJMA: That was Swahili. Aferit Ingleze kebel Inta Inat? *That* was Arabic.

MUHAMED: Nam. Shaweya.

NAJMA: Muzboot. Inta min el jazeera.

ESL TEACHER: Okay! First of all, Zeinab and Muhamed should not be having private conferences with Najma during class time, and second (*to all*) what do we speak in this class?

CHILDREN: English only.

ESL TEACHER: English only. If you have something to say please share it with *everyone* in *English*.

MUHAMED: She asked her, You know English before you came here?

NAJMA (*shaking her head no*): Only Somali. Only Swahili. Only Arabic.

BAO (*to* MUHAMED): Qu'est ce qu'elle a dit?

ESL TEACHER: No French! All *right* today we have a short class. Does anyone know why?

ALICIA: Half-day.

ESL TEACHER: We have a half-day *please* raise your hand Alicia and why do we have a half-day?

CHILDREN: Thanksgiving.

ALICIA: Thanksgiving is tomorrow.

NAJMA: What's Thanksgiving?

ALICIA: When the white people stopped killing the Indians and ate them.

ESL TEACHER: When the *Pilgrims* sat down to eat *with* the Indians.

ALICIA (*puzzled*): They wasn't white?

ESL TEACHER: Yes, but—Manuel! Is that gum? Give me that gum!

ALICIA: Yo creía que ellos eran blancos.

ESL TEACHER: Sh! Thanksgiving is tomorrow and we only have a half-day today so let's review the one hundred words. If we know these one hundred words, what do we know?

Hands shoot up.

ESL TEACHER: Muhamed?

MUHAMMED: Half of English.

ESL TEACHER: Half of all American spoken English.

ZEINAB: Soomaaliya miyaad ka timi?

NAJMA: Haa. Lokerkayga waxa ku jira gooryaan?

ESL TEACHER: Zeinab. Najma, no one else can speak Somali so what are you being when you speak Somali privately with Zeinab?

NAJMA: Rude.

ESL TEACHER: Rude. *(To all.)* You read, I'll repeat.

Slowly, as ESL TEACHER *shows cards:*

CHILDREN: A. (Uh.)

ESL TEACHER: A.

CHILDREN: The.

ESL TEACHER: The.

CHILDREN: And.

ESL TEACHER: And.

CHILDREN: Feend.

ESL TEACHER: Find. Long *i*.

CHILDREN: Find. Stop.

ESL TEACHER *(correcting)*: Stop. The Hispanic students want to put an *e* at the beginning, the Somali students want to put an *e* at the end. Stop.

CHILDREN: Stop.

ESL TEACHER: Very good.

CHILDREN: People.

ESL TEACHER: People. Excellent.

CHILDREN: As.

MANUEL: ¡Quiero dibujar! Me gusta dibujar. ¿Por qué no podemos dibujar?

ALICIA: Porque nosotros sabemos leer.

MANUEL: ¡Yo no quiero leer! Yo quiero dibujar.

ESL TEACHER: ¡Manuel! ¡Alicia! ¡Están interrumpiendo la clase! Ustedes no están permitidos hablar entre sí durante las lecciones. ¿Me entienden? ¡Y cuántas veces les tengo que repitir que en esta clase sólo hablamos inglés! ¿Cómo piensan que Muhamed y Najma y Marta y Bao y Marta y Zeinab se sienten al ser excluidos? Ellos no hablan español. *Muhamed stop pulling her hair!* En esta clase aprendemos inglés escuchando y hablando unos con los otros y si ustedes insisten en hablar español, no sólo están excluyendo a Najma y Zeinab y Bao y Muhamed, sino que también estén malgastando el tiempo de todos. ¿Creen que éso es justo? No, no es justo y ¿saben qué les pasa a los niños como ustedes? ¿Saben? Les damos un *time-out*. ¿Eso es lo que ustedes quieren? (MANUEL *and* ALICIA *shake heads a vehement no.*) Ya me imaginaba que no, así que yo les sugiero que dejen de interrumpir y pongan atención y recuerden que en esta clase hablamos *English only!*

Bell. The CHILDREN *exit, walking in twos.*

ZEINAB: Ma arki karaa gooryannka?	MANUEL: Voy a dibujar en la próxima clase.	MUHAMED: Tu veux venir chez moi après l'école?
NAJMA: Miyaad ka baqdaa gooryaanka?	ALICIA: Yo también.	BAO: Je dois demander à Maman.
ZEINAB: Maya.	MANUEL: Tú vas a dibujar después del almuerzo.	MUHAMED: On peut jouer avec ma Play Station.*
NAJMA: Waan hubaa inaad ka baqdo.	ALICIA: Yo voy a dibujar las *Power Puff Girls.* *	BAO: On peut regarder *Power Puff Girls*.
ZEINAB: Waxba kama baqo waxaan ahay Power Puff Girl!	MANUEL: Después del almuerzo.	MUHAMED: Okay.
NAJMA: Waa slimy.	ALICIA: ¡Ahora!	BAO: Maman me fera finir mes devoirs d'abord. Je peux venir chez toi après mes devoirs.
ZEINAB: Dadka way cunaan.	MANUEL: Yo voy a dibujar ahora.	MUHAMED: Okay . . .
NAJMA: Ma cunaan.	ALICIA: Yo también.	
ZEINAB: Fransiisku way cunaan . . .	MANUEL: ¡Qué no!	

* May be replaced with any popular children's game.

Scene 4

Cemetery. TAY C *studying a tombstone, her bike parked against another.* NAJMA *enters.*

TAY C: Whadju follow me for?

NAJMA *just stares at* TAY C. TAY C *rolls her eyes. Quiet awhile,* TAY C *back to studying the stone.*

NAJMA: That your sister?

TAY C: Look how old these gravestones are. My sister died two years ago this grave place no vacancy since 1941. *(Beat.)* How'dju follow me? You don't got a bike.

NAJMA: Walked. You stopped, looked at the building they gutted, stopped, looked at the pond, ice melted, stopped, go in the store, candy bar.

TAY C: That's just why I need a rear-view mirror. I asked her for it, my birthday, need to know what's behind me.

Silence.

NAJMA: This your quiet place? Secret place?

TAY C: *Was.*

Pause.

TAY C: I like to figure it out. It's okay to add to it. Like this one, "Loving mother, born December 3, 1900, died October 15, 1921," and with hers "Emily Elaine, born October 15, 1921, died October 17, 1921." Childbirth, that's easy. But try this: Timmy, 1932–1939 that's seven, Jessica five, Landis two. At first I thought TB or somethin' but all took the same date: May 29, 1939.

Pause.

NAJMA: Tornado!

TAY C: Right! Somethin' sudden, accident or act of nature. I say drowned. Took the rowboat out, unfortunately downriver it gets choppy. Too little they knew no better. *(Beat.)* You ever see so many dead people?

NAJMA: War. When my mother left Hargeisa she said dead everywhere.

TAY C: Thought you were from Mogadishu.

NAJMA: Am. But my mother born Hargeisa. Too many dead, they just stayed there. Not buried.

TAY C: Did not.

NAMJA: Did. (Pause.) My father. Shot dead.

TAY C: They just leave his body? In the open?

NAJMA: That was Hargeisa, he died later, my home. Mogadishu.

TAY C: Oh. (Pause.) Where he get it? The back?

NAJMA: Belly.

TAY C: Was there like blood? Like sticky red all over him?

NAJMA: Uh huh.

TAY C: Was there like guts? Like meat his liver or muscle or kidney pokin' through?

NAJMA: Uh huh.

TAY C: Was his body like—?

NAJMA: Uh huh.

Pause.

TAY C: Use to play here. Ghosts in the Graveyard. Hide and Seek, the flashlights.

NAJMA: Flashlight? *Night?*

TAY C: 'Course.

NAJMA: Uh uh.

TAY C: Yep.

Beat.

NAJMA: My sister died in childbirth.

TAY C: Your sister was five.

NAJMA: My little sister Qalin five years old, her belly balloon up, stick arms skinny skinny. I say to my aunt, "She having a baby? That a baby in there?"

NAJMA *giggles. Then stops.*

NAJMA: No baby. Just hungry.

TAY C *(sings)*: "There was an old woman all skin and bones. Oo oo oo oo. She lived down by the old graveyard. Oo oo oo oo."

NAJMA: Came with my aunt to the refugee camp, they only took six, no room for my mother.

TAY C: One day she thought she'd go for a walk. Oo oo oo oo.	NAJMA: One day we're packing, I'm crying, "I don't want another refugee camp!" But my aunt said, "We're going to America. In America it'll be different.

TAY C: She saw the bones all layin' around. Oo oo oo oo.

NAJMA: "In America eat and eat and eat and eat!"

TAY C: She went to the closet to get a broom. Oo oo oo oo.

NAJMA: "America: The more you eat, the smaller your tummy."

TAY C: She opened the door and BOO!

TAY C *grabs* NAJMA. NAJMA *screams.* TAY C *and* NAJMA *both laughing hard. When it subsides:*

TAY C: They didn't just leave the dead bodies there. Layin' on the ground.

NAJMA: Did.

TAY C: "She opened the door and BOO!"

TAY C *grabs* NAJMA *again. Both squealing.*

Scene 5

Bedroom. NAJMA *practicing her kaman; she's a relative beginner. Trying to sing a Somali song with her playing.* TAY C *walks in. Obnoxiously blasts rap music.* NAJMA *gradually gets up and expertly raps with the rapper.* TAY C, *surprised, cracks up.* LAINE *enters the house, races up to the bedroom. She screams, but they can't hear.* TAY C *finally turns down the music.*

TAY C: Huh?

LAINE: I SAID YOU CAN HEAR THAT ALL THE WAY DOWN THE STREET TURN IT *OFF!*

TAY C *turns it off. Starts giggling again.*

TAY C: I never pegged you for it. Rap head, spit back every syllable perfect.

NAJMA: Just memorization, easy. Somali never written 'til the '70s, doesn't mean history wasn't recorded. Poetry.

They stare at her, confused.

NAJMA *(still standing):*   *Baraar habarti loog ka ma furto gawrac kama baajo*
Bil saddex ihi galabtii hadday beelo kaa bixiso
Beladkaad u jeeddiyo iftiin beelo ku ma geyso
In kastoo la baabuuniyoo baayac lagu doono
Bisinkiyo karaamada haddii loo burannburiyo

Hear the buh buh buh? That's how Somalis do it. You rhyme. We alliterate.

LAINE: What's it mean?

NAJMA: An old poet speaking to a young poet in a poetry duel. I don't know all the words all the words we don't say anymore. It's a million years old it's Beowulf. Everyone's a poet. Politicians out-poeting each other for office.

Beat. LAINE *staring at* NAJMA.

LAINE: Wait.

LAINE *goes downstairs to the living room. Pulls out of a drawer a few photo albums, flips through, searching. Meanwhile* TAY C *takes a piece of notebook paper, making a cutout as she speaks.*

TAY C: You were cryin' in your sleep last night.

NAJMA: Wasn't.

TAY C: You were talkin' in your sleep, cryin' "Hooyo! Hooyo!" That means "Mommy," right?

NAJMA: I wasn't talking in my sleep.

TAY C: You don't really think she's comin' for ya, do ya.

NAJMA: She's coming.

TAY C: How your cousin gonna pay for it? Lotta money, bring your hooyo here. Look.

TAY C *shows the cutout:* NAJMA'S *kaman.* NAJMA *stares.*

TAY C: It's your guitar.

NAJMA: Kaman.

TAY C: You can put it on your wall if you want, I got some tape.

TAY C *tapes the cutout to* NAJMA'S *wall.*

TAY C: Like it?

NAJMA *nods.* LAINE *enters with an album.*

LAINE: Found the one I was looking for.

LAINE *opens it.*

NAJMA *(reads)*: "Poetry Slam Finals."

TAY C: Here we go.

NAJMA: I see you! *(Meaning* LAINE.*)* Blue dress.

TAY C: This should go on all night I'm ridin' my bike.

Exits.

LAINE: She just doesn't want you to see how cute she was little.

NAJMA: What's a poetry slam?

LAINE: What you said about your politicians. One poet stands, tries to outdo the others. Get the most votes. Or loudest applause.

NAJMA (*photo*): You won that trophy?

LAINE *nods.*

NAJMA: Where is it?

LAINE (*shrugs*): Attic. Somewhere.

NAJMA: You were good.

LAINE: Well. Tell the truth, inherent flaw in the system is sometimes style outweighs the words. Why I finally got out of it. Year I took the championship, second place went to someone whose poem was better. I know better when I hear it. Just shy, he couldn't woo the crowd. Wooing's my forté.

NAJMA: Can I hear?

LAINE: Don't know I even remember any. (*Turns page.*) See him? Red tie, third from the left?

NAJMA *nods.*

LAINE: Cam and Tay C's daddy. See how the fingertips barely meet the drum? I had the words, he the perfect accompaniment touch.

NAJMA: Is that Cam?

LAINE: No, she was too little to come to the slams then. But look.

Turns a few pages.

NAJMA (*reads*): "Mother and Daughter Night."

LAINE: Sponsor it every Mother's Day.

NAJMA: She's cute!

LAINE *smiles.*

NAJMA: Where's Tay C?

LAINE: Tay C never took an interest, always chose apple pie at Grandma's over slam nights. Cammy loved the piano, so poetry just an extension of the music, I guess.

NAJMA *(turns the page)*: She's so little!

LAINE: First recital. Just turned eight. Started her lessons at five.

NAJMA *(turns page)*: Cam again?

LAINE: Mm hm. This bed. And who's that?

LAINE *points.* NAJMA *looks closer, stunned.*

NAJMA: *Tay C?*

LAINE *nods.*

NAJMA: That little girl? giggle girl? *(Beat.)* I've never seen Tay C smile like that! Let someone hold her like that! *(Beat.)* The room looks different.

LAINE: Cam's piano posters. Chopin. Scott Joplin. Stevie Wonder.

NAJMA: Where are they?

LAINE: Attic, I guess. Like everything else.

NAJMA: You didn't have to take them down cuz I moved in.

LAINE: Tay C took 'em down. Long before you moved in.

Turns the page.

NAJMA *(laughing)*: What a mess!

LAINE: We always let 'em dive into their cake and ice cream. That was Tay C's birthday, second, but look at Cam: strawberry face!

NAJMA: Cam loved ice cream, right? Sometimes Tay C dreams I hear her mumble. Only words I can make out: "Cam." "Ice cream."

Pause.

LAINE: She died like that. Gang wars Cam and Tay C heard the ice cream truck, Cam ran out to get it. Stray gunfire.

Pause. Then LAINE *suddenly stands.*

LAINE: Played with her goat
           Jump with her sister
           Sister saw the boat
           Then turned and kissed her.

           Ship on the coast
           Man on the ship
           White as a ghost
           With chain and whip

It goes on like that I don't remember what came next but you can
pretty much guess the rest.

NAJMA: It's good! *(Beat.)* Sometimes I write in English. Somali
    poem in English. American words, Somali alliteration, Somali
    scansion. *Hard!* Harder than rhyme. *I* think.

LAINE: Let's hear.

NAJMA *(stands)*:   Sister says let's play the game where sticks swing
                     I say let's play the game of stepping stones
                     Our stomachs so round suggests something new
                     "Stomach jump!" says she

Hear it? the sss sss sss?

Pause.

LAINE: You were hungry.

NAJMA: My sister sleeps long My sister stays sleep
           Her starving is past Suffering is past
           Some place in the sun Some place happiness.

Pause.

NAJMA: It's a happy poem.

LAINE: I know. It's okay to be sad, too.

NAJMA: I'm not. Wanna hear another?

LAINE *nods.*

NAJMA: Well. It's not really a poem, more like a poem thing, like a help for me, learn my capitals. Test Friday.

LAINE: Slam me.

NAJMA: Ida Ho gets coysy
            Whenever she sees a Boise.

LAINE *(laughs)*: Very good! *(Thinks.)*
            Turned up the tune on the stereo
            And two little girls stroll in and go
            (Dancing.)
            Go go gogo Go go gogo

LAINE *stops.* NAJMA *waits.*

LAINE: That's it.

NAJMA *giggles. Dances:*

NAJMA: *Go go gogo Go go gogo*

LAINE: I wrote that when Cam and Tay C were little. We used to dance to it, your turn!

NAJMA: Where I stay I'd say's quite nice
            If you love the snow and ice
            I'll be happy when I call ya
            From the airport in Somalia.

LAINE *(sings)*: Oh beautiful for spacious skies
            For chocolate shakes and jumbo fries
            For study hall, lunch, recess

NAJMA: And a blizzard the night before the test.

LAINE: We used to say "And being the teacher's number one pest."

NAJMA: I just made it up.

LAINE: Really?

NAJMA *nods.*

LAINE: Good rhyme! Here's a game we played in school:
> Little Miss Muffet
> Sat on her tuffet
> Eating her curds and whey

NAJMA *stares.*

LAINE: Finish it.
NAJMA: What's "whey"?
LAINE: Nobody knows.
NAJMA:
> Little Miss Muffet
> Sat on her . . . tuffet?
> (LAINE *shrugs.*)
> Little Miss Muffet
> Sat on her tuffet
> Eating her curds and whey
> (*Slower, as she makes it up.*)
> The curds made her sick
> The whey didn't stick . . .
> No!
> Little Miss Muffet
> Sat on her tuffet
> Eating her curds and stuff
> She knew things weren't sound
> When the meal going down
> Tasted better when it came back up.

They giggle. TAY C *appears in the doorway, looking in on them, observing their camaraderie. She does not smile. They don't notice her.*

NAJMA: What was that one, "go go"?
LAINE:
> Turned up the tune on the stereo
> And two *big* girls stroll in and go

LAINE and NAJMA: Go go gogo Go go gogo

LAINE: And two big girls stroll in and go

LAINE and NAJMA: Go go gogo Go go gogo

Laughing, touching. Somewhere during NAJMA'S *next poem,* TAY C *exits unnoticed.*

NAJMA: Hey!
           Little Miss Muffet
           Sat on her tuffet
           Eating her curds and whey
           The curds gave her gas
           She let it all pass . . .

Pause.

LAINE: Which is why she's still "Miss" to this day.

Giggle giggle: time of their lives.

Scene 6

TAY C *on the couch, relaxed, remote control in hand, staring blank at the blasting TV.* NAJMA *enters from school. Goes to the table where the mail has been put. She finds a letter and is happy, a second, a third. She opens one, sits and reads it. Then puts it down, starting her homework, writing in her notebook.* TAY C *glances at her.* TAY C *back to staring at the TV;* NAJMA *working. Eventually* TAY C *looks at* NAJMA *again. Remotes off the TV. Strolls over to stand at the table, staring at* NAJMA. *Finally* NAJMA *looks up.*

NAJMA: What?

TAY C: You just leave the letter open, I could read it if I was nosy.

NAJMA: Read it.

TAY C: I know Somali! think I don't? (TAY C *stares at the letter.*) Haye Najma: Dear Najma.

NAJMA: It means "hello."

TAY C: Same thing.

NAJMA (*corrects pronunciation*): Haye.

TAY C (*better*): Haye.

NAJMA *goes back to writing.*

TAY C (*muttering to herself*): Haye haye haye. (*Beat.*) How come you only open one letter at a time?

NAJMA (*shrugs, not looking up*): Save 'em.

TAY C: Why?

NAJMA: Enjoy a little now, enjoy a little later.

TAY C: What if it's important?

NAJMA: It is. But not urgent.

TAY C: Why she gotta write you three letters same day?

NAJMA: I dunno. She thinks of other stuff to say.

TAY C: If I went away and my mother wrote three letters the same day I'd tell her Are you crazy? I'd probably be like you, save 'em 'til later, *if* I got to 'em at all. She won't get in 'til 7:30, doin' the AIDS hotline.

NAJMA: Your mom's a saint. (TAY C *stares at her*). My cousin Damac says. AIDS hotline, literacy program, homeless shelter.

TAY C: She useta be normal, only became Betsy Busy Bee after my sister died. She calls, tell her I'm on my bike, back before dark.

TAY C *grabs her backpack and heads for the door.* NAJMA *doesn't look up. At the door* TAY C *turns to* NAJMA.

TAY C: I know where your cousin lives. I bike by there every day. You ever see *Mary Tyler Moore*? old show? Mary Tyler Moore lived in an apartment in a house with Rhoda and Phyllis but then, halfway through the show, Mary moves to a high-rise. You can see the outside of it when the show comes on. She musta moved out when the show got canceled though cuz she's not there anymore, your cousin is. All your country people, Mary moved out and the Somalis moved in.

TAY C *exits.* NAJMA *walks to the stereo, blasts a rap CD, sits back down and writes in her notebook a few moments.* LAINE *enters.* NAJMA *quickly runs to turn the music off.*

NAJMA: Sorry, Laine!

LAINE *(cheery)*: You almost gave me a heart attack. When I heard the music I mistook you for Tay C—*studying*! The shock surely'd killed me.

NAJMA: I thought you were doing the AIDS hotline.

LAINE: First time this happened: more volunteers than phones. So came home to grab the grocery list, check that chore off now instead of Sunday, I got a better idea for Sunday. Wanna do the Mother's Day slam?

NAJMA *startled.*

LAINE: Of course you're not my daughter but I'm your guardian, right? For now? I think they'll let it pass. They still do it! I called, I just got this inspiration, they said, "Yes, the annual All Ladies Brawl," you've such natural poetic instincts, it just came to me, Why waste our co-talent?

Pause.

NAJMA: I have a local history test on Monday—

LAINE (*grabs grocery list taped to fridge*): Well! If not this Sunday next, we've got time. Or how about Thursday after I get back from the peace rally? You have a spare hour between homework and bed, right? Mother's Day not 'til May and it's barely February, write, read, rehearse, we'll get there.

LAINE gone. NAJMA stares after her a few seconds, then turns back to her notebook. Finishes what she's writing, then stands to read to the audience, as if she is standing before the class.

NAJMA: Chapter 4. When things got bad bad, we left. My aunt claimed us with her kids, our mother didn't make the lottery. Walking miles and miles, then the long hard bus ride. We were at the refugee camp in Kenya for fourteen months. It was hot, it smelled. We played games.

Simultaneous: NAJMA makes a few gestures, e.g., taps her head, snaps her fingers, does several crisscross hops as QALIN enters and walks to NAJMA. Just as NAJMA finishes the routine, QALIN will make the same exact gestures. NAJMA does it again, this time a little more elaborate. QALIN does the same. Now NAJMA does a hugely complicated series, and QALIN follows, almost gets it right.

NAJMA: You only tapped your foot twice. I did three.

QALIN: You did two.

NAJMA: Three.

QALIN: Why you always leader?!

NAJMA: Cuz you're five and I'm eight.

QALIN: I'm telling Abdi! Where is he?

NAJMA: Trying to find us a new tent. The old one got ripped, remember?

QALIN: Why he gotta do it?

NAJMA: We need a tent! And he's our big brother he's the grown-up. Fourteen.

QALIN: I'm telling Hooyo. I want Hooyo!

NAJMA: Mommy'll come, meet us. Sometime.

QALIN: *When?*

No answer.

QALIN: I want Hooyo! I want Hooyo!

NAJMA *gets on her hands and knees and humps her back.*

NAJMA: Camel!

QALIN *happily jumps on* NAJMA's *back.* NAJMA *gives* QALIN *a ride, moving her back up and down.* QALIN *squeals, thrilled. Then suddenly* QALIN *falls silent, despite* NAJMA's *continued entertaining bumpy ride. Eventually:*

QALIN: I'm hungry.

In one fell swoop NAJMA *jumps up (*QALIN *jumping or falling off) and reads from her paper to the audience.*

NAJMA: Sometimes there was school in the camp and sometimes
there wasn't. Either way Qalin had to keep up her studies. (*Turns
to* QALIN.) Write "Qalin."

QALIN *finger-writes on the ground.*

NAJMA: What's seven plus eight?

Rapidly, expertly, QALIN *adds with her fingers hidden behind her back.*

QALIN: Fifteen.

NAJMA: What's the capital of Ethiopia?

QALIN: Addis Ababa.

NAJMA: What makes up matter?

QUALIN: Solid liquid gas.

NAJMA: How are you? Answer in Swahili.

QALIN: Sijambo.

NAJMA: When did Somalia gain independence?

QALIN: Old old days Somalia traded with Egypt with Phoenicia with Persia with Greece with Rome, then the Suez Canal opens and in fly the Europes. But July 1, 1960, Somalia's declared independent, we give the Brits and Italians the boot. It wasn't easy but it wasn't awful either. 'Til the drought.

NAJMA: What's three times six?

QALIN (*rapidly finger-adding behind her back*): Eighteen.

NAJMA: Say it in Arabic.

QALIN: Thamâniyaᶜashra.

NAJMA: When was Mohammed born?

QALIN: The Year of the Elephant.

NAJMA: What color's the rainbow?

QALIN: Red orange yellow green blue indigo violet.

NAJMA: Hold out your hands.

QALIN, *puzzled, does.* NAJMA *snatches them.*

NAJMA: What's eleven minus three?

QALIN, *panicked, tries adding in her head.*

QALIN: Seven . . . eight!

NAJMA: Conjugate "dhis."

QALIN: Dhísayaa dhísaysaa dhísayaa dhísaysaa dhísaynaa dhísaysaan dhísayaan.

NAJMA: Conjugate "keen."

QALIN: Keénayaa keénaysaa keénayaa keénaysaa keénaynaa keénaysaan keénayaan.

NAJMA: Conjugate "akhri."

QALIN: Cúnayaa cúnaysaa —

NAJMA: I said "akhri"!

QALIN: I don't wanna read I wanna eat I wanna conjugate "eat"!

NAJMA: Read!

QALIN: Eat!

NAJMA: Read!

QALIN: Eat! Eat! Eat! Eat! Eat! Eat! Eat! Eat! Eat! Eat! Eat! Eat! Eat!
   Eat! Eat! Eat! Eat! Eat! Eat!

QALIN *jumping around the room and yelling. Then* NAJMA *starts jumping right behind her, also yelling "Eat!"* QALIN *starts giggling,* NAJMA *giggling. Suddenly* NAJMA *and* QALIN *turn to something they see offstage.*

NAJMA and QALIN: Dinner! Dinner! Dinner!

They stand in line, QALIN *before* NAJMA. *Silence. After awhile they take a step forward. Silence.*

NAJMA *(as if reading from her paper)*: When mealtime finally came, we
   could be in line for hours.

Finally they are at the front and happily, eagerly take their imaginary plates, sit on the ground. Now they both stare at their own plates, disappointed. Then NAJMA *looks at the audience.*

NAJMA: It isn't much. It very very very isn't much.

Now NAJMA *looks at* QALIN's *plate.* QALIN *has not looked up from it.*

NAJMA: But it's more than Qalin got.

QALIN *looks at* NAJMA's *plate, then up at* NAJMA. NAJMA *suddenly starts scarfing down her food, not looking at* QALIN, *who continues to stare at her. Eventually* QALIN *stands, picks up the notebook and pencil, places it in front of* NAJMA.

QALIN: Write it.

NAJMA *stops eating but without looking at* QALIN *slowly shakes her head no.* QALIN *continues staring at* NAJMA. NAJMA *looks at* QALIN. NAJMA *writes. Stands. Reads.*

NAJMA: I always got more than Qalin. I was bigger and always always always got more. Then Qalin died.

NAJMA *turns back to* QALIN. *They stare at each other. Then* NAJMA *suddenly, violently, erases what she just wrote and scrawls new text in its place. Then reads.*

NAJMA: Food Food Food!

NAJMA *opens a nearby cabinet. It is stuffed with all manner of junk food: chips and Oreos and cheese puffs and Twinkies. She grabs the stuff by the armload and puts it in front of* QALIN, *who digs in.* NAJMA *keeps going back for more, piling the junk in front of* QALIN. *As she does:*

NAJMA: Plenty. Meat and cheese, vegetables and every dessert, gallons of water we waited and waited, and it was provided!

NAJMA *sits, gazes contented at gorging* QALIN.

NAJMA: I didn't have anything myself. Who needs it I got fat just watching my baby sister eat.

NAJMA *laughs heartily, grabbing handfuls of cheese puffs and tossing them high in the air, letting them rain down.* QALIN *laughs as she continues eating everything in sight.*

Scene 7

TAY C *and* NAJMA *asleep.* TAY C *wakes: beautiful, sophisticated jazz piano music.* TAY C *races downstairs.* CAM *at the piano.*

TAY C: You were never that good.

CAM: 'F I'd lasted, I woulda been.

TAY C *listens awhile. Then:*

TAY C: Chopsticks!

TAY C *plays "Chopsticks" while* CAM *accompanies with her brilliant stuff: masterpiece.* TAY C *laughs. When* CAM *speaks, she may periodically turn to* TAY C, *her hands still flawlessly beating out the notes.*

TAY C: Can we go to the park after school tomorrow?

CAM *(shrugs)*: Mom says so.

TAY C: Can we feed the ducks?

CAM: If Mom says we can go.

TAY C: Mom don't get home 'til 5:30 she won't know.

CAM *plays music, ignores* TAY C.

TAY C *(mutters)*: I'll go if I want you're not my boss. (CAM *gives her a look.*) Okay.

CAM: I'm twelve you're ten, think I am.

TAY C: *Okay!*

CAM *switches to another piece.*

TAY C: Cam.

CAM *ignores her, still playing.*

TAY C: Cam. *(Ignored.)* I'm not ten anymore. Twelve. Twelve like you.

CAM *(still not looking up from piano)*: I know that. Dontcha think I know that? I know this is your dream.

TAY C: Don't worry. This is it, I'm not havin' my next birthday. Next birthday make me pass you, thirteen, forget it. Weird enough we're the same age.

CAM *keeps playing.*

TAY C: She ain't that wild about me anymore. She liked me enough when you were alive, when there was both of us, but now she volunteers every second she got away from me.

CAM: She liked me.

TAY C: Which I figure I use to my advantage. If I don't advertise my birthday, she'll forget. If my own mother forgets, no one'll know. If no one knows, I'll stay twelve.

CAM: She liked me.

Ding ding.

CAM: Yes!

TAY C: I'm goin'.

CAM: *I'm goin'.* You want a vanilla cone dipped in that red crap, right?

TAY C: Cherry.

CAM *(counting change)*: Grrr-ross, looks like blood.

TAY C: So? what's chocolate dip look like? Poop!

CAM: Yeah, right.

TAY C: Right.

CAM: So mature.

TAY C: Right. I'll get it.

CAM: No, she calls and neither of us answers the phone she'll think we snuck off without askin'.

TAY C: How come you always—?

CAM: *Argue?* Keep it up we'll stand around miss it altogether!

TAY C: So I'm stuck here. Waitin'.

CAM: Back in a flash.

Exits.

TAY C *(sulk)*: I'm stuck here. Waitin'.

TAY C *waits.*

End of Act One.

Scene 1

Bedroom. NAJMA *is taping up* CAM's *music posters all over her own side of the room.* TAY C *enters downstairs with the mail. She wears headphones, bouncing to the music.* NAJMA *quickly rushes to sit on her own bed, grabs a book, opens it.* TAY C *comes up and enters the bedroom. Tosses a letter at* NAJMA *without looking at her, goes directly to her own bed, throws her backpack on it, starts to exit without looking up.*

NAJMA (*yelling above the headphones*): HI!

TAY C *vaguely glances in* NAJMA's *direction, catches a glimpse of the wall, stops in her tracks.*

NAJMA (*jumps up to look at the posters with* TAY C): I found—

NAJMA *sees* TAY C *can't hear with headphones.* NAJMA *takes them off* TAY C's *ears, letting them drop around her neck.*

NAJMA: I found 'em! The attic. All I had was my prayer rug so there was plenty of room. Thought you'd like it, little bitta Cam here. (*Laughs.*) You almost walked out and missed it!

NAJMA *now realizes* TAY C *is not smiling.* TAY C *moves to the pictures.*

NAJMA (*a plea*): Don't tear 'em.
TAY C (*barely containing anger*): They're not yours don't tell me what to do with 'em.

TAY C *takes them all down without damaging them; then, holding them, heads for the door and on the way out quickly—before* NAJMA *can register it—picks up* NAJMA's *letter, tears it in half and drops it back on* NAJMA's *bed. Exits.* NAJMA *sits on her bed. Takes the two halves of letter out of the two halves of envelope, puts the pieces together and reads.*

Scene 2

LAINE *and* DAMAC *drinking coffee while* LAINE *polishes an old poetry slam trophy. Two other newly polished ones on the table.* DAMAC *holds money out to* LAINE. LAINE *stops rubbing, stares at it. Doesn't take it.*

DAMAC: Laine. (LAINE *shakes her head no. Beat.*) I was an engineer, Somalia. If I were an engineer here getting a place for Najma and my kids and me would be easy. But no one will hire me as an engineer here, I'm a janitor. Still. She's my cousin. I'll contribute.

LAINE: Your situation. (*Beat.*) Did a bit of overtime, my paycheck little fatter this month—

DAMAC: Not enough overtime for a whole other person the deal was Najma would stay here, my apartment so small but never intended you to strain your budget: food. Clothes. Notebooks. (*Beat:* LAINE *still doesn't touch the money.*) Take it! You need it, right? Tell me the truth: Hardship without it. Right? (LAINE *reluctantly nods.*) Take it. You've given Najma a bed, space. Generosity enough. (LAINE *takes the money.*)

LAINE: Thank you, Damac.

DAMAC: Thank *you*, Laine.

LAINE: Thank *you*, Damac, this wasn't your idea. When did you start thinking this was your idea? Remember that Saturday I picked you up for the bake sale, when I met Najma? And you showed me those cookies she made. Cam used to love to bake It made me think of my Cam. And then she came along with us I was so surprised! I'd never think of asking Tay C she'd just roll her eyes, or come and be bored stiff, but Cam . . . Cam was a mama's girl. Najma's good grades and Najma playing her kaman and I thought of Cam's piano and honor roll report cards and what a nice influence Najma could be on Tay C, and how they could help each other, two girls each with a sister loss I did it for them. So when you brought up your overcrowded rooms—

DAMAC: Hinting! Shameless.

LAINE: Really? (DAMAC *nods, ashamed.* LAINE *laughs.*) I didn't even notice. If you thought you were laying some trap I didn't even pick it up cuz I was laying my own I wanted her! For Tay C. And for Najma I wanted them to help each other I did it for them. I did it for them.

NAJMA *enters from the outside.*

NAJMA: Damac!
NAJMA *runs and hugs* DAMAC.
DAMAC: Najma, you act like you haven't seen me in five years!
NAJMA: You're never here Thursdays, only Saturdays when you pick me up to go to prayers. (*Sees trophies, wonder:*) These were your poetry slam trophies?
LAINE: Found them in the attic. Hold it from the bottom.

NAJMA *picks one up from the bottom.*

NAJMA: Heavy! You must've been good, Laine. (*Suddenly puts trophy down, worry, turns to* DAMAC.) You're never here Thursdays, only Saturdays when you pick me up to go to prayers Is Hooyo okay? Hooyo sick?
DAMAC: No she's not sick.
NAJMA (*suddenly bright*): Is she coming?! You came over to say she's on her way?

DAMAC *shakes her head no.* NAJMA *stares at her.*

DAMAC: Have you ever heard of the al-Barakat company? (NAJMA *shakes her head no.*) It was a money transfer station. Somali people ran it. Somali people here sent money to relatives back home. We took the money to al-Barakat, and al-Barakat sent it to family in Somalia, your hooyo. (*Beat.*) They shut down al-Barakat.

Pause.

NAJMA: Who?

DAMAC: The United States.

Pause.

NAJMA: The United States shut down al-Barakat? *(*DAMAC *nods.)*
   Why?

DAMAC: After 9/11, the United States government claimed that al-
   Barakat had ties to al-Qaeda. These ties were never proven, but
   because of the suspicion, al-Barakat was closed, and I haven't
   been successful with any other money transfer sources so I
   haven't been able to send money to your mother.

Pause.

NAJMA: Since *9/11?*

DAMAC *(to* LAINE*)*: Some of the cash I've heard went to the warlords,
   and if that's true, good! Glad they closed them down! *(Beat. To*
   NAJMA.*)* But they were the biggest. They were the ones I trusted.

NAJMA: *You haven't sent money to Hooyo since 9/11?!*

DAMAC: She is resourceful, she's managed to get by, not starve. I
   write her, tell her it won't be long, it will blow over.

NAJMA: You didn't tell me before. Why are you telling me now?

DAMAC: It won't blow over. I heard today about a Somali man who
   was imprisoned for assisting his uncle in running an al-Barakat
   station, and who recently appealed his sentence. His sentence
   was stiff on the grounds of al-Barakat's suspected ties to al-
   Qaeda. He appealed on the grounds that he knew nothing about
   al-Barakat's suspected ties to al-Qaeda. The court considered
   this new information and resentenced the man for four times
   the original term.

Beat.

NAJMA: When is she coming? *(No answer.)* *When is she coming?*

DAMAC: I don't know what it means, Najma, if I can send your mother a plane ticket, if they'll let her in the country. Anyway she needs money to prepare to leave.

NAJMA: Who owns al-Barakat?

DAMAC: Somalis. In this country.

NAJMA: So how did the U.S. shut it down? It's not theirs.

DAMAC: The U.S. government has the power—

NAJMA: I thought possession was nine-tenths of the law: it's not theirs.

DAMAC: Najma—

NAJMA: My mother's not a security risk! They think my mother's a security risk? What's my mother got to do with the security of the United States?

DAMAC: I know—

NAJMA: They think my mother'll come here with a bomb? She can barely afford food, how she afford a bomb?

LAINE: We're gonna find out what's going on. We're not gonna let them—

NAJMA: I love America! Somalis love America, why they pick on *us*?

LAINE: Not right—

NAJMA: I love America! Except the snow and freezing rain.

LAINE: Your mother—

NAJMA: I love America! Except dodge ball they throw too hard and my throws always miss. Except a couple of buildings fall New York, and suddenly people here look at me funny, my veil. Except that old Somali man they killed because "they hate Muslims."

Pause.

NAJMA: Is my mother hungry?

DAMAC: No! I don't think so, she—

NAJMA: Because she didn't tell *me* about any of this in her letters I don't know anything.

DAMAC: She's okay—

NAJMA: What if she isn't telling *you*? Lying to you, too?

DAMAC: She's not lying—

LAINE: She didn't want to worry you—

NAJMA: IS MY MOTHER HUNGRY?!

DAMAC: NO! *(Pause.)* Not yet.

Silence.

NAJMA: Don't even know why I read her letters they're nothing. Tell me nothing a hundred letters I have and I'm all ignorant in the dark, just words all they ever say is "I love you." "I love you."

NAJMA *exits.*

Scene 3

Bedroom. NAJMA *on her knees, forehead on the floor, in prayer.* TAY C *enters to get her walkman off the bed. She starts to exit. Then, for fun, she walks over and kicks* NAJMA *in the butt, knocking her over.* NAJMA *flies at* TAY C, *screaming, punching, and kicking, completely surprising* TAY C, *who runs out.* NAJMA *slams the door behind* TAY C *and walks back. Though* TAY C *is too far gone to hear,* NAJMA *mutters, finishing the fight.*

NAJMA: And stay out.

NAJMA *goes back to prayer position on the floor.*

Scene 4

NAJMA, *lying on the living room couch reading a comic book.* TAY C *enters from school. Each girl wears a big "Earth Day" button.* TAY C, *no pause, drops her backpack and heads for the kitchen.*

TAY C: So they gimme detention for bein' late for detention, I oughta just move in there. *(Stops. Notices* NAJMA's *comic book.)* That don't look like homework.

NAJMA: What are you, a narc?

TAY C *looks at her, then goes to the kitchen. Searches through cabinets.*
Finds an empty Girl Scout cookie box, rushes back into the living room.

TAY C: *Hey!* We got Oreos we got ginger snaps we got Chewy Chips
   Ahoy, remember that for your midnight kitchen raids! In future
   direct your overnight pig-outs to any a the above Girl Scout
   cookies available only once a year *valuable!*
NAJMA: I didn't—
TAY C: *Lie?* You think I'm deaf? I hear you slip out three a.m., hear the
   fridge door open, close, open, close. But daytime: oh little light
   eater Najma. Fronta *her*: Oh eats like a bird, what a little dainty.
NAJMA *(shame)*: Sorry!

TAY C *goes to the kitchen again, returns with Oreos and milk. A few*
moments, then she walks over and turns on the TV. As soon as she goes
back to take her seat, NAJMA *takes the remote, hidden beneath her, and*
turns the TV off.

TAY C: Hey!
NAJMA: I can't concentrate.
TAY C: You useta concentrate fine, homeworkin' while I caught the
   WWF finals now you can't read a stupid comic book without
   silence?

NAJMA *goes back to reading her comic.* TAY C *rushes over to retrieve the*
remote and NAJMA *hides it under her body.* TAY C *reaches.*

NAJMA: NO!

TAY C *gets it and turns on the TV, this time blasting it. In the struggle*
NAJMA *had gotten up, and now* TAY C *slams her own butt on the couch*
and quickly stretches out, blocking NAJMA. NAJMA *flies up the stairs.*
Starts tearing up TAY C*'s bed. Throws* TAY C*'s pillow down the stairs.*

TAY C: That better not be *my* bed!

NAJMA *throws* TAY C*'s blanket down the stairs.*

TAY C: HEY!

TAY C *flies up the stairs, snatching her pillow and blanket along the way. Throws the stuff on her own bed, then begins tearing up* NAJMA*'s bed,* NAJMA *trying to hold her back and failing.* TAY C *suddenly looks at* NAJMA*'s wall.*

TAY C: Hey. Hey I know, I know how to decorate your wall since you were so considerate about *my* sister, lemme get some Christian Children's Fund posters, Starvin' babies and flies and big eyes, then you can thinka *your* sister.

NAJMA: I was trying to be nice! Stupid! I was trying to get along!

TAY C: I thought Somalis didn't know how to get along. Oh your great-great-grandfather killed my great-great-great—oh you stole a chicken from my fourteenth cousin mother's side gotta kill ya now wah wah wah.

NAJMA: I *try* to give up the clan think but kind of hard, come here, you people clan away from us!

TAY C: *What* people?

NAJMA: African Americans you all about as African as George Bush.

TAY C: *A* student, all As. And your autobiography's total fiction but no worry you can always fool 'em. They always A you even though it's garbage. Happy happy, where's your sister dyin'? oh! Suddenly the refugee camp got its shipment a Fruit Loops. Where's your father dead? My mother said bad men did bad things to your cousin in the war her fifteen, didn't hear nuthin' 'bout that.

NAJMA: Thanks for all your help but I generally make it a practice not to take advice from D students.

TAY C: Where's your mother? Not here, the Congress sure ain't gonna let her kind cross the border.

NAJMA *suddenly snatches down the kaman cutout, balls it up, and hurls it to the floor.*

TAY C: Now there's a shame, at least that one didn't hurt my ears like everything you pick on that other one, you ever thinka takin' lessons? Someplace else?

NAJMA: You may not be the sharpest tack in the pack but you're not a total idiot I don't *think*, I'll benefit of the doubt you'd at least score the occasional B if you weren't so lazy, why're Americans so lazy? Free education you don't even appreciate free school waste it away skippin' or not studyin' lazy, lazy African American you didn't even plant a tree today take off that badge!

NAJMA tears TAY C's button off.

TAY C: *You* take it off!

TAY C tears NAJMA's button off. Naturally this has them pulling and punching and kicking and screaming all over the room. Eventually they pull away from each other, panting and glaring.

TAY C: SEE? Ain't that Somali? Solve everything with your fists.

NAJMA: Oh *that's* right, you took Conflict Resolution let's hear all your newfound wisdom. All three classes since you cut the rest.

TAY C: Clan mad Clan mad boo hoo Jeez! Aren't you all Somali? When you gonna kiss and grow up? Bygones?

NAJMA: When I see you kissing the guy gunned your sister.

They stare, stunned, at each other. Then TAY C pulls her fist back, about to punch NAJMA in the face, when LAINE enters downstairs.

LAINE (*calls*): Hello?

No answer. LAINE heads for the kitchen. She carries a bakery cake box, takes the birthday cake out, and puts on candles. TAY C pulls back her fist and, still glaring at NAJMA, flops down supine on her bed. LAINE hears.

LAINE: Who's home?

LAINE *quickly puts the cake in the fridge and walks into the living room.*

LAINE *(calling upstairs)*: Hello?

NAJMA *comes to the top of the stairs.*

NAJMA: We're up here.

LAINE: Najma! Come on down. I wrote something today we'll have our first rehearsal!

As NAJMA *reluctantly descends the stairs,* LAINE *prepares: pulls two papers out of her bag, pushes back furniture, etc.*

LAINE: It's a little rough it's the first draft. Whenever I had a spare minute I jotted down a line, then lunch hour this outpouring of creativity, at five I stayed after to type it, copy it, here's yours. Just read through it.

NAJMA *stares at it.*

LAINE: Aloud.

NAJMA: In the mall in the line for the latest movie, it's a G all . . . It's a . . . What's a "G all"?

LAINE: I'll read it, you'll get the hang. Like I said, rough draft I'm open to criticism. Listen.

> *In the mall in the line for the latest movie*
> *It's a G*
> *G like rated G.*
> *It's a G all these kids so I think "fam-i-lee."*
> That's my part. Then you say
> *There's a Mexican woman and a black man, dreadlocks*
> *With a boy boy and girl look like a Xerox*
> Then I say *(points to herself)*
> *And a blonde pulls out cash as the register rings*
> *Popcorn for adopted child born south of Beijing*

(Points to NAJMA.*)*
There's two dads and no mom There's a mom and no dad
There's a grandma only parent those boys ever had
(Points to herself.)
And a girl in my house same age as my girl
Born another woman's house other side of the world
And I think "Can we work it? Not blood fam-i-lee"
Then she stands and her lips spout the pop poetry
This is where you do your poem.

LAINE *stares at* NAJMA. NAJMA *confused. Then, cautious:*

NAJMA: *Baraar habarti loog ka ma furto—*

LAINE: Yes! So you go through the poem or part of the poem, I don't
    want to cut you off but we want to keep the audience on the
    edge of their seats and they may get restless not knowing the
    translation, so you'll do part of your poem and I'll come back with

> *I say "What?" She says "Hey, that's how we play*
> *When we string the words together the Somali way"*
> *(Points to* NAJMA.*)*
> *So we work and we word, practice 'til we all spent*
> *(Points to herself.)*
> *Connecting Africa with African descent*
> *(Points to* NAJMA.*)*
> *And if one thing we learned through the blood, sweat,*
>   *and fun*
> *It's the world's a small place*

LAINE *quickly puts her arm around* NAJMA'S *shoulder, points to the line
on the page. They say it together,* LAINE *slowing it down dramatically and*
NAJMA *awkwardly trying to follow.*

LAINE and NAJMA: *And We Are One.*

LAINE *turns to* NAJMA.

LAINE: Like it? (NAJMA *nods obediently.*) You don't have to love it yet it's a start. We can change things but I think we should start practicing, get a sense of the rhythm. And don't feel like it's my poem, I want your input, *need* your input or it's not a team effort and we are a team. I'll start with the first two lines—

NAJMA: Won't we get disqualified? *(Beat.)* I'm not your daughter.

LAINE: But that's the point, what I talk about in the poem. Who can define "family"? Changes situation to situation. You, Tay C, and I make up a kind of family, I'm not dismissing your cousin Damac, I'm just saying we've *formed* a family—

NAJMA: I have a mother.

LAINE: Of course—

NAJMA: Tay C's your daughter.

LAINE: I'd love to have Tay C get up in front of all those people and beat down a poem with me now how likely is that? *(Pause.)* I don't want to make you if you don't want to. It's just . . . we had such a great time that day. I think we'd be great together.

Silence.

LAINE, NAJMA: Okay.

Resigned NAJMA *has refused.*

LAINE: O*kay?*

NAJMA *nods.*

LAINE: Okay! let's do it.

LAINE *gestures: 1, 2, 3—about to jump into it.*

LAINE and NAJMA: *In the mall—*
LAINE: oh no the first part's mine, see?

LAINE *points to the paper.* NAJMA *nods.*

LAINE: Ready?

NAJMA *nods.*

LAINE: *In the mall in the line for the latest movie*
            It's a G all these kids so I think "fam-i-lee"
NAJMA: *There's a boy* I'm sorry!
            There's a Mexican woman and a black man, dreadlocks
            With a boy
            (NAJMA *confused.*)
            With a boy boy
LAINE: *With a boy, boy, and girl*
            It's the woman and man's three kids.
NAJMA: *With a boy, boy, and . . . and girl looks just like a—*
LAINE: "Look," no *s.* (NAJMA *confused.*) Like to say "a boy, boy, and
    girl *who* look like a Xerox." "Xerox," like a copy.
NAJMA: I know.
LAINE: Don't put in "just": "look like a Xerox." Try again.
NAJMA: *There's a Mexican woman and a black man, dreadlocks*
            With a boy, boy, and girl looks—
LAINE: Look.
NAJMA: *With a boy, boy, and girl look just like—*
LAINE: No "just."
NAJMA: *With a boy, boy, and girl look like a Xerox*
LAINE: *And a blonde pulls out cash as the register rings*
            Popcorn for adopted child born south of Beijing
NAJMA: *There's two dads and no mom There's . . . There's a mom and no*
    dad—
LAINE: I'll say it, you repeat. (*Just speaks without the rhythm.*) There's
    two *dads* and no *mom,* There's a *mom* and no *dad* There's a
    grandma only parent those boys ever had
NAJMA: *There's two dads and no mom, There's a mom and no dad*
            There's a grandma only parent those boys ever had

LAINE: *Very* good! *And a girl in my house same age as my girl*
Born another woman's house other side of the world

LAINE and NAJMA: *And I think—*

LAINE: No that's my line.

NAJMA: Sorry!

LAINE: Easy mistake! I threw you. We've been doing two lines and two, then suddenly I take four don't worry. That's what rehearsal's for.

And I think "Can we work it? Not blood fam-i-lee"
Then she stands and her lips spout the pop poetry

NAJMA, *finally at ease, immediately stands and recites. Meanwhile* TAY C *descends the stairs.*

NAJMA: *Baraar habarti loog ka ma furto gawrac kama baajo*
Bil saddex ihi galabtii hadday beelo kaa bixiso

TAY C (*walking without stopping to the kitchen*): Bubba bubble boo boo blub blub.

LAINE: Quiet! Go on.

TAY C *getting more Oreos. Eventually will open the fridge door, stare awhile, take something and put it in her pocket, then close the door.*

NAJMA: *Beladkaad u jeeddiyo—*

LAINE: Oh! idea. Let's break up the next two lines so I say "I say *'What?'* She says" and then you say "Hey that's how we play / When we string the words together the Somali way." Then I'll take the next two lines, "So we work and we word, practice 'til we all spent / Connecting Africa with African descent" and the rest is the same: "And if one thing we learned" blah blah here, write it down. (*Newer idea.*) *And!* Okay, you go so far in your poem then I'll interrupt with my line and you stop in the middle of your line to pick up with "Hey, that's how we play" okay? (NAJMA, *totally confused, nods.*) This is gonna be great. HEY!

LAINE *suddenly rushes into the kitchen.*

LAINE: Did you get in the fridge? (TAY C *shakes her head no.*) Okay,
cuz it's . . . I need to clean it.

TAY C: I didn't get in the fridge.

TAY C *exits with Oreos, heads for the stairs and up to her bedroom.* LAINE
reenters the living room.

LAINE: Okay! let's try it. Top of your poem.

NAJMA: *Baraar habarti loog ka ma furto gawrac kama baajo*
      Bil saddex ihi galabtii hadday beelo kaa bixiso
      Beladkaad

| NAJMA: *u jeeddiyo iftiin beelo ba* | LAINE: *I say "What?" She says* |
| *ma geyso—* | |

LAINE: No, you need to stop your poem and jump in. When you hear
me say "She says," I'll always start around the same place in your
poem, after that word. What's that word?

NAJMA: "Beladkaad"?

LAINE: Yes! right after . . . (*Beat.*)

NAJMA: "Beladkaad."

LAINE: Yes! right after "beladkaad" (*poor pronunciation*)

NAJMA: "Beladkaad."

LAINE: "Beladkaad." (poor pronunciation)

NAJMA: "Beladkaad."

LAINE: Yes, right after that I'll start, so you listen, and as soon as you
hear "She says" cut your poem off wherever you are and come
in with "Hey, that's how we play / When we string the words
together the Somali way." Okay? (NAJMA *shakes her head no.*)
What's the matter?

NAJMA: That's not how we string the words together the Somali way.
You rhyme, we alliterate.

LAINE: I know you do your poem your way. Then tell me, *my* way, you
did it *your* way. Okay? (NAJMA *stares at her.*) Okay. Your poem.

TAY C *descends the stairs. Grabs her backpack and starts to go back up.*

NAJMA: *Baraar habarti loog ka ma furto gawrac kama baajo*
         Bil saddex ihi galabtii hadday beelo kaa bixiso
         Beladkaad

NAJMA: *Hey, that's how we play—*	LAINE: *I say "What?"* No! you have to wait 'til I say "She says."*

TAY C, *who has stopped at the foot of the stairs, is laughing.*

LAINE: Stop it! she's just learning.

NAJMA *(no sarcasm)*: You wanna do it?

TAY C: No!

LAINE: Then keep your comments to yourself.

NAJMA: You can do it if you want.

TAY C: No, but I'll come, see when they give you the award: "Biggest Fools."

LAINE: Ignore her, let's try again. Now you don't start 'til you hear what?

NAJMA: "She says."

LAINE: Right. Let's go.

NAJMA: *Baraar habarti loog ka ma furto gawrac kama baajo*
         Bil saddex ihi galabtii hadday beelo kaa bixiso
         Beladkaad

NAJMA: *u jeeddiyo iftiin—*	LAINE: *I say "What?" She says*

TAY C: *"Hey, that's how we play!"*

LAINE: Tay C! (TAY C *rolling in laughter.*)

NAJMA: Maybe we should do it the way you said the first time, Laine. *You* do those lines, then I won't have to interrupt myself.

LAINE: That's so boring compared to this, *this* is competitive. There'll be two trophies. You'll get one.

NAJMA: Maybe I should finish my whole poem first—

LAINE: No! we can do this, we just need to practice. Now where do you cut yourself off?

NAJMA and TAY C: After "She says."

LAINE: Tay C! (TAY C *laughing again.*) I mean it. (TAY C *tries to suppress giggles.*) Go on.

NAJMA: *Baraar habarti loog ka ma furto gawrac kama baajo*
Bil saddex ihi galabtii hadday beelo kaa bixiso
Beladkaad

NAJMA: *Hey, that's how—*	LAINE: *I say* Najma!

NAJMA: Sorry!

LAINE: Just pay attention!

TAY C: She can't do it.

LAINE: She can it just takes practice. Patience. Look we'll just do that line. Start with . . . *(Beat.)*

NAJMA: "Beladkaad."

LAINE: Start there. And be ready for "She says."

NAJMA: *Beladkaad*

NAJMA: *u jeeddiyo iftiin—*	LAINE: *I say "What?" She says*

NAJMA: *"Hey, that's how we play*
When we string the words together the Somali way"

LAINE: *Yes!* I knew we could do it, teamwork! Again.

NAJMA: *Beladkaad*

NAJMA: *u jeeddiyo iftiin—*	LAINE: *I say "What?" She says*

NAJMA: *"Hey, that's how we play*
When we string the words together the Somali way"

LAINE: That's it! Again.

NAJMA: *Beladkaad*

NAJMA: *u jeeddiyo iftiin—*	LAINE: *I say "What?" She says*

NAJMA: *"Hey, that's how we play*
When we string the words together the Somali way"

LAINE: We got it! Top of the poem.

NAJMA: *Baraar habarti loog ka ma furto gawrac kama baajo*
Bil saddex ihi galabtii hadday beelo kaa bixiso
Beladkaad

NAJMA: *Hey, that's how—*	LAINE: *I say*

LAINE *screams in frustration.*

NAJMA: I can't do it, Laine.

LAINE: Yes you can.

NAJMA: I can't!

LAINE: You are a very smart little girl with musical talent, poetic talent you *can*.

TAY C: She says she can't.

LAINE: I'm not deaf, Tay C.

TAY C: If she can't, she can't.

LAINE: "Can't" is a four-letter word! She just needs to practice.

NAJMA: I don't wanna practice!

TAY C: She says she doesn't wanna practice!

LAINE (*to* TAY C): YOU'RE NOT A PART OF THIS!

NAJMA: I don't wanna go out there! Mothers and daughters we're not that! We're not that!

LAINE: I know—

NAJMA: I have a mother!

LAINE: Of course—

NAJMA: I have a mother!

LAINE: Najma—

NAJMA: I have a mother and I have a brother and I had a sister.

LAINE: I know, I never intended—

NAJMA: I HAD A SISTER!

TAY C: She's not her.

LAINE: Honey, if you don't want to do it, I won't—

TAY C: SHE'S NOT HER!

LAINE: WHAT!

TAY C: NEXT WEEK GUESS YOU MAKE HER LEARN THE PIANO!

The phone rings. A second. Third. Finally LAINE *picks it up.*

LAINE: Hello? (*to* TAY C.) It's Mrs. Shepard from the Art Club. (TAY C *doesn't react.* LAINE *listens.*) Why weren't you in Art Club?

TAY C: Detention.

LAINE (*mutter*): There goes the one A—

TAY C: Art club's extracurricular! No grade.

LAINE: She wants everyone to bring a baby picture for their collages tomorrow. (*No answer. Into receiver.*) I'll make sure she has it. Thank you, Mrs. Shepard.

LAINE *hangs up and opens a cabinet. She is out of* TAY C*'s line of vision, but* TAY C *hears.*

TAY C: What are you doing?

LAINE: Looking for your baby picture.

TAY C: *Don't.* I wanna find the one I want.

LAINE *(pulls out a photo album)*: You're not gonna "forget" that picture, you're not failing art—

TAY C: DON'T!

TAY C *runs to snatch it out of* LAINE*'s hands but it's too late:* LAINE *gasps. Snatches it back. Turns pages: frantic. Quickly grabs other photo albums, flips through them, catastrophe. Looks at* TAY C.

LAINE: What did you do?

Brief silence.

TAY C: I—

LAINE: WHAT DID YOU DO TO YOUR *SISTER?*

Silence. LAINE *holds up an album, rapidly flipping the pages.*

LAINE: CUT HER OUT! CUT HER OUT EVERY PICTURE HOW COULD YOU *DO* THAT?

A long silence. Then, suddenly:

TAY C: Always yelling at me! What about her? What about her?

LAINE: What *about* her?

TAY C: Perfect all perfect she the *perfect* one—

TAY C *interrupts herself with a scream and shoves* NAJMA.

LAINE: HEY!

TAY C: ONLY DAUGHTER LEFT HOW COME I STILL NOT THE FAVORITE?

Silence. Then LAINE *makes the slightest move toward* TAY C.

TAY C: NO! NO HUG! no hug no hug no hug no hug no hug no hug no hug no hug no hug . . .

TAY C *quickly takes the mantra out of the room and up the stairs, sits on her bed, pulling her knees to her chest and rocking. Meanwhile* LAINE *stares at the albums: despair.* TAY C *suddenly stops muttering. Pulls out of her pocket the birthday candle she'd taken off the cake.*

TAY C: Mom?

It is loud enough for LAINE *to hear, but she does not answer.*

TAY C: Mommy?

Silence.

TAY C: I took off a candle. Okay? I took off a candle cuz I'm stayin' twelve. I took off a candle I'm not turnin' thirteen. Not 'til Cam does. Okay?

TAY C *goes back to rocking.*

Scene 5
NAJMA *and* TAY C *slumped over the living room furniture, staring blank at the TV.* LAINE *standing with fridge door open.*

LAINE: Cook you some eggs? *(No answer.)* Tay C?
TAY C: I had cereal.
LAINE: Najma?
NAJMA: I had instant apples 'n' cinnamon oatmeal, thank you.

LAINE (*stands in the living room doorway*): Rare opportunity, all us here, Sunday morning. Bit a bacon? (NAJMA *reacts.*) Sorry, pancakes.

As LAINE *turns back to the kitchen, the doorbell sounds.* NAJMA *and* TAY C *don't take their eyes off the TV.* LAINE *walks through the living room, past the girls, to answer the door.*

LAINE: Damac.

NAJMA *glances at the door, then turns back to the TV.* DAMAC *and* ABDI *step in.*

Tay C (Amanda Granger) and her mother (Marie-Françoise Theodore) watch as Najma (Sonja Parks) is reunited with her brother, Abdi (Darien Johnson), and her cousin, Damac (Marvette Knight). Photograph by Rob Levine.

DAMAC: And Abdi.

NAJMA *quickly looks up.*

NAJMA: Abdi! (NAJMA *runs to him.*)
ABDI: Najma! *(hugging her)* Iska waran? Xagaad ka dhacday!
NAJMA: Adigu xagaad ka dhacday!
ABDI: Waad weynaatey.
NAJMA: Adiguba. (ABDI *laughs.*) Wax fiican baan keenay iskuulka.
    Straight As!
ABDI: Gabar fiican!
DAMAC: Najma! Aren't you going to introduce?

TAY C *has turned off the TV and slowly strolled over to the others.*

NAJMA: Abdi. Waa Laine iyo Tay C. Laine, Tay C. This is my brother.
    Abdi Salaam.
LAINE: Hello. *(Shakes hands.)*
ABDI: Hello, Laine. Thank you for taking care of Najma.
LAINE: My pleasure. She's a good girl. (NAJMA *embarrassed.*)
ABDI *(turns to* TAY C): It's nice to meet you, Tay C.
NAJMA: Why didn't you tell me he was coming?!
DAMAC: I didn't know 'til three this morning, he shows up my
    doorstep!
ABDI: Damac was going to call first light this morning but I wanted to
    surprise. Damac said, "No more secrets from Najma!" so anyone
    to blame, blame me.
TAY C: Haye!

All surprised by TAY C*'s interruption and her sudden bilinguality.*

ABDI and DAMAC: Nabad! (TAY C *confused. Looks to* NAJMA.)
NAJMA: You say "Haye," they answer "Nabad." *(Turns to* DAMAC.)
    Peace.

NAJMA *and* DAMAC *smile.*

ABDI: Poor Damac! Driving around with me hours, searching high and low: "For Lease." *(To* NAJMA.*)* Got us a place. Closet, but it's ours.

NAJMA *jumping, laughing, and clapping.*

LAINE: To*day*?
DAMAC: Yes. Is that an inconvenience?
LAINE: No, just . . .

Pause: LAINE *stares at* NAJMA, *moist eyes.*

NAJMA: I'll miss you too. *(Eyes on each other. Then, new thought.)*
    Hooyo. Where will Hooyo sleep? "Closet," where's Hooyo's bed?
ABDI: When Hooyo comes, we'll have to find a bigger place.
NAJMA: We'll have to find it soon! Cuz she's coming! Soon! Right?
ABDI: Not soon.

NAJMA *sad.* ABDI *gets close to her.*

ABDI: She'll come. One day, or we'll go home to her.
DAMAC: Laine. If you don't mind, we were hoping to take Najma out for lunch, return for her stuff later.
LAINE: Of course.
ABDI: Please join us.
LAINE: How long since you seen your sister? I think you all need a little alone-time. But thank you.
ABDI: Sure? Tay C?
DAMAC: Going to that new Vietnamese place. *(*TAY C *shakes her head no.)*
LAINE: If we're not here when you get back, Najma has a key.
ABDI *(pulls out a camera)*: Najma. Stand with Laine.

LAINE *puts her arm around* NAJMA. *Snap.*

DAMAC: Now the girls.
ABDI: Yes, Tay C.

NAJMA *and* TAY C *reluctantly put their arms around each other. Snap.*

ABDI: Okay. Mother and daughter.

There seems to be a moment of confusion as to whom ABDI *refers. Then awkwardness as* LAINE *puts her arm around* TAY C. *Snap.*

DAMAC: Beautiful.
NAJMA: You came, Abdi. I didn't know you would.
ABDI: What have I been saving for? Car, gas and an apartment.
    (Beat.) I have a present for you.

ABDI *hands* NAJMA *a little beaded bracelet.* NAJMA *stares at it.*

LAINE: Pretty. But . . . small for you?
NAJMA: Qalin.
ABDI: Najma made this bracelet for Qalin. They were little. All our
    moving, I kept it, didn't want it to get lost. But you're settled
    now, *we*'re settled. I wrote to Hooyo, she wrote back, "Give it to
    her, Abdi. She's a big girl now." (NAJMA *looks up at* ABDI.)
NAJMA: It's not mine. I made it for Qalin, it's hers.
ABDI: She'd want you to have it. Her big sister. One she knew always
    take care of her.

ABDI *puts his arm around* NAJMA. *They exit with* DAMAC. *After a moment*
TAY C *moves back to the couch.* LAINE *goes to kitchen, pulls bacon out of
the freezer, sets it down. Comes back into the living room.*

LAINE: No pancake? Sure?

TAY C *nods, eyes on the TV.*

LAINE: When you and Cam were little, and I was on call at the old
folks' home: lucky. (TAY C *has looked up.*) Steady work they called
all the time but always a different shift, felt like I was never not
sleepy. Still, every night I read you your stories. The miracle was
nursing home just three blocks away from Grandma's, so when
you stayed there on my overnights I could easily pull out the
book for your eight o' clock bedtime before my eleven to seven
shift. But even when they gave me the afternoon, three to eleven,
my seven to eight dinner break didn't I rush home to spend it
with you and Cam and *The Berenstein Bears*? You remember?

TAY C: Kinda.

LAINE: Then Cam got older: didn't wanna share the same story,
wanted her own book. Sometimes I tried, sometimes the
tiredness just too much. "You're a big girl now, you can read to
yourself." She was six and you were four. I was still saying it when
she was nine and you seven, I never once told you to read to
yourself even though by now you were a bigger girl than Cam was
when I started calling her "big girl." One day Cam says, "Why she
the favorite?!" I say, "I have no favorites, I love both my babies
the same." But it was a lie.

I did have favorites. Sometimes the favorite was Cam.
Sometimes the favorite was you. At the time I thought lying was
the right thing, but how can lying be the right thing? I should
have just said, "I'm sorry."

Pause.

LAINE: I'm sorry.

TAY C *stares at* LAINE. *Then* TAY C *slowly nods.*

LAINE: Would you like to come with me today? Reading to the kids?

Pause. TAY C *surprised.*

TAY C: Little kids? In the shelter? (LAINE *nods.*) Okay! (*Beat.*) Can *I* read to 'em?

LAINE: They'd love that.

TAY C: Okay!

LAINE: We can ride our bikes over there—

TAY C: *Really?*

LAINE: And on the way back, detour for a little bike hike 'round the park.

TAY C: OK, but today's Sunday. Don't you have your kickboxing after the shelter?

LAINE: Spring, finally spring. I need to be outside. With my daughter. (*Pause.*) And pizza dinner. All that: Sound good?

TAY C: Delivery?

LAINE: Or go out. Which?

TAY C: Go out.

LAINE: Okay.

TAY C: Okay! *Oh!*

LAINE: What!

TAY C: Last chance. That's what she said, I gotta turn in three pages a my autobiography tomorrow or flunk.

LAINE: Better order in dinner then, save time.

TAY C: No story.

LAINE: Next week. Promise. (TAY C *still disappointed.*) Start your homework now, by the time I get back time for a pre-dinner break. Still do that bike ride.

TAY C *smiles a little, starts toward the stairs. Then stops.*

TAY C: Mom. (*Pause.*) Yesterday I was lookin' for my tire pump, and it wasn't in my room, and it wasn't in the garage, and it wasn't in the attic. The basement, but before I found it there I looked in the back closet. Found somethin' else.

TAY C *goes to the closet, reaches in to retrieve a packet of photos. Pulls out the negatives. Hands them to* LAINE, *who slowly takes them.*

TAY C: Hold 'em to the light. (LAINE *does.*) Christmas, three years ago. Remember? You kept talkin' 'bout global warming, and we got a new backboard and ball. Fifty out, me and Cam shootin' hoops twenty-fifth of December.

LAINE *pulls out more strips, looking at them.*

TAY C: Negatives, 'course they're redevelopable so you won't have to always have a close-by lamp to view 'em.

LAINE *holding another strip to the light. Another. Another.* TAY C *heads for the stairs as* LAINE *continues looking at pictures. In her bedroom,* TAY C *pulls out a notebook, thinks aloud.*

TAY C: Chapter 1. My mother holds my sister and me to the light.

TAY C *starts to write.*

Scene 6
Sound: loud hip-hop. TAY C *on her bike (stationary?), equipped with the rearview mirror she'd requested for her birthday. Speed demon: pedaling like mad. Happy. In the wind, streamers attached to her handlebars fly back horizontal—these streamers are a collage of some sort. She wears headphones: the hip-hop the audience hears is what she is hearing. Hip-hop out, and immediately the soft sound of* NAJMA *playing her kaman and singing the song she had sung in Act I, Scene 5.*

On another part of the stage she sits on the stoop outside of her building, her backpack beside her. Back to hip-hop and speed demon TAY C. *Back to* NAJMA's *song. She is getting bolder, louder. Hip-hop.* TAY C. NAJMA's *song. Around this point she may be standing, reaching some sort of crescendo—then suddenly sees something in the distance. She gasps, snatches her backpack, and sprints. SMASH.* NAJMA *collides with* TAY C *on her bike.*

NAJMA: I'm sorry! I'm sorry!	TAY C: *Hey!* watch where you're— Hey!

Now they recognize each other. Sudden uncontrollable laughter. When it finally subsides:

TAY C: What're you runnin' for? Never seen you do the sprint before, outside a gym. Soccer.

NAJMA: The bus. (NAJMA *points.* TAY C *looks.*)

TAY C: What bus?

NAJMA: *Yeah.*

TAY C: Oh. What now? walk?

NAJMA: Too far. City bus, not the school bus, so another'll come. Eventually.

TAY C: You're gonna be tardy? (NAJMA *nods.*) Wow. Never saw detention hall my school but looks like you'll be finding the way your new place.

NAJMA: Uh huh.

TAY C: Like it?

NAJMA: New school? (TAY C *nods.* NAJMA *shrugs.*) It's okay.

TAY C: You should come back and visit sometime. Make sure you tell me though so I'll know to come in that day.

NAJMA: Okay. (*Beat.*) Hey. What're you doing, my neighborhood? Your school's way over—(*Dawns on her.*) Cutting?

TAY C: You gonna tell?

NAJMA *gives* TAY C *a look.* TAY C *smiles.*

NAJMA: What're you doing? My neighborhood.

TAY C *looks down, embarrassed. As she speaks,* NAJMA *notices the two streamers. Toward the end of* TAY C's *speech,* NAJMA *reaches for one of them.*

TAY C: I dunno. Lookin' for someplace new to ride, I guess. I dunno maybe just wondered where you were stayin'. Come by a couple times before you weren't around *hey!*

TAY C snatches the streamer back. NAJMA *startled. Looks from* TAY C *to the streamer. It hits her.*

NAJMA: Cam?
The streamer is a collage of the cutout photos of CAM. TAY C *looks at the pictures, glances at* NAJMA: *a decision. She shows a photo.* NAJMA *giggles.*

TAY C: Street fair. They painted our faces.
NAJMA: Leopard.
TAY C: Cam was that. I was a tiger. *(Another photo:* NAJMA *laughs hard.)* We were makin' mud pies. She was probably too old for that. I think . . . I didn't know then but now I think sometimes she played down. Played games my age. So we could play together.
NAJMA: Who does she have her arms around?
TAY C: Me.

TAY C stares at the photo. A lengthy stillness before she nods, eyes on the picture.

NAJMA *(another photo)*: I thought these were all Cam.
TAY C: They are.
NAJMA: Uh uh. You.
TAY C: That's Cam. Twelve, like us. Her last school picture.
NAJMA: You look alike!

TAY C surprised.

TAY C: Nuh uh . . .
NAJMA *(putting the photo next to* TAY C*'s face)*: Hold it.

TAY C holds the picture next to her face.

NAJMA: C'mere.

NAJMA *brings* TAY C *over to* TAY C's *bike mirror.* TAY C *stares at the reflection of herself and* CAM.

NAJMA: I have something. (TAY C *nods in wonder.*) Wait.

NAJMA *goes inside her building.* TAY C *continues staring at herself and the picture in the mirror.* NAJMA *returns. Now she seems hesitant.* TAY C *stares at her.* NAJMA *holds out a photo.* TAY C *takes it. Smiles.*

TAY C: You look cute.
NAJMA: *You* look cute. Abdi takes nice pictures. We have doubles
    so . . . you want it?

TAY C *looks at* NAJMA. NAJMA *shyly holds out a pair of scissors. After a momentary confusion,* TAY C *understands: takes the scissors and cuts out the picture, ties it to her streamer.*

TAY C: We'll be the tail end in the back so we'll really fly. (TAY C
    straddles her bike.) What time's school?
NAJMA (*looks at watch*): Last bell's fifteen minutes.
TAY C: How far?

Tay C (Amanda Granger) and Najma (Sonja Parks) finally connect as friends. Photograph by Rob Levine.

NAJMA *(shrugs)*: Three miles.

TAY C: Know the way?

NAJMA: Sure.

TAY C: Hop on.

At first NAJMA *does not understand, then gets it: hops on the bike seat behind* TAY C. *They take off, laughing as the streamers fly in the wind.*

END

TRANSLATIONS

Act I, Scene 1

ARABIC	*Allah hu akbar.*	God is most great.
	Ashahadu an al allah il Allah.	I testify there is no god except God.
	Ashahadu Muhammed el rasool Allah.	I testify that Muhammed is the messenger of God.
	La Allah il allah.	No god but our God.

Act I, Scene 2

SOMALI	*Wáa maxay, ESL?*	What is "ESL"?

Act I, Scene 3

SPANISH	*¿Y ella no tiene que contestar?*	She doesn't have to do it?
HMONG	*Kuv yuav ntses.*	I want the fish.
FRENCH	*Pourquoi je'n peux pas avoir le poisson?*	Why can't I have the fish?
	Elle laisse seulement les nouveaux déssines.	She only lets the new ones color.
SWAHILI	*Ume sema Kiingereza kabla ya kuja hapa?*	Did you know English before you came here?

ARABIC	*Aferit Ingleze kebel Inta Igget?*	Did you know English before you came here?
	Nam. Shaweya.	Yes. A little.
	Muzboot. Inta min el jazeera.	Right. You're from Algeria.
FRENCH	*Qu'est ce qu'elle a dit?*	What did she say?
SPANISH	*Yo creía que ellos eran blancos.*	I thought they were white.
SOMALI	*Soomaaliya miyaad ka timi?*	Are you from Somalia?
	Haa. Lokerkayga waxa ku jira gooryaan?	Yes. I have a worm in my locker, wanna see?
SPANISH	*¡Quiero dibujar! Me gusta dibujar ¿Por qué no podemos dibujar?*	I wanna draw! I like to draw, why can't we draw?
	Porque nosotros podemos leer.	Because we have to read.
	¡Yo no quiero leer! Yo quiero dibujar.	I don't wanna read! I wanna draw.

¡Manuel! ¡Alicia! ¡Están interrumpiendo la clase! Ustedes no están permitidos hablar entre sí durante las lecciones. ¿Me entienden? ¡Y cuántas veces les tengo que repitir que en esta clase sólo hablamos inglés! ¿Cómo piensan que Muhamed y Najma y Bao y Zeinab se sienten al ser excluidos? Ellos no hablan español. Muhamed stop pulling her hair! *En esta clase aprendemos inglés escuchando y hablando unos con los otros y si ustedes insisten en hablar español, no sólo están excluyendo a Najma y Zeinab y Bao y Muhammed, sino que también estén malgastando el tiempo de todos. ¿Creen que éso es justo? No, no es justo y ¿saben qué les pasa a los niños como ustedes? ¿Saben? Les damos un time-out. ¿Eso es lo que ustedes quieren? Ya me imaginaba que no, así que yo les sugiero que dejen de interrumpir y pongan atención y recuerden que en esta clase hablamos* English only!

Manuel! Alicia! You are interrupting the class! You are not supposed to speak during class. Do you understand? And how many times do I have to tell you this class is English only! How do you think Muhamed and Najma and Bao and Zeinab feel? They don't speak Spanish. *Muhamed stop pulling her hair!* In this class we learn English by listening and speaking it with each other and if you keep speaking Spanish, you are not only excluding Najma and Zeinab and Bao and Muhamed but you are also wasting everybody's time. Do you think that's fair? No it's not fair, and do you know what happens to children who do that? Do you? They get a time-out. Is that what you want? I didn't think so I suggest you stop interrupting the class and pay attention and remember in this class we speak *English only*!

SOMALI	*Ma arki karaa gooryaanka.*	Can I see the worm?
	Miyaad ka baqda gooryaanka?	Are you scared of worms?
	Maya.	No.
	Waan hubaa inaad ka baqdo.	I bet you are.
	Waxba kama baqo waxaan ahay Power Puff Girl!	I'm not scared of anything, I'm a Power Puff Girl!
	Waa slimy.	They're slimy.
	Dadka way cunaan	People eat them.
	Ma cunaan.	They do not.
	Fransiisku way cunaan.	The French eat them.
SPANISH	*Voy a dibujar en la próxima clase.*	I'm gonna draw in the next class.
	Yo también.	Me, too.
	Tú vas a dibujar después del almuerzo.	You're gonna draw after lunch.
	Yo voy a dibujar las Power Puff Girls.	I'm gonna draw the Power Puff Girls.
	Después del almuerzo.	After lunch.
	¡Ahora!	Now!
	Yo voy a dibujar ahora.	I'm gonna draw now.
	Yo también	Me, too.
	¡Qué no!	No!
FRENCH	*Tu veux venir chez moi après l'école?*	Do you wanna come to my house after school?
	Je dois demander à Maman.	I have to ask my mom.

FRENCH	*On peut jouer avec ma Play Station.*	We can play with my Play Station.
	On peut regarder Power Puff Girls.	We can watch *Power Puff Girls*.
	Maman me fera finir mes devoirs d'abord. Je peux venir chez toi après mes devoirs.	My mom will make me do my homework first. I can come over after I do my homework.

Act I, Scene 5

SOMALI	*Hooyo.*	Mommy; Mother.

Act I, Scene 6

SOMALI	*Haye.*	Hi.

Act II, Scene 5

SOMALI	*Iska waran? Xagaad ka dhacday!*	How are you? I missed you! Where've you been?
	Adigu xagaad ka dhacday!	I missed you! Where've you been?
	Waad weynaatey.	You've gotten so big!
	Adiguba. Wax fiican baan keenay iskuulka.	You too! I did great in school!
	Gabar fiican!	Good girl!
	Waa Laine iyo Tay C.	This is Laine and Tay C.
	Nabad.	Peace.

ELISSA ADAMS is director of new play development at Children's Theatre Company. She has overseen the commissioning and development of more than twenty new plays since 1998, including *Esperanza Rising, Brooklyn Bridge, Once upon a Forest, A Very Old Man with Enormous Wings, Reeling, Five Fingers of Funk, Snapshot Silhouette, Korczak's Children,* and *Anon(ymous).* She received a McKnight Foundation Theater Artist Fellowship, is a frequent guest dramaturg at the Sundance Theatre Lab, and has served on numerous panels for Theatre Communications Group.

LYNNE ALVAREZ went to New York in 1977. She had great success as a poet and served as vice president of the board of directors for Poets & Writers for ten years. In 1978 she turned to playwriting after attending a gathering of Hispanic writers at Miriam Colon's Puerto Rican Traveling Theatre. She wrote two plays through this workshop, which premiered at the St. Clements Theatre in 1983 and won her a National Endowment for the Arts fellowship and entry into New Dramatists. She wrote several plays as a New Dramatist, including *Hidden Parts,* which won a Kesselring Award in 1983 and premiered at Primary Stages in 1987, and *The Wonderful Tower of Humbert LaVoignet.* She also translated three plays by the contemporary Mexican playwright Felipe Santander. Lynne Alvarez passed away in 2009.

PETER BROSIUS has been artistic director of Children's Theatre Company since 1997. Under his leadership, CTC established Threshold, a new play laboratory that has created world premiere productions with leading American playwrights. He directed the world premieres of *Bert and Ernie, Goodnight!*, *Iqbal*, *Iron Ring*, *Madeline and the Gypsies*, *Average Family*, *The Lost Boys of Sudan*, *Anon(ymous)*, *Reeling*, *The Monkey King*, *Hansel and Gretel*, *The Snow Queen*, and *Mississippi Panorama*, all commissioned and workshopped in Threshold. He has received Theatre Communications Group's Alan Schneider Director Award as well as honors from the Los Angeles Drama Critics Circle Award and Dramalogue.

KIA CORTHRON is often called a "political" playwright. Most of her plays deal with African American issues yet skirt the realm of all human consciences. Her large commissioned body of work includes *Light Raise the Roof*, *Slide Glide the Slippery Slope*, *The Venus de Milo Is Armed*, *Breath Boom*, *Force Continuum*, *Splash Hatch on the E Going Down*, *Seeking the Genesis*, *Digging Eleven*, *Life by Asphyxiation*, *Wake Up Lou Riser*, *Come Down Burning*, and *Cage Rhythm*. Among her awards for playwriting are the AT&T On Stage Award, the Daryl Roth Creative Spirit Award, the Mark Taper Forum's Fadiman Award,

National Endowment for the Arts/TCG, Kennedy Center Fund for New American Plays, the New Professional Theatre Playwriting Award, and the Callaway Award. She is a resident of New Dramatists.

LARISSA FASTHORSE (Rosebud Sioux Tribe, Lakota) grew up in South Dakota. She was a ballet dancer and choreographer, but she always loved to write and began her writing career by working in feature film and TV development with a production company at Paramount Studios. Since leaving development, she has received the Sundance/Ford Fellowship and the Fox Diversity Writers Initiative Fellowship; attended the ABC/IAIA Writers Program; and was an inscribed delegate at the United Nations in Geneva, where she spoke on the power of film for Indigenous peoples. Her next piece for Children's Theatre Company, *Fancy Dancer,* is part of the National Endowment for the Arts: Distinguished New Play Development Projects.

MELISSA JAMES GIBSON's plays include *[sic]* (OBIE Award for playwriting; Kesselring Prize; and The Best Plays of 2001–2) and *Suitcase, or Those That Resemble Flies from a Distance* (NEA/TCG Theatre Residency Program for Playwrights). She received fellowships from the Jerome Foundation and the MacDowell Colony, and her work has received development support from the National Endowment for the Arts, the Rockefeller MAP grant, the New York State Council on the Arts, Theatre Communications Group, and the Greenwall Foundation. She received a Whiting Writers Award, is a graduate of the Yale School of Drama, and is a proud member playwright of New Dramatists.